D0223759

My Night at Maud's

Rutgers Films in Print

Charles Affron, Mirella Jona Affron, and Robert Lyons, editors

My Night at Maud's

Eric Rohmer,

director

English Showalter, editor

Rutgers University Press

New Brunswick, New Jersey

My Night at Maud's is volume 19 in the Rutgers Films in Print series

Library of Congress Cataloging-in-Publication Data

My Night at Maud's: Eric Rohmer, director /
  English Showalter, editor.
      p.   cm.—(Rutgers films in print; v. 19)
  "Rohmer filmography, 1950–1992": p.
  Includes bibliographical references.
  ISBN 0-8135-1939-X (cloth)
  ISBN 0-8135-1940-3 (pbk.)
  1. Ma nuit chez Maud. 2. Rohmer, Eric,
1920– —Criticism and interpretation.
I. Rohmer, Eric, 1920– . II. Showalter,
English. III. Series.
PN1997.M153M9   1993
791.43′72—dc20   92-31724
                                      CIP

British Cataloging-in-Publication information available

The script for *My Night at Maud's* first appeared in *L'Avant-Scène Cinéma* 98 (December 1969) and is reprinted by permission of Eric Rohmer and *L'Avant-Scène Cinéma*.

The stills on pages 41, 42, 46, 52, 54, 57, 61, 70, 75, 76, 77, 79, 82, 88, 96, 100, and 104 are reproduced courtesy of the Museum of Modern Art/Film Stills Archive.

The preface from *Six Moral Tales* by Eric Rohmer, translated by Sabine d'Estrée, copyright © 1974 Editions de L'Herne, translation copyright © 1980 by Viking Penguin is used by permission of Viking Penguin, a division of Penguin Books USA Inc. The interview with Eric Rohmer, "Nouvel Entretien avec Eric Rohmer," from *Cahiers du Cinéma* 214 (April 1970): 46–55, and the review by Pascal Bonitzer, "Maud et les phagocytes," from *Cahiers du Cinéma* 219 (July-August 1969): 59, are reproduced courtesy of *Cahiers du Cinéma*. The interview with Eric Rohmer by Graham Petrie, from *Film Quarterly* 24, no. 4 (Summer 1971): 34–41, copyright © 1971 by the Regents of the University of California, is used by permission of the University of California Press Journals and by permission of the author, Graham Petrie, McMaster University, Hamilton, Ontario, Canada.

The review by Jean de Baroncelli is reprinted from *Le Monde*, June 7, 1969, p. 11, by permission of *Le Monde*. The review by Henry Chapier is reprinted from *Combat*, May 16, 1969, p. 13. The review by Frantz Gevaudan is reprinted from *Cinéma 69* 138 (July-August 1969): 26. The review by Martin Tucker, "The Screen: Maud's Place," is reprinted from *Commonweal* 92 (May 1, 1970): 169–170, copyright © 1970 by the Commonweal Foundation, with permission. The review by Richard Schickel is reprinted from *Second Sight,* published by Simon & Schuster, 1972, copyright © 1972 by Richard Schickel, by permission of Simon & Schuster. The review by Peter Cowie is reprinted from *Focus on Film* 1 (January-February 1970): 11–13, by permission of the author.

The excerpts from chapter 6 of Marion Vidal's book are reprinted from *Les "Contes moraux" d'Eric Rohmer* (Paris: Lherminier, 1977), pp. 83–105. The excerpts from the essays by Jean Collet are reprinted from *Le Cinéma en question* (Paris: Éditions du Cerf, 1972), pp. 172–183, by permission of Les Éditions du Cerf. The excerpts from chapter 5 of *Eric Rohmer: Realist and Moralist* by C. G. Crisp (Bloomington and Indianapolis: Indiana University Press, 1988), pp. 52–53 and 56–59, are reprinted by permission of Indiana University Press. The excerpts from "Pascal's Wager and the Feminist Dilemma in Eric Rohmer's *My Night at Maud's*" by Frank R. Cunningham are reprinted from *The Kingdom of Dreams in Literature and Film,* edited by Douglas Fowler (Tallahassee: Florida State University Press, 1986), pp. 83–89, by permission of the Florida State University Press.

Acknowledgments

First of all, I would like to thank Leslie Mitchner for giving me the opportunity to do this book, on a subject close to my heart but not so close to most of my scholarship, and for her patient advice and help. The series editors—Charles Affron, Mirella Jona Affron, and Robert Lyons—also gave me sympathetic and constructive criticism, for which I am very grateful. The staff and librarians of the British Film Institute, the Museum of Modern Art, and the Princeton University Library were unfailingly helpful and courteous. Some of my research was partly supported by the Rutgers University Research Council. My students at Rutgers, Camden, have kept strong my conviction that French films in general, and Rohmer's films in particular, appeal to a much broader audience than usually gets to see them. The best discussions of the movies I have ever heard take place when Michael, Vinca, and Elaine get going; from *Viridiana* to *Night on Earth,* they have been my source and inspiration, and this book is for them.

Contents

Introduction

My Night at Maud's: Moral Choices, Realistic Chances

English Showalter

I t was a surprise to everyone, including Eric Rohmer, that the public liked *Ma Nuit chez Maud* (*My Night at Maud's*). One of his producers, Pierre Cottrell, remarked later, "When we made *Maud,* I didn't think it could ever be shown outside of France or that it could ever attract a large audience. Now I believe 'all is possible.'"[1] It violated almost all the rules of popular filmmaking: it had no crime, no explicit sex, no violence, no action; in fact, it even had very little plot. A good half of the film was spent on one scene in which three characters talk and talk and talk. And what about? Religion, philosophy, Catholicism, Pascal, morality, mathematics—not the sort of subjects calculated to appeal to the average movie-goer. Moreover, the story apparently ends with the reaffirmation of traditional and conventional values—fidelity, chastity, piety, the family. How could that interest an audience at the end of the 1960s?

Rohmer's name certainly did not carry sufficient prestige to draw a crowd. Despite his early association with the great New Wave directors, he had not shared in their successes between 1958 and 1962, and in the 1960s his ideas diverged ever more sharply from theirs. When a team of interviewers from *Cahiers du Cinéma* discussed *My Night at Maud's* with Rohmer in 1970, the first line of their article was: "Everything, in this conversation with Eric Rohmer, opposes us to him."[2] In fact, Rohmer's style bears little resemblance to that of New Wave filmmakers. Where they deliberately intruded themselves into their works, he maintained a sober detachment. They went out of their way to destroy the illusion of reality, to call attention to the artificiality of film, to play with the conventions of film

1. Melton S. Davis, "Boy Talks with Girl, Boy Argues with Girl, Boy Says . . .," *New York Times Magazine,* November 21, 1971, p. 88.
2. Pascal Bonitzer, Jean-Louis Comolli, Serge Daney, and Jean Narboni, "Nouvel Entretien avec Eric Rohmer," *Cahiers du Cinéma* 219 (April 1970): 47; this introductory paragraph is not included in the selection reprinted in this volume.

genres; he was a self-proclaimed realist, who believed in film as an instrument for revealing truth. Godard, for example, had also included a long conversation in *Breathless,* but Godard's frolicsome camerawork and bravura editing called attention to the comic surrealistic incoherence of what was being said; Rohmer, by contrast, strove to create an illusion of presence and intimacy, so that the *Cahiers* interviewers charged him with reviving the "fourth wall" technique of late-nineteenth-century naturalist playwrights. The New Wave directors almost always included a sly wink at their audience in the form of an homage, a specific allusion to another film, like Michel's imitation of Bogart in *Breathless* or Antoine Doinel's theft of the poster for Bergman's *Monika* in *The 400 Blows;* the characters of *My Night at Maud's* are just the sort of people who might go to the movies, but instead they go to a concert of classical music and a midnight mass.

Rohmer even passed up some of the best established devices of the cinema. Nestor Almendros, his cameraman, had already proved to him during the making of *La Collectionneuse* (*The Collector*) that color filming was not much more expensive than black-and-white, but Rohmer regarded black-and-white filming as an artistic necessity, to the initial dismay of his producers. Likewise, Rohmer refused to add a musical soundtrack as background, because "it is merely the means to help a weak scene."[3] Critics regularly began their reviews by commenting that *My Night at Maud's* is "not at all what a movie is supposed to be, since it takes minimal advantage of what the camera can do"[4] or that Rohmer "flies in the face of the prevailing film aesthetic."[5] Immediate audience response, critical acclaim, several awards, and the continuing interest of film lovers have long since vindicated Rohmer's stubborn individualism; but his films pose unusual problems.

Six Moral Tales

Perhaps the first context one should use to understand *My Night at Maud's* is the series of six films called *Six Contes Moraux* (*Six Moral Tales*), in which it figures as number 3, although it was the fourth to be filmed. Rohmer conceived the project just after the failure of his first feature film in 1962. It was deliberately modest and out of the mainstream, intended to let him "go on filming, no matter what."[6] He described the common theme of the moral tales in these terms: "While the narrator is in search of one woman, he meets another, who absorbs his

3. Davis, "Boy Talks with Girl," p. 90.
4. Robert Hatch, Review, *The Nation* 210 (April 27, 1970): 509.
5. Richard Schickel, *"My Night at Maud's,"* in *Second Sight* (New York: Simon & Schuster, 1972), p. 306; reprinted in this volume; see p. 152.
6. Graham Petrie, "Eric Rohmer: An Interview," *Film Quarterly* 24, no. 4 (Summer 1971): 36; this passage is not included in the selection in this volume.

attention until he finds the first one again."[7] The first two tales were filmed in 16mm with mostly amateur casts and volunteer crews, and have never been in general release. In the first, *La Boulangère de Monceau* (*The Baker's Girl from Monceau*), a young man sees a girl on the street but does not know how to meet her. While he is looking for her, he meets and flirts with a salesgirl in a bakery. When he finds the first girl again, he discovers that she lives in an apartment over the bakery, has seen him going to the bakery every day, and thought he was going there to impress her. In the second, *La Carrière de Suzanne* (*Suzanne's Career*), Bertrand admires Sylvie but is pursued by Suzanne, one of the girlfriends of his best friend Guillaume. She is flirting with Bertrand only to stay close to Guillaume, who has tired of her and passed her on to Bertrand; he goes along unhappily with the arrangement because he is afraid of displeasing Guillaume. In the end, the hero never finds the chance to approach Sylvie and loses both girls.

In *The Collector,* made in 1966, the hero, Adrien, is on the Riviera, where he is both attracted to and repelled by a hedonistic and sexually promiscuous girl, Haydée, who "collects" lovers. He comes perilously close to succumbing to her, but an accident—she breaks a priceless vase—causes him to tear himself away just in time and fly off to his true love in London. *My Night at Maud's* was completed in 1969. The nameless narrator, like the hero of *The Baker's Girl from Monceau,* sees a woman he does not know and sets out to meet her. In the process he meets Maud, a sensual and attractive woman like Suzanne, Haydée, and the baker's girl, who tries to seduce him but fails. He then finds and eventually marries Françoise, the one he had seen by chance.

The success of *My Night at Maud's* enabled Rohmer to complete the last of his two tales in quick succession: *Le Genou de Claire* (*Claire's Knee*) in 1970 and *L'Amour l'après-midi* (*Chloe in the Afternoon*) in 1972. In the former, Jérôme is engaged to a Swedish woman we never see; the story takes place in Annecy, where he is vacationing surrounded by three women, the novelist Aurora Cornu and two adolescent girls, Laura and Claire. Abetted by Aurora, he flirts with the two girls and becomes obsessed by the beautiful and unresponsive Claire; in the end, he departs to rejoin his fiancée, and it is not entirely clear whether he has resisted temptation or simply been ignored. In *Chloe in the Afternoon,* the happily married and successful Frédéric dreams of erotic adventure (with the women from the previous films, who appear in a dream sequence) and is drawn into a relationship with Chloe, another seductress, another shopgirl; but an unexpected glimpse of himself in a mirror brings him to his senses and he returns to his wife, Hélène.

Obviously, these stories not only repeat each other but also follow a circular pattern, ending more or less where they began. One of the recurring motifs

---

7. Michel Bellot-Antony, "Les Constantes d'un genre: Le Conte moral de Marmontel à Eric Rohmer," in François Marotin, ed., *Frontières du conte* (Paris: CNRS, 1982), p. 82.

discussed by C. G. Crisp (see the "Commentaries" section of this volume) is the hole in time—a vacation, an interval of idleness—when the temptation occurs. Outside their normal routines, the men go astray. The temptresses are usually associated with the appetites, especially with food and drink, and with the night. And the structure represents for Rohmer a kind of morality play, in which the man may take either the path of virtue or the path of vice. As he explained it, "when there is any possibility of choice, it is the first woman that he chooses—that is, he chooses morality rather than vice, virtue rather than vice."[8] The condition is important; the subject of the film is often not the making of a choice, but whether the possibility of choice exists.

The term "moral," moreover, has connotations in French rather different from its standard English meaning. In an interview Graham Petrie asked Rohmer to explain his use of the term, and he answered in part that "moral" can also refer to people "who like to bring their motives, the reasons for their actions, into the open, they try to analyze, they are not people who act without thinking about what they are doing."[9] In other words, the *Moral Tales* portray people dealing with moral problems, about which Rohmer has an opinion just like anyone else; but he is not concerned with persuading us, or even telling us, what is right and what is wrong. Instead, he is interested in showing how people decide for themselves, and how they go about adjusting their actions to their beliefs, and vice versa.

It should be noted, finally, that the genre of moral tales has existed in France since the eighteenth century. Jean-François Marmontel is usually credited with the first use of the title *Moral Tales,* and he published several volumes of short stories under that collective title beginning in the 1750s. It is characteristic of Rohmer to ally himself with tradition—in fact, with an archaic tradition; he is a classicist, following the stylistic principle that one says less to say more, and seeking always the permanent and universal elements rather than the fashionable and ephemeral. "For me what is interesting in mankind is what is permanent and eternal and doesn't change, rather than what changes, and that's what I'm interested in showing," he told Graham Petrie.[10] Typically, even in the ultramodern genre of film, he clung to the obsolescent black and white in making *My Night at Maud's,* as he had originally preferred silent films to the talkies. He regularly injects references to French classical culture into his films—Denis Diderot in *Chloe in the Afternoon,* Jean Jacques Rousseau in *Claire's Knee* and in *The Collector,* and of course Blaise Pascal in *My Night at Maud's.*

8. Quoted by C. G. Crisp, *Eric Rohmer: Realist and Moralist* (Bloomington and Indianapolis: Indiana University Press, 1988), p. 33.
9. Petrie, "An Interview," pp. 38–39; see p. 125.
10. Ibid., p. 39; see p. 126.

Blaise Pascal

Anyone educated in the French schools would have little difficulty following the conversations among Maud, Vidal, and the narrator concerning Pascal. When his name is raised, Maud instantly responds with a pair of proverbial phrases, and Vidal chimes in with a third: "Man is a thinking reed"; "the two infinites"; "Cleopatra's nose" (shot 85). These are from the *Pensées,* an unfinished and posthumously published book of related fragments intended as a defense of Christianity:

> Man is but a reed, the weakest thing in nature; but a thinking reed.
>
> For I ask, what is man in Nature? A cypher compared with the Infinite, an All compared with Nothing, a mean between zero and all.
>
> Cleopatra's nose—had it been shorter, the whole face of the earth would have changed.[11]

In the short-story version of *My Night at Maud's,* the narrator tells in the opening sequence how, while looking for a book on mathematics, he noticed and bought a copy of the *Pensées.* "I hadn't read the book since high-school days. . . . I thought I knew his work by heart; as I reread it, however, though I found the text familiar, it was no longer the same one I remembered. The one I recalled had taken to task human nature as a whole. The text I was reading now, after all these years, struck me as uncompromising and extreme, passing judgment on me, on both my past and my future. Yes, a text written for and aimed specifically at me."[12] In some respects, the encounter with Pascal resembles the encounters with women: while looking for one book, he finds another. The narrator is an engineer, who enjoys mathematics as a pastime; his profession and his tastes form part of his character, that of a man who lives by reason and logic, who plans and controls. Pascal's picture of humanity at the mercy of chance profoundly disturbs the narrator; and the conclusion Pascal drew from his analysis of the human condition bothers him still more: "Between the extremes of the ungodly and the saintly Pascal left no room for the man of goodwill that I earnestly wanted to be."[13]

Now it is not just Pascal's book that Rohmer brings into play. The film is set in Clermont-Ferrand, which was Pascal's hometown; this fact leads to the discussion of his failure to appreciate the local wine. It also suggests a deeper parallel to Pascal in the narrator's own experience, for Pascal, like the narrator, began his career as a mathematician and engineer. A precocious genius, he wrote a treatise

11. Blaise Pascal, *Pensées,* trans. and ed. M. F. Stewart (New York: Pantheon, 1965), pp. 83, 21, 51; a longer excerpt following the first passage is reprinted at the end of the Cunningham article, p. 175.
12. Eric Rohmer, *Six Moral Tales,* trans. Sabine d'Estrée (New York: Viking, 1980), pp. 70–71.
13. Ibid., p. 71.

on conic sections at the age of sixteen, and two years later constructed a calculating machine that is generally regarded as the distant ancestor of computers. (It is in honor of this invention that one of the most popular programming languages is named Pascal.) In 1648 he devised the experiment to prove that air has weight, by means of a barometer carried to the top of the Puy de Dôme, one of the volcanic mountains near Clermont-Ferrand. In short, from 1623 to 1654 Pascal followed a career much like the narrator's, including an agreeable social life spent in Parisian salons with worldly aristocrats like the celebrated *moraliste* Duc François de La Rochefoucauld and freethinking men of letters. This phase of Pascal's life ended in November 1654 when he was almost killed in a carriage accident—a motif that recurs in *My Night at Maud's*—and felt that his survival was a providential miracle. From then until his death in 1662 he devoted almost all his energy to religious causes.

Pascal belonged to a particularly austere school of thought within Catholicism, known as Jansenism, which was in fact declared heretical and suppressed in the early eighteenth century. The name comes from an early seventeenth-century bishop, Cornelius Jansenius, who advocated a return to a strict Augustinian doctrine of salvation: God is all-powerful and mortals are completely powerless without God's grace; one cannot deserve or earn salvation, one receives it from God according to His inscrutable wisdom. The moral consequences of this belief, as the Jansenists interpreted it, were that one should devote one's whole being to worship. All occupations, all pleasures only served to distract one's attention from the profound misery of the human condition. Perhaps the most famous of all Pascal's thoughts is the wager, an argument by which he hoped to persuade his erstwhile friends, who shared the century's passion for gambling, to convert to his faith. Either God is, or He is not, argues Pascal, but reason cannot decide the question. Therefore, one must wager. And, concludes the argument: "Let us weigh gain and loss in calling heads that God is. Reckon these two cases: if you win, you win all; if you lose, you lose naught. Then do not hesitate, wager that He is."[14] Rohmer's narrator recognizes that this argument has no force for a genuine atheist but, being a Christian, he is troubled by Pascal's logic.

Settings

Rohmer has always attached great importance to settings, to space, to geography, to architecture. One of his major works of criticism deals with space in the films of the silent film director F. W. Murnau, and one of his first critical articles was entitled "Cinema, the art of space" (1948). Moreover, as he declared emphatically when challenged by the *Cahiers* interviewers, he regarded the cinema as a tool

14. Pascal, *Pensées*, p. 119.

with which to reveal the beauty of the real world. In many of his films, characters play themselves, like Aurora Cornu in *Claire's Knee,* and in others the actors wrote their own lines, like Antoine Vitez in *My Night at Maud's,* who told Rohmer he was interested in Pascal and developed the Marxist interpretation on his own. Similarly, the places are real, and affect the films.

As has already been noted, Clermont-Ferrand was Pascal's birthplace. The places where the film's action occurs can be easily identified: there is a village called Ceyrat outside of town, a Romanesque church of Saint-Nicolas-du-Port, in a neighborhood of old and narrow streets; there is a cathedral, a municipal theater, a Place de Jaude, and a Michelin factory. Although Rohmer contests the notion that he creates a filmic space, it is nonetheless clear that he selects which aspects of the site to put on screen, and that he organizes what he shows to bring out a certain sense of the place. In this case, he makes the entire region a vast metaphor for Pascal's either/or wager.

Even the choice of black-and-white film relates to this theme. In part, as Rohmer stressed when asked about it, the region itself lacks color. The native stone is black lava and the old city is noticeably dark; Rohmer dressed the actors and decorated Maud's apartment in gray. He avoided the few dashes of color, like hoardings and road signs. "I was concerned above all with exploiting the contrast between black and white, between light and shadow," he told Graham Petrie.[15] He went on to mention a sheet and the snow as being white "in a positive way." The bleakness of the landscape thus reflects the bleakness of a Pascalian vision of human life, or of the narrator's feeling of being pushed to choose.

In similar fashion, the rest of the settings seem to form pairs, between which one must choose. The narrator lives in the country, and commutes into the city every day; it will turn out that Françoise also lives out of town. Their preference for rural solitude may again allude to the Jansenists, who withdrew from Parisian society to the Abbey of Port-Royal, where they were known as the "solitaires." Maud, of course, lives in town, as does Vidal. To the rural/urban polarization may be added an opposition between heights and valleys. The rural villages, Ceyrat and Sauzet, are on hills; driving into Clermont-Ferrand, one looks down into the city. After his humiliating night with Maud in the city, the narrator appears much more at ease and in control the next day, hiking on the Puy de Pariou, one of the many peaks of the region. Indoor and outdoor scenes reinforce the same contrasts; key moments occur in the open air—the narrator's first contact with Françoise, his recovery of his composure with Maud, Françoise's confession, and the epilogue scene at the beach. In Maud's room, in Françoise's rooming house, although the narrator avoids the sin of fornication, it is not so certain that he avoids lust, and he is certainly sorely tempted. This may be yet another discreet nod to Pascal, who

---

15. Petrie, "An Interview," p. 37; see p. 124.

wrote "I have often said that man's unhappiness arises from one thing only, namely that he cannot abide quietly in one room."[16]

Contrasts in time play a similar role. Maud is associated with the night, as well as the indoors and the city, Françoise with the day, outdoors, the country. The season is Christmas, one of those vacation periods when normal routines cease and empty periods provide opportunities for going astray. It is the time of year when nights are longest, by contrast to the final summer scene on the beach. It is finally the time of the year for snow, the natural "accident" that gives Maud a pretext to keep the narrator in her apartment overnight, that gives the narrator a pretext to offer Françoise a ride, that is evoked by Maud as the cause of her lover's death, and that in fact causes the narrator's car to slide off the road so that he has to stay overnight with Françoise. Unwelcome to Vidal, who finds it phony and childish, fatal to Maud's happiness, snow serves the narrator and Françoise. Its pure, "positive" whiteness transforms the varied grays of the landscape into a single dazzling light, congenial to the moral absolutism of the narrator.[17]

It would be wrong to make this dichotomy schematic and absolute, however. As we will see, Rohmer insists on the fact that his film is a first-person narrative. The binary vision of the world is the narrator's, not necessarily Rohmer's, and it is not reality itself. Everywhere there are small lapses in the system, which point to a larger ambiguity. For example, the final scene shows the narrator and Françoise, married and parents of a son, on a beach, outdoors, in the sun, with white sand and glimmering sea—in short, a setting not unlike their other symbolic places; but in this scene, it is Maud who goes up the hill and looks down on them, for she knows a truth about them that they can never tell each other. Or again, the narrator attends mass in the city, despite living in the country. It is in church that he sees Françoise for the first time, thus indoors and in the city. He is disappointed not to see her at midnight mass on Christmas Eve, and we might think it appropriate for her not to be among these night people; but we will eventually learn that she has her own night story, which may well explain her absence. Christmas can be taken as a symbol of the ambiguities in the setting: it is both the dead of winter and the rebirth of the year. Nothing Rohmer shows us is ever as simple as it first seems.

Characters

The film involves four characters, who are contrasted as sharply as are the elements of the setting: two men, the narrator and Vidal; two women, Maud and Françoise. Of the two men, Vidal is a Marxist professor of philosophy, the narrator

16. Pascal, *Pensées*, p. 59.
17. See Marion Vidal, *Les "Contes Moraux" d'Eric Rohmer* (Paris: Lherminier, 1977), p. 85; reprinted in this volume, see p. 161.

a Catholic engineer. Of the two women, Maud is a nonbelieving pediatrician, Françoise a Catholic graduate student in biology. There are subtle ironies even in these superficial identities, the scientist and the engineer being devout believers in revealed religion, the teacher and the doctor doubting the validity of the ethical system in the name of which they act.

Of the four, Vidal has the smallest part and seems the least complicated. The *Cahiers* interviewers attacked Rohmer for the conception of this character, claiming that he was no Marxist at all. His Pascalian view of Marxism, that he must wager his life on it because it gives a meaning to history and thus to his life, undermines the fundamental pretension of Marxism to being a science. Rohmer retorted that he did not care whether Vidal was an orthodox Marxist or not. In fact, he fits better into the cast as a hesitant or wavering Marxist, for the others, too, have difficulty reconciling their beliefs and their lives. His attitude toward Marxism puts him in parallel to the narrator, although he lacks the self-doubt of Trintignant's character. One might say that, just as a real Christian ought to shun the world, so too a real Marxist ought not to be going to concerts, escorting pretty blondes to cafés and dinner, or spending long evenings eating and drinking with Maud.

Vidal's main function in the film, however, is to introduce the narrator to Maud, and to introduce the themes of chance and providence. Rohmer has said that the original idea of this tale was simply a man forced to spend the night in a woman's room.[18] It came to him in 1945, and in the first version the wartime curfew was responsible. Twenty years later, that pretext seemed too historically limited; the snowstorm was more universal. The storyteller has expended considerable ingenuity in establishing the plausibility of an unlikely situation: how could an intelligent and experienced thirty-four-year-old man find himself trapped in the bedroom of a woman he has just met? It is the setup for a farce, and indeed the film has many comic moments. Vidal plays a major part in bringing the narrator into this trap, for reasons that seem not only credible but at times even touching.

He had known the narrator when they were lycée students together some fifteen years earlier. A chance encounter reunites them, at a time when neither has pressing engagements. Vidal has been Maud's lover, and he still feels a strong attraction to her. On the surface, Vidal and Maud make a good couple; they have similar beliefs, they are both unattached, and they seem to get along well. Toward the end of the film, we learn that Vidal has accompanied Maud to Toulouse, where she intends to establish a new medical practice, to help her with the move. But there is no real love between them, and both recognize it. Vidal invites the narrator to go to Maud's with him in part to avoid the temptation of sleeping with her: "If I told you to come, it's because I know very well what we would do if you didn't

---

18. Bonitzer et al., "Nouvel Entretien," p. 49; see p. 117.

come. . . . We'd make love . . . casually, . . . out of boredom" (shot 75). Which doesn't stop him from making suggestive remarks to her when they go there.

Maud, however, is drawn to the narrator instead, and when Vidal realizes it, he gets drunk, eggs Maud on, and invents a pretext—the snow will come in his open windows—to leave them alone. In short, he colludes in the seduction. Maud tries to explain his behavior to the narrator, who thinks he was drunk and wanted to go home. It was out of bravado, she says; Vidal is in love with her, but understands that they are not well matched, so he is looking for reasons to be hurt, to despise her: "He's one of those people who want to believe the worst" (shot 122). As with most of the characters' analyses, one cannot be sure whether Maud is sincere in all she says, but the last remark seems to fit Vidal quite well, and to place him in marked contrast to the narrator, whose optimistic wish to believe the best borders on complacency.

Vidal has seemed to critics a minor but likable character. If his masochism and hopeless attachment to Maud hint at psychological depths, what we see of him alleviates any concern: he is with a pretty blonde when the narrator meets him, he is with another the day after that night at Maud's. Françoise, on the other hand, has received a fairly negative press. Unluckily for her ratings, she seems to incarnate the narrator's preconception of an ideal woman—young, blonde, beautiful, practicing Catholic—and he claims to have decided to marry her before ever speaking to her, on the basis of a furtive glance in church. As Jean Collet puts it, "Françoise is presented right away as an image . . . while the second woman, Maud, bursts in and imposes herself as a very carnal being, with her weight of experience and life, her past."[19] Or Frank Cunningham: "She is a lesser woman than Maud."[20] Maud and the narrator joke about his search for a woman to meet his specifications, and imagine advertising for her in the personals: "Engineer, thirty-four, Catholic, five nine, good-looking, with car, seeks blond, practicing Catholic" (shot 125).

Her blond hair, her association with the snowy outdoors, and her innocent look conjure up terms like "pale," "frigid," and "remote." Her entrance is delayed and muted; although she is glimpsed in the opening sequence, her first real lines come two-thirds of the way through the film, after Maud has deployed the full range of her sophisticated personality and voluptuous charms. After the first scene in the church, where the narrator's stare fixes Françoise's image in close-up shots, she is repeatedly shown in the far distance or in the margins of the frame, fleeing on her motorbike, as in shots 20–24, when the narrator pursues her in vain; shot 42, when she pulls alongside his car and then disappears again; shot 147, when she rides by the café; and shot 172, when he encounters her at night.

---

19. Jean Collet, *Le Cinéma en question* (Paris: Cerf; 1972), p. 172; reprinted in this volume; see p. 167.
20. Frank R. Cunningham, "Pascal's Wager and the Feminist Dilemma in Eric Rohmer's *My Night at Maud's*," in Douglas Fowler, ed., *The Kingdom of Dreams in Literature and Film* (Tallahassee: Florida State University Press, 1986), p. 87; reprinted in this volume; see p. 177.

In all her scenes, Françoise is timid, withdrawn, embarrassed: when the narrator accosts her on the street (shot 153), when he offers her a ride home (shot 173), when he has to spend the night in her rooming house, especially when he returns to her bedroom to ask for matches (shot 209), when he tells her the next morning that he loves her (shot 217), when they meet Vidal by chance (shots 225 and following), when she confesses to him that she has had a lover (shots 233–235), and finally after they meet Maud at the beach (shots 250–252). Several times, she exits the frame, escaping the narrator's embrace or a threatening presence (shots 153, 217, 229, 231, 241); at others, the camera pans to follow her anxious look (shots 225, 240, 252). Her eyes are often downcast and Rohmer reinforces the feeling of her humility by photographing her from slight high angles in shots 209 and especially 250 and 252. In shot 234 the camera focuses on Françoise closely enough to require small movements to follow her agitated gestures; the instability creates a sympathetic anxiety in the viewer. At the end, almost the only extreme close-up in the film shows Françoise's hands nervously twisting her wedding band, as she listens to the narrator recount his talk with Maud.

Françoise's scenes bring the film to a rapid close, and the last two sequences contain the surprising revelation that Françoise had a lover who was none other than Maud's husband. In terms of the plot and the interpretation of the film, this information has a crucial importance, which we will consider later. For Françoise's character, it explains her awkwardness and shyness: she knew Maud because of her lover, she knew Vidal because of Maud. Whereas every corner of Clermont-Ferrand seems to offer the narrator the chance of some new providential encounter, the same corners harbor mainly risks for Françoise: that her guilty secret will be exposed, that the narrator will stop loving her when he knows who she really is.

Of the four characters, Françoise is the most tormented and perhaps the most complex. If Vidal is a doubtful Marxist, she is even more falsely represented as the icon of female perfection. That is the narrator's view of her, not her own. The first words she says, in her fleeting appearance as a member of the congregation in the opening sequence, are: "Lord, I am not worthy that you should come under my roof." How easy it is to lose them in the general murmur of the throng, how easy to equate "practicing Catholic" with "virtuous virgin." It is as easy for us as for the narrator to confuse the image with the person. Retrospectively we understand that Françoise's comings and goings in Clermont-Ferrand have more to do with her lover's being in town than with her job in a laboratory. In her case, the protagonist of the moral tale returns to the first woman, only to find that she is also the second woman.

Maud, by contrast, makes her entrance with a good deal of advance notice; Vidal has already described her as a doctor, a divorcée, a remarkable woman, very beautiful, and approachable. The long, central scene takes place in her apartment, where she is completely at home. She enters first in the center of the frame and advances confidently, smiling and facing the camera; then the same commanding

entrance is repeated when she returns from putting Marie to bed, from changing
into her middy, and from showering the next morning. Her first exchanges with
Vidal show her bantering, restraining his puppyish affection, deflating his exaggerated remark, "We haven't seen each other for an eternity," and gently mocking
the narrator as well, when she says "You look like arrested adolescents, both of
you" (shots 78 and 79). She sets the tone and directs the flow of conversation,
eventually silencing Vidal and encouraging or teasing the narrator to say more.
When she provocatively changes into the middy and gets into bed, retaining her
false eyelashes and snuggling under a white fur rug, with prints of male nude
anatomical studies on the wall just overhead, she even compares herself humorously to the Marquise de Rambouillet, the most famous of the seventeenth-century
salon hostesses, who similarly presided from her couch over the conversations of
her era's wittiest men and women. By her situation and by her manner, Maud is a
strong woman, in control.

Marion Vidal (see "Commentaries" section) suggests that the camera, too, is
captivated by Maud: "While Vidal and [the narrator] exchange repartee off-
camera, a 'fascinated' camera, complicitous with their desire, follows her movements."[21] This effect is most noticeable in the sequence after dinner, when Maud
serves coffee: while the two men are locked in a debate over Pascal, Maud enters
and draws the camera, and in five of the seven shots in the sequence she attracts or
holds the camera. Moreover, near the end of the sequence, she comes to sit facing
and almost touching the narrator, to challenge him to answer Vidal's question
about what he would do if Maud offered to sleep with him (shot 100). Maud also
gets more than her share of long close-up shots, as she first challenges the narrator,
then tells him her own story (shots 116, 122, 124, and 126).

For Marion Vidal, Maud is honest, sincere, loyal; other critics call her a free spirit.
Frank Cunningham regards her as "a strong woman mourning the lack of strong men"
and praises her "ceaseless creation of value, her spontaneous and perennial openness
to risk and social and intellectual involvement."[22] Jim Hillier thinks "perhaps the best
expression of Maud's qualities and attitude to life is her reaction to the appearance of
her daughter halfway through the evening. Maud is gentle, tolerant, loving, amused."[23]
Penelope Gilliatt, turning Pascal on his head, reckons that for the narrator the "possibility of making love to her represents a bet in which there is nothing to be lost and
maybe a kingdom to be won."[24]

Obviously, *My Night at Maud's* simply would not work if Maud were not
desirable, if most spectators did not more or less share Gilliatt's analysis, that the

21. Vidal, *Les "Contes Moraux,"* p. 102; see pp. 165–166.
22. Cunningham, "Pascal's Wager," pp. 88, 89; see p. 178.
23. Jim Hillier, "Ma Nuit chez Maud," *Movie* 18 (Winter 1970–1971): 19.
24. Penelope Gilliatt, "A Good Night" [review], in David Denby, ed., *Film 1970–71* (New York: Simon & Schuster, 1971), p. 126.

man was risking nothing and stood to gain something fabulous. To call it "a kingdom" may overstate the case, though; Rohmer's own view was that "if he'd had an affair with Maud it would have lasted a week and then it would have been over."[25] Moreover, although she is certainly no prude about sex, she has no more desire than the narrator to sleep with just anyone—witness her attitude toward Vidal. Maud is not another *collectionneuse* like Haydée in the previous film, but her motives are one of the film's mysteries. She carries out a strategy of seduction in which no tactic seems beneath her—erotic self-display, challenges, appeals to sympathy, shaming, hints of rivalry with Vidal, lies—but why?

Marion Vidal ticks off some possible reasons: Loneliness? Love? To toy with Vidal? As a challenge, to prove the atheist can overcome the believer's scruples? To get revenge on the hypothetical blonde?[26] No one can answer for sure, but it is hard to imagine an answer that does Maud much honor. If it is just loneliness, why prefer the narrator to Vidal, especially with such cruel obviousness? Can one seriously believe in a love born on such short acquaintance? And if love it be, does she not rush the courtship in a spectacularly insensitive way? And give up on it with equal haste? Is there any way to condone her flinging herself at the narrator simply to play games with poor Vidal? Or to play some other game—especially the game of undermining the narrator's moral principles? Suppose she guesses the shallowness of those principles; what makes it her responsibility to force him to an embarrassing choice?

Of all the motives, something like revenge is perhaps the most human, the most plausible, and even the most honorable. For the target is purely theoretical: the narrator has not yet spoken to Françoise. The narrator has no real person to be faithful to, and Maud has no real person with whom to get even by seducing him. It would no doubt be more accurate to think in terms of regaining self-esteem, by seducing someone symbolically like the rival; someone, that is, who shares the rival's values; someone, in fact, who could be the rival's husband; someone, ironically, who becomes the rival's husband. Maud frankly admits to hating the still unnamed Françoise and claims as a good action her success in making her husband break off the affair. During their long evening's conversation, it is mostly Maud who obsessively insists that the narrator has a pretty blonde practicing Catholic girlfriend. She invests the narrator with the qualities he needs to be a suitable means for her to even the score; but in one of the odd twists of fate that Rohmer loves, she fails in her seduction, while the imaginary qualities she gave him come true.

Maud, although she has more time on screen and tells more about herself, remains, like Françoise and Vidal, a character refracted through the narrator's vision. We see only what he sees of her. For that reason if no other, some of her

25. Petrie, "An Interview," p. 37; see p. 123.
26. Vidal, *Les "Contes Moraux,"* p. 98; see p. 164.

mystery must remain intact. Not all the comments have been favorable to her; Crisp, for example, takes the symbolism of light and dark, day and night, blonde and brunette at face value, and regards Maud as a temptress with "dark powers." Paradoxically, her naturalness is unnatural, her freedom constricting. Ultimately "Maud's world, of desire, appetite, and animality . . . comes to seem artificial, perverse, a prison ruled by mechanistic logic."[27] This may be too harsh; the narrator's last word for her is a kind one—"sympathique," that is, likable, or nice. She seems genuinely glad to see the narrator again, and appears forgiving even toward Françoise. If at moments she has been cruel to Vidal and the narrator, they both like her anyway. If her desires and even her revenge have been frustrated, she bears no grudges.

At the same time, her life has not gone well. Her first marriage ended in divorce, her second is not going smoothly. Her lover died in an accident, she and Vidal do not get along, she fails to seduce the narrator. The plot, at least, does not reward her for any of her good qualities, except to the degree that her maturity, honesty, and courage promise to see her through. She is resilient, not defeated. When she and the narrator meet on the beach, he comments that she has not changed, and, even though we know this is just a courtesy (she says the same of him), it shows that nothing dramatic has befallen her. Maud is neither a heroine nor a villain, simply a human being with the usual complexities and enigmas of human beings. She passed through the narrator's life, became part of his story, and then passed out of it again. Her life would require its own story, but *My Night at Maud's* belongs to the Catholic engineer from Michelin who lays his claim in the first word of the title: "My."

The narrator is simultaneously the most exposed and the most hidden of the characters. He is in every scene, although not always on screen, and he talks a lot about himself. His thoughts, especially about himself, constitute the core of the film; Rohmer is very clear about that. In the short-story version, the narrator says a lot to the reader, as well as reporting his conversations. In the film these first-person interventions have been reduced to two: near the beginning his voice says, "That day, Monday the 21st of December, the idea came to me, sudden, precise, definitive, that Françoise would be my wife" (shot 42). The shooting script describes this as "interior monologue," but it would be more accurately described as a retrospective summary of an interior monologue. And in the final scene, signaled by a near freeze-frame, the voice explains the narrator's sudden realization of the truth about Françoise, that she had been Maud's husband's mistress: "I was about to say: 'Nothing happened,' when, all at once, I understood that Françoise's uneasiness wasn't coming from what she was hearing about me, but from what she guessed I was hearing about her, and which I discovered at that moment, and only at that moment. . . . And I said, quite to the contrary: 'Yes, that

---

27. Crisp, *Eric Rohmer*, pp. 58, 59; see p. 174.

was my last fling!'" (shots 251–253). Rohmer explained that he wanted the spectator to know with certainty that the narrator's plan to marry Françoise was not a mere game, and that his realization of the truth came only at the end.[28] But this device relates more to the narrative technique than to the character; most of his self-revelation comes through his response to the three other characters, Vidal, Maud, and Françoise.

Rohmer has compared several of his characters, including this one, to Don Quixote: "My heroes, somewhat like Don Quixote, think of themselves as characters in a novel, but perhaps there isn't any novel."[29] They derive their world view from some fictional or philosophical abstraction, and then encounter the "real" world. As with Don Quixote, their adventures expose their self-delusion and subject them to ridicule; but at the same time they attain a certain grandeur because of their loyalty to an ideal and their effort to think through their conduct. The narrator believes in a comfortable form of Catholicism not far removed from the optimism satirized by Voltaire in *Candide* or, closer to Rohmer, by Albert Camus in "Jonah, or the Artist at Work" and *The Fall*. Whatever happens to the protagonists of these fictions, they attribute it to a benevolent providence. This naive faith justifies a profound spiritual lethargy; the characters can be passive and indifferent, trusting in the divine order to take care of them. Rohmer's protagonist has lived well, enjoying good food and fine wine, travel, a car (in an era when not everyone had one), and women. In his view, his love affairs have posed no moral problems because in each case he intended to marry the woman, although it never worked out; that, too, he regards as providential, because not working out actually worked out to everyone's advantage. Vidal claims, however, that one of his former mistresses, Marie-Hélène, entered a convent, raising the possibility of more painful outcomes, for which the narrator evades any responsibility.

At the start of the story, and throughout the evening with Maud, the narrator struggles with the challenge posed to his complacency by Pascal. He may be troubled, but he is not converted. He declares himself opposed to Pascal's conception of Christianity, its rigor, its refusal of what is good in life. He rejects the argument of the wager, because he dislikes the idea "of giving in exchange, of buying a ticket like in a lottery" (shot 94). Vidal accuses him, not without justice, of being jesuitical. To Pascal the Jesuit casuists represented the worst perversion of Christianity; their rationalizations made a mockery of morality, he argued in the *Lettres provinciales*. One example was the direction of intention, which held in effect that the end justified the means, and that a bad action was not necessarily a sin if one's intention was good. It could be applied to the narrator's love affairs, where his intention to marry authorized his fornication. As noted before, the

28. Bonitzer et al., "Nouvel Entretien," p. 55; see p. 122.
29. *Six Moral Tales*, preface, p. viii; see p. 133.

narrator's contact with Pascal seems like a spiritual diversion from his real belief, almost a parallel to the man-between-two-women plot.

Maud is a temptation of a different and more dangerous sort. Prodded by a tipsy Vidal and a flirtatious Maud, the narrator confesses that once upon a time he would have accepted a proposition like Maud's (shot 98). When it actually comes, he has no convincing reason to turn it down. He has disclaimed moral reasons (shot 96) and when Maud presses him, he finds himself defending a general choice about life, to be faithful to one's beloved, and yet he also claims not to be in love. This scene is richly comic, and depends on the same cultural assumptions that underlie Henry Fielding's description of Joseph Andrews's defense of his virtue against the predatory Lady Booby. When Rohmer's narrator tries to settle down for the night in a chair, Maud whispers "Idiot," and many a viewer would agree. It requires an actor with all the urbanity and charm of Trintignant to survive this scene without appearing a complete wimp. Maud's invitation pits his masculinity against his principles and forces him to define them.

When he admits that in the past he might have succumbed, he claims to have been converted, and, although he defends the idea of conversion by citing Pascal, it is clearly not a conversion to Pascal's puritanical Catholicism. The sermon he hears at midnight mass comes closer to his experience: "Each man and each woman is called this evening to believe that an unknown joy can invade them, for at the heart of this night is given unto us the pledge of our hope" (shot 70). The narrator is converted to a new sense of himself, generated by the vision of Françoise. If he is Don Quixote, she is his Dulcinea.

The narrator is not only a man of faith, however; he is also an engineer. He contrives to authorize his passivity by science as well as by belief in providence. The calculation of probability especially fascinates him and seems to rationalize his constant good luck. The chances of meeting an old friend, of seeing the girl on the bicycle again, of escaping temptation seem to him to depend on mathematical laws. If he could ascertain all the facts, he could write the formula for the likelihood of two people meeting by accident. Rohmer begins and ends the film with two such random encounters, the first with Vidal, the second with Maud. Both meetings illustrate the paradox the narrator proposes to Vidal: "Our ordinary paths never cross, . . . so it's in the extraordinary that our points of intersection are situated" (shot 57). Therefore it is normal for them to meet in a café neither one frequents regularly.

Such a small deviation from everyday routine can open up the hole in time, the space of adventure, where Rohmer's heroes are repeatedly tested. The narrator resists such interruptions; the pattern of his life, as he describes it, has been prudent. Amazingly, he has lived the bourgeois life even in exotic locales like Vancouver and Valparaiso. Françoise exposes the mainspring of his character: he puts his principles ahead of everything, even love. He, however, is ignorant of this side of his psyche. It appears to him that he has always been spared the need to make hard moral choices by the intervention of external forces—what the engineer would call probability, what the Christian would call providence, what others would call luck. He does not like to inject such considerations into moral debates and does not want to accept the idea that choice may entail sacrifice, pain, and loss. He denounces Pascal's wager for its element of exchange values, and one thing he dislikes about the Church is "the accounting for actions, sins, . . . or good deeds" (shot 124).

The glimpse of Françoise, however, galvanizes him to action, albeit in a way that preserves his illusion of irresponsibility. He sets out first to alter the odds; he changes his normal habits, so as to be more likely to see Françoise again. As the short-story version makes clear, that is his motive for spending time with Vidal, who is a professor and therefore has contacts among students. He frequents cafés and prowls the streets, attends the concert and midnight mass, hoping that she will be there too. It is nonetheless, in a sense, a chance occasion that gives him his first opportunity to talk to her, when she passes by while he is on his way to meet Maud to go hiking in the mountains. Again, Françoise sees through the narrator's pretense. "You don't look like somebody who likes to rely on chance," she tells him; he retorts, "On the contrary, my life is only made up of chance events," and she ends the exchange, "That's not my impression" (shot 153). At the end of *My Night at Maud's,* the narrator will have to reconsider his belief in chance, too. He has been ensnared in an unpredictable web of coincidences and accidents, which require him to choose between his principles and his love, Françoise; and he chooses Françoise, twice. In doing so, he overcomes his distaste for moral accounting at the same time: "this way we're even," he tells her (shot 235).

The choice between love and principles suggests melodrama. Françoise, no doubt thinking of her own dilemma with Maud's ex-husband, proposes a melodramatic test case to the narrator: if one of the women he loved had wanted to leave her husband and children for him, would he have married her? But that was Françoise's problem, not the narrator's. He dodges the issue by saying he was lucky and it never happened. His adventure is no life-and-death cliff-hanger, but an amusing tale of false assumptions and eventual enlightenment, in which everything ends for the best. Rohmer's story, as others have pointed out, reminds us of comedies of manners. Marivaux's title, *Le Jeu de l'amour et du hasard (The Game of Love and Chance)*, could easily be applied to *My Night at Maud's.* But this is an endless game, in which the play never stops, and the narrator is not one to stake everything on a single bet.

The Tale

A tale, or "conte," differs from a story, or "histoire," in its emphasis on the teller and the telling. A tale is less a sequence of events forming a plot than a voice narrating. Rohmer himself stressed the importance of that aspect of the films in his preface to the text of the short stories:

My intent was to film not raw, unvarnished events but rather the account of them as given by one of the characters. The story, the selection and arrangement of the facts, as well as the way they were learned, happened to relate very clearly and specifically to the person relating them, independently of any pressures I might exert on that person. One of the reasons these tales are called "moral" is that they are effectively stripped of physical action: everything takes place in the narrator's mind. The same story, told by someone else, would be quite different, or might well not have been told at all.[30]

We have just seen how the other three characters, Françoise, Maud, and even Vidal, live stories with more emotional drama than does the narrator, although if he had felt more sympathy and more involvement in his previous love affairs, he too might appear as a psychologically tormented person.

Rohmer faced a complex problem in filming first-person narratives. On the printed page, the reader never sees more than the narrator chooses to tell, and in a realistic narration the narrator may seem to remain transparent. The cinema imposes different conditions on the author: the screen must be filled with something, even if it is only the white space of snow or the black space of night. Moreover, the narrator himself has to be embodied: we will see him from the outside, with clothes, an expression, and gestures, much as Maud, Françoise, or Vidal see him; and we will hear him, with a tone, an accent, a timing, and not just a semantic content to his speeches. The camera's intervention is so continuous and so complicated that it would be virtually impossible to give a full account of it; some of the most striking elements will be cited in the next section, after the narrative method itself has been explored.

The most obvious first-person device has already been mentioned: the narrator speaks directly to the spectator on two occasions in a voiceover. In the interview with *Cahiers du cinéma,* all the discussants agreed that the effect was, unexpectedly, to make it harder for the audience to identify with the narrating character. When the narrator is engaged in conversation with other characters, he is structurally indistinguishable from them; all of them use the first person, all of them are exposed to each other's and our gaze. Only when he speaks to us as a disembodied voice do we recognize his privileged position. Then we strongly feel our distance from him. The *Cahiers* interviewers suggest that while the illusion of reality persists, we occupy the privileged position, sitting in the directorial chair, hidden by the imaginary fourth wall, controlling and creating the action. But when a character speaks from outside the diegetic space, from some place not within the range of the camera's eye, but alongside the director, then that character becomes our rival. We resist his challenge to our autonomy; far from relaxing into complete identification with the narrator, we rebel against his authority. Having recognized

---

30. Ibid., see p. 133.

this phenomenon, Rohmer kept this narrator's direct interventions to a very discreet minimum, and eliminated them altogether from the next film, *Claire's Knee:* "In my next film, there won't be any narration, or commentary, but a character present in all the scenes. Will he be taken for the 'narrator'?"[31]

The first voiceover comes very early in the film. The narrator has seen Françoise in church but lost her in the winding streets afterward. The next day he sees her again on her motorbike and honks his horn, and she turns and waves. In the short-story version, this unexpected second sighting confirms in the narrator's mind his confidence of eventual success in meeting her. It is, in other words, a providential meeting. In the story he says, "I had the impression that in that brief second I had seen her smile."[32] In the film, obviously, Marie-Christine Barrault must have an actual expression on her face, and although the photography can make it ambiguous, there is no way to ensure that the viewer will interpret it as the narrator does. At best, the filmmaker can be sure we know how the narrator interprets it, by telling us in so many words "That day, Monday the 21st of December, the idea came to me, sudden, precise, definitive, that Françoise would be my wife" (shot 42). The fact that he tells us, moreover, gives it great authority; when he talks about similar topics to Maud and Vidal, they doubt his sincerity, joke with him, and press him to change his story.

In fact, what he tells them contradicts what he has told us, and raises the possibility that we are dealing with an unreliable narrator, one who misunderstands and therefore misrepresents, or else who deliberately lies. Unreliable narration is widely used in written genres of fiction but remains a minor element in most film interpretations (despite some notable exceptions like *Rashomon*).[33] The cinema gives such a powerful impression of reality that viewers have difficulty accepting the idea that what they have seen was only a mediated version of reality, if it is called to their attention. Rohmer does not in fact exploit the possible unreliability of the narration in *My Night at Maud's;* the discrepancies between the engineer's view of himself and the impression he makes on others are displayed in full on the screen. They do not in any noticeable way affect the way the narrator delivers the story. The most important misunderstanding is his ignorance of Françoise's involvement in Maud's life. What actually makes a story of these events is his belated realization of the truth.

The first voiceover does, however, establish clearly that *My Night at Maud's* is a retrospective story. The narrator knows the outcome from the start, but is going to relive the events, letting us repeat the process of discovery he went through. The first line of the short story is, "In this story I'm not going to tell

31. Bonitzer et al., "Nouvel Entretien," p. 54; see p. 121.

32. Rohmer, *Six Moral Tales,* p. 61.

33. James Monaco says that viewers reacted angrily when Hitchcock had a character narrate a flashback, and lie, in *Stage Fright; How to Read a Film* (New York: Oxford University Press, 1981), p. 173.

everything."[34] In any story, the dénouement is likely to be concealed; this hardly
counts as unreliable narration, unless the narrator misrepresents the events along
the way. The skill of the storyteller consists largely of the ability to give all the
information necessary for the final revelation but to offer it so matter-of-factly, so
camouflaged by the context, that the reader or spectator shares the narrator's
blindness until the very last moment. Looking back from the end, we can see the
clues we missed; and the entire narrative acquires a new meaning. In the short
story, the narrator goes on to say, "Besides, there isn't any story, really: just a
series of very ordinary events, of chance happenings and coincidences of the kind
we have all experienced at one time or another in our lives. The deeper meanings
of these events will be whatever I choose to endow them with."[35]

   The most obvious clues to the truth come late in the film, in rapid succession;
this compression helps prevent the spectator from guessing the revelation too
early. In particular, three quick scenes point quite strongly to Françoise's affair
with Maud's ex-husband: first, the chance encounter with Vidal, during which she
is embarrassed; second, her own confession to the narrator that she had been in
love with a married man; and third, the unexpected meeting with Maud at the
beach, when it is revealed for the first time that the two women know one another.
Once the connection is made, we recall that Maud had described her husband's
mistress as "a girl a little bit of your type . . . very moral, very Catholic" (shot 127).
Moreover, her insistence that the narrator's ideal woman should be a pretty young
blonde seems in retrospect to be motivated by her own hurt. Françoise's presence
in Clermont-Ferrand during the Christmas holiday seems probably the result of
her lover's visit.

   The net effect of the narrator's concluding realization is an ironic reversal of his
interpretation of almost all that went before. What has seemed luck or providential
coincidence to him has been brought about by actions contrary to his principles.
Maud the predatory temptress has in fact lost two men to Françoise the innocent
girl: her husband and the narrator. The most comic irony comes from the fact that
the fidelity the narrator struggled so hard to preserve during his night with Maud
must be twice denied; it is not simply that he might as well have slept with her, his
happiness actually depends on making Françoise believe that he did. These rever-
sals remain comic, however; the narrator's very shallowness saves him. Whatever
he believed about Françoise, he does not express shock when she first confesses to
him, nor when he learns her lover's identity. The ending has been compared to the
dramatic revelation at the heart of *Les dames du Bois de Boulogne* (*Ladies of the
Park*), a film based on a story by Diderot, in which the hero discovers that he has

---

34. Rohmer, *Six Moral Tales,* p. 57.
35. Ibid. If one tells this sequence without Françoise's secret, it appears quite pointless, not unlike the
skeleton plot Rohmer used for all six of the *Moral Tales*. If the narrator penetrated the secret any
sooner, it would raise entirely different problems for him.

married a whore. But Françoise is far from being a prostitute; the narrator finds out she had a lover while he could still leave if he wanted to, but in fact he never shows any desire to do so. The situation allows him once again to transmute misfortune into good luck, by claiming to be more of a sinner than he is. The film ends with the united family, the narrator, Françoise, and their son, running happily into the water—a common symbol of cleansing and rebirth.

Narrating in Film Images

Rohmer makes it very plain that the character played by Trintignant is the narrator of *My Night at Maud's;* that is to say, the story is told as this thirtysomething Catholic engineer at Michelin would remember and reconstruct it. In film, however, a narrator's role differs from that of a narrator writing or speaking a story. First-person narrators, who write their memoirs or relate incidents from their past and tell everything from their own point of view, are commonplace in written fiction. For Rohmer, the narrator's role is more flexible, and corresponds more nearly to what literary critics would call a limited third-person narrator. The narrator is present in every scene, although not necessarily on the screen, and so only what he witnesses is shown; what the narrator sees and thinks may be shown or told directly, but similarly subjective representations of other characters' thoughts and perspectives are theoretically forbidden; the narrator may nonetheless be presented from an outside perspective, either the point of view of another character or that of a disembodied gaze, the director's. There is only one minor infraction of this technique in *My Night at Maud's:* in shot 109, we see snow falling from Vidal's perspective, before the narrator comes and looks at the same scene.

Most films do not respect this literary purity, which even in literature is only one of many narrative techniques. Having adopted the method, however, Rohmer obeys its corollaries: the author-director's presence must remain discreetly hidden behind the narrator's point of view, and the narrative must reflect the character of the narrator. In *My Night at Maud's* the narrator entertains no unusual views of anything; he interprets the world from an exceptionally rational and commonsensical ideology. His delusions are pretty much those of an average successful man, a bit self-satisfied and egotistical, but not incapable of sometimes recognizing his mistakes or of adapting to new circumstances.

As a result, both the individual shots and the editing of *My Night at Maud's* are very straightforward. In practice, this technique is easier to define by what it does not include: there are almost no unusual angles, almost no extreme close-ups, almost no disconcerting cuts from one shot to the next, almost no distracting elements in the composition of the scenes. One must compare Rohmer's direction to that of his fellow New Wave directors to appreciate how classically old-fashioned it is: for example, Alain Resnais's *Last Year at Marienbad* (1961), Louis Malle's *Zazie in the Subway* (1960), Jean-Luc Godard's *Weekend* (1967), and

François Truffaut's *Jules and Jim* (1962), with their dazzling use of jump cuts, match cuts, cross cuts, voiceovers, intense close-ups, intertitles, long tracking shots, odd angles, framing devices, split screens, and assorted fantasy sequences. Even though the point of view is the narrator's, it corresponds closely to Rohmer's own; he has said that the filmmaker's main task is to enable the real world to reveal its own coherence and meaning.

It is one mark of Rohmer's conventional shooting that at a staged event, like the Léonide Kogan concert, he simply frames the two musicians and allows them to play Mozart for two minutes; it seems almost a refutation of Godard's concert scene in *Weekend,* in which the camera circles the players in slow and attention-grabbing 360° pans. The three religious services in *My Night at Maud's* are treated with equal respect. The narrator's perspective is represented in the pans over the congregation, but the prayers and sermons are heard to a meaningful closure, and for long stretches the priest is framed within the frame, right in the center. In other words, the narrator has a long attention span, and when the narrator attends to something, the camera also gives it full attention.

Outside Maud's apartment, the narrator's point of view is generally a free-ranging and curious gaze. The film opens with his long panoramic view of the Forez mountains at dawn; twice we share the scenic look at Clermont-Ferrand from the highway, as he drives into town from Ceyrat. In town as well we ride in his car, peering out at Christmas lights, shop windows, and above all, of course, the passersby. In the church and in the concert hall, he stares around the crowd, desperately seeking Françoise, but in doing so he is only repeating the survey of the crowd that singled her out in the beginning. In the cafés and in the bookshops, he is always looking over what, or who, is available.

The tracking shots that interpret the narrator's search seem a sort of pun on his tracking Françoise. After spotting her in the church, he chases her four times in the street. On the third attempt, he makes contact; on the fourth, he draws her into his car and quickly thereafter into his life. The most menacing scene in the film occurs in the boardinghouse where she lives: having been shown his room, he goes back to hers on the pretext of needing a light. We see him slip from his room, wait in the darkened hall, creep down to her door. A tempting line of light shows around the edges; watching over his shoulder we see the dark silhouette of a head and a hand tapping. When he goes in, she is vulnerable, wary. With pulsing music, this sequence would unmistakably suggest imminent rape. Such is not the narrator's purpose, although in the short-story version he confesses that he wanted to learn how far he could go, and he is relieved to detect fear in her chilly reaction to his reappearance. The narrator's relentless tracking gaze is the counterpoint and symbolic cause of Françoise's anxiety, which has already been described.

Maud, as has also been shown, appears exactly the opposite of Françoise: centered, equal to the narrator, returning his gaze, looking and speaking straight into the camera for long periods. She succeeds even in disorienting the narrator. His confinement in her apartment blocks his sweeping look. At moments of discomfiture, he paces back and forth. As Maud reaches the most painful moment in her own story, he once again gets up and goes to the window. When he discovers that there is no spare room, he looks anxiously around, but his gaze is powerless: only Maud and her bed are there.

His forced acceptance of a share of Maud's bed concludes a long seduction scene, in which Maud patiently draws him toward her. The camerawork provides a visual accompaniment to this strange dance. In the early part of the night at Maud's, the shots are long, with numerous pans in which the camera follows one character and is then intercepted or distracted by another; meanwhile, the conversation continues partly on and partly off screen. It is a kind of exposition, as the three characters move from polite formulas to teasing banter to a serious relationship. At dinner, the narrator holds center stage, expounding his views of religion and Pascal, even sitting silent while Maud and Vidal joke off-screen. After Marie's interruption—treated, incidentally, with solemn attention by Rohmer, despite its negligible narrative contribution—Maud begins her flirtation with the men and with the camera, described earlier. She then takes full control of the action by announcing her intention of getting into bed, and doing it. Once again, the camera pans this way and that, as in the beginning, as if trying to reorient itself. Eventually Maud asks Vidal to open a window, and seizes on the pretext of the snow to invite the narrator to stay the night; Vidal, obviously aware of her purposes, promptly leaves.

At this point the narrator and Maud are alone together, but he is reluctant and awkward. She is in bed and he is in a chair nearby, but they are on opposite edges of the frame. In the next sequence he paces nervously. Although no really long shots could be taken inside the rather small space, he gets as far away as possible, and stands with his arms folded or his hands in his pockets. Maud lures him onto the bed the first time by asking for her cigarettes; increasingly, her face occupies the frame and she does the talking. For a moment the narrator seems about to succumb, as he stretches out toward her and they whisper to each other. When he backs off again, she entices him once more by asking for a glass of water, and then tells the story of her marriage and her lover in extended close-up shots. As Vidal had said, she is a woman of great beauty, scantily clad, in bed; she tells an emotional and seductive story, in a moderate close-up, aimed straight at the camera, the narrator, and the viewer. But if viewers have often fallen under her spell, the narrator in fact resists, gets up, and asks about the other bedroom, only to learn that there is none. Maud's charm has worked indirectly if not directly; the narrator has been held in thrall long enough so that he can no longer leave and has nowhere to go but into Maud's bed.

Toward the end of the long sequence at Maud's, the speeches are almost as long as the shots; but for most of the evening the shots are relatively long even though the conversation is flying rapidly from one character to the other and they themselves are moving about. Paradoxically, the continuity in the shot produces an effect of disorientation. It is as though the viewer could not quite find the thread of meaning, which may be in the words, the glances, or the movements, and thus partly off-screen. By contrast, when the narrator begins to establish his relationship with Françoise, Rohmer reverts to editing more in the classic Hollywood style, angle-reverse angle, for example in the sequence in her room. The visual message is stability, security, confidence; with Françoise, unlike with Maud, the narrator knows what he wants and feels in control.

Unobtrusive though he is, Rohmer does allow himself the two voiceovers, a rapid fade at the end of Françoise's confession, and a few rather blatant expository shots—the clock in shot 145, and the pages of the books in shots 44, 47 and 48, and 200. The most continuous sign of his presence, however, is a sort of discreet signature ending certain shots: the action ends, the narrator exits, and the camera lingers on a closed door or an empty space. It happens as he leaves his chalet for the first time (shots 3 and 4), as he gets up the next morning (shot 27), as he follows Maud out of bed (shot 138), as he drives away (shot 142), as he runs out of the café after Françoise (shot 149), as he leaves Maud's apartment the second day (shots 168 and 169), and as he and Françoise leave her room for church (shot 217). Ever so subtly, it reminds us of a directorial authority independent of the narrator, an intelligence that comprehends his actions and is not contained within his intelligence, a force that maintains order and coherence in the story.

Interpretations

The strong contrasts between Françoise and Maud and the plot placing the narrator between them have led many critics to conclude that the movie advocates the qualities Françoise apparently represents—religion, fidelity, family, caution—and of course condemns what Maud represents—nonbelief, openness, independence, risk. Such an interpretation is also suggested by Rohmer's own characterization of his plot formula: "[the hero] chooses morality rather than vice, virtue rather than vice."[36] Rohmer made this remark in 1964, however, and this opposition is not what he stressed in interviews after the release of *My Night at Maud's*. It is important to bear in mind that his definition of "moral" has to do with an intellectual attitude, not with specific rules of conduct; as he put it in 1971, "What matters is what they *think* about their behavior, rather than their behavior itself."[37] In other words, what Rohmer meant was that the hero has thought about his behavior and followed the guidelines he set for himself. As we have seen, Françoise does not make a very convincing symbol of religion, fidelity, family, and caution. Nevertheless many commentators share the judgment formulated by Crisp: "*despite appearances,* true liberty lies with Françoise rather than with

---

36. Crisp, *Eric Rohmer,* p. 33.
37. Petrie, "An Interview," p. 39; see p. 125.

Maud; *despite appearances,* to give way to animality is perverse rather than natural. In a sense, these paradoxes echo another and older paradox: only by sacrificing yourself can you attain the Kingdom of Heaven, only by losing your life can you hope to gain life."[38] For example, Peter Sourian claims that *My Night at Maud's* "comes down on the side of a belief"[39] and Martin Tucker that it "romanticizes *la vie bourgeoise.*"[40]

One sign that Rohmer's message is by no means clear is that several critics have drawn a directly opposite conclusion. In their view, the narrator's initial choice of Françoise, when she was still only an image of the ideal woman, was ridiculous to begin with, and its folly is borne out by her eventual confession. Her scandalous past does nothing to raise her to Maud's level of human dignity and authenticity, however, since she remains guilt-ridden and self-denying, like the narrator. In the end, their happy marriage depends on sustaining the lie of the narrator's last fling with Maud. Perhaps the most outspoken proponent of this interpretation is Frank Cunningham, who reads the final scene as follows: "Hand in hand, holding their child, they run from the prying camera's eye into the sea, secure in their illusions, their conventional marriage, their need not to be honest with one another, far from the moral struggle and ambiguity faced daily by Maud. Their institutional Christianity is sterile when compared to Maud's ceaseless creation of value."[41] But many others also find the narrator's marriage flawed, such as Marion Vidal, who describes it as "founded on lies and secrecy . . . a union that apparently can survive only thanks to the illusions and the climate of duplicity maintained by the couple."[42]

Rather than look for such a clear-cut message, it is no doubt preferable to take Rohmer's theoretical statements more seriously, and accept his image of himself as opening a window onto the real world. To be sure, he has an interpretation of reality, which he has described succinctly to the *Cahiers* interviewers: "Not only is there a beauty, an order in the world, but there is no beauty, no order, except in the world."[43]

Yet it is the mark of Rohmer's artistry to trust the real world. He says that his characters are free—a paradoxical claim often made by authors, to which he has given some substance by letting the actors collaborate in creating the characters. More to the point, he feels no compulsion to make the world seem more beautiful or more orderly than it is, by making his heroes role models and his villains monsters, or by making the ending always turn out well. Tragic endings are

38. Crisp, *Eric Rohmer,* p. 59; see p. 174.
39. Peter Sourian, "Eric Rohmer: Starring Blaise Pascal," *Transatlantic Review* 48 (Winter 1973–1974): 141.
40. Martin Tucker, Review, *Commonweal* 92 (May 1970): 170; reprinted in this volume; see p. 151.
41. Cunningham, "Pascal's Wager," p. 89; see p. 178.
42. Vidal, *Les "Contes Moraux,"* p. 106; see p. 166.
43. Bonitzer et al., "Nouvel Entretien," p. 52; see p. 119.

unknown in Rohmer's work but melancholy is pervasive. Petrie asked him, "Would you agree that the endings of your films tend to be rather sad?" and his reply can serve as the best statement about his purpose as a filmmaker:

> They are not what one is expecting to happen, they are to some extent *against* the person concerned. What happens is against the wishes of the character, it's a kind of disillusionment, a conflict—not exactly a failure on his part but a disillusionment. The character has made a mistake; he realizes he has created an illusion for himself. He had created a kind of world for himself, with himself at the center, and it all seemed perfectly logical that he should be the ruler or the god of this world. Everything seemed very simple and all my characters are a bit obsessed with logic. They have a system and principles, and they build up a world that can be explained by this system. And then the conclusion of the film demolishes their system and their illusions collapse. It's not exactly happy, but that's what the films are all about.[44]

One may say, then, that Rohmer's message is an appeal to question one's beliefs, to resist the tendency to self-delusion. In this regard he follows Pascal, who analyzed the human soul and found it irresistibly drawn to self-deception: "Man then is only disguise, falsehood, and hypocrisy in himself and towards others. He does not want to be told the truth; he avoids telling it to others; and all these tendencies, so far removed from right and reason, are naturally rooted in his heart."[45]

But Rohmer did not follow Pascal into pessimism, despair, and renunciation of the world; he also admired other more worldly moral philosophers, including some of the great thinkers of the Enlightenment, such as Diderot and Rousseau. In *My Night at Maud's* the narrator responds to disillusionment with an affirmation of the possibility for human happiness; it is a modest lesson, but one repeated throughout Rohmer's career.

---

44. Petrie, "An Interview," p. 41; see pp. 127–128.
45. Pascal, *Pensées,* p. 79.

Eric Rohmer:
A Biographical
Sketch

Eric Rohmer is an internationally renowned director. He has been writing film criticism since the 1940s, making films since the 1950s, and reaching a wide audience since the late 1960s. He has often been interviewed by cinema journals and by the popular press. His ideas on the cinema, his works, and the major events in his career are well known. His personal life, however, has been sheltered from the public eye. One sign of his wish for privacy is that he has masked his identity behind a pen name since his early days as a critic; his real name is Jean-Marie Maurice Schérer. Even his associates are kept at a distance; Aurora Cornu, the Romanian novelist who appears as herself in *Claire's Knee*, claimed in 1971 to be the only one who had ever been to his home.[1] Melton Davis, the same reporter who talked to Cornu, quotes Rohmer himself as saying, "I prefer not to talk about other things than my films."[2] When reporters have asked about his private affairs anyway, he has mischievously given different answers to different interviewers, and has, for example, deliberately maintained a certain confusion about his birth and early years.[3]

He was probably born in Nancy in 1920, and it seems certain at least that the Schérer family[4] was Catholic and that Rohmer has never abandoned his childhood

1. Melton S. Davis, "Boy Talks with Girl, Boy Argues with Girl, Boy Says . . .," *New York Times Magazine,* November 21, 1971, p. 92.
2. Ibid., p. 38.
3. April 4, 1920—C. G. Crisp, *Eric Rohmer: Realist and Moralist* (Bloomington and Indianapolis: Indiana University Press, 1988), p. 14; December 1, 1920, in Nancy—Davis, "Boy Talks with Girl," p. 38; December 1, 1920, or April 14, 1923—*Current Biography;* March 21, 1920, in Tulle—Joël Magny, *Eric Rohmer* (Paris, Rivages, 1986), p. 9, and *Who's Who in France,* 1990; April 4, 1923, in Nancy—Graham Petrie, "Eric Rohmer: An Interview," *Film Quarterly* 24, no. 4 (Summer 1971): 34.
4. According to *Current Biography,* his parents' names were Lucien Schérer and Mathilde Bucher; according to *Who's Who in France,* they were Désiré Schérer and Jeanne Monzat.

faith. He earned a degree in history, and, during the difficult years of the German occupation and the immediate postwar period, he taught history, geography, and literature in Parisian high schools.[5] In 1946 he published a novel, *Elisabeth, ou les vacances* (*Elisabeth, or the Holidays*), signed with yet another pseudonym, Gilbert Cordier. The name Eric Rohmer first appeared on an article he wrote in 1950 for a short-lived periodical, *Gazette du Cinéma;* when C. G. Crisp asked him in 1974 about his reasons for adopting it, "he simply plunged his head in his hands and groaned 'personal reasons,'"[6] although various explanations have been offered, some emanating from Rohmer himself.[7]

A reporter learned from one of Rohmer's colleagues that he was married to a woman named Thérèse[8] and had two young sons, but was warned, "He's a fanatic about his privacy. . . . Don't ask him personal questions. He'll just make up what he thinks you want to hear."[9] Aurora Cornu confirmed the information about Rohmer's family in 1971, adding that the sons were then ten and twelve, healthy and mischievous.[10] Only where the cinema is concerned has he been more open about his early experiences. Compared to many of his colleagues and contemporaries, he discovered movies rather late, as a student. Although initially he "despised the cinema,"[11] Marcel Carné's *Quai des brumes* (*Port of Shadows,* 1938) first revealed to him the potential of the medium, and he then came to appreciate other classic films like René Clair's *A nous la liberté* (*Liberty for Us* or *Give Us Liberty,* 1931), and G. W. Pabst's *Dreigroschenoper* (*The Threepenny Opera,* 1931).[12] He went regularly to the Cinémathèque and developed an enthusiasm for silent films. It was after the war, however, that American films fully converted him to the art of the cinema.

Paris in the late 1940s was full of film clubs, several of which Rohmer joined and helped run. Two especially marked his career, the Ciné-Club du Quartier Latin and Objectif 49. Through his association with these clubs, Rohmer came into

5. Eric Rohmer, *The Taste for Beauty* (Cambridge: Cambridge University Press, 1989), p. 4.
6. Crisp, *Eric Rohmer,* pp. 15–16.
7. "It was a name I chose just like that, for no particular reason, only because I liked it"; Davis, "Boy Talks with Girl," p. 38. He used the false name to conceal his moviemaking from his aged mother, who was living in the provinces and thought that her son was still teaching, in a lowly job in a second-rate lycée; Michel Mardore, Review, "Rohmer: l'anti-Vadim," *Le Nouvel Observateur* 242 (June 30–July 6, 1969): 40; similarly, Pierre Billard, "Sous le signe de Pascal," *L'Express* (June 9–15, 1969): 52. Rohmer wanted to distance himself from a brother who was active in militant leftist and gay movements; Magny, *Eric Rohmer,* p. 9.
8. *Who's Who in France* gives her full name as Thérèse Barbet and the date of the marriage as August 22, 1957.
9. Paul Gardner, "My Night with Rohmer," *New York Magazine* (November 8, 1976): 66; the information was obtained in 1966 or 1967.
10. Davis, "Boy Talks with Girl," p. 92.
11. Petrie, "An Interview," p. 34.
12. Crisp, *Eric Rohmer,* p. 14.

contact with some of the most influential older critics, notably Jean-Georges Auriol, who was editing *Revue du Cinéma,* and André Bazin, who would soon found *Cahiers du Cinéma.* He also met and joined a remarkable group of younger men, who would form the nucleus of the New Wave about ten years later: François Truffaut, Claude Chabrol, Jean-Luc Godard, Jacques Rivette. Rohmer was in fact almost ten years older than the others, and in many respects his style and ideas belong to a tradition older than theirs.

In 1948, however, they were united in their enthusiasm for American directors like Alfred Hitchcock, Howard Hawks, and George Cukor, and in their contempt for the French "cinéma de qualité" of directors like Claude Autant-Lara and René Clément. They already aspired to make films themselves in a new style, but, lacking the financial means, they made their professional debuts as critics. Rohmer began his career with an article entitled "Cinéma, art de l'espace (Cinema, the Art of Space)," which appeared in *Revue du Cinéma* in June 1948 and argued for greater emphasis on *mise en scène,* or composition of the image, as opposed to montage, or editing. In the years that followed, he contributed to *Les Temps Modernes, Combat,* and *Opéra.* When *Revue du Cinéma* ceased publication, Rohmer himself founded *Gazette du Cinéma,* which lasted only five issues, from May to December 1950. In 1951 *Cahiers du Cinéma* began publication, under Bazin's guidance; throughout the decade it would be the house organ for the emerging New Wave directors. No doubt the most memorable article it published was Truffaut's "Une certaine tendance du cinéma français (A Certain Tendency of the French Cinema)" (1954), a devastating attack on the traditional style of filmmaking in France. Rohmer contributed regularly, including a series of five articles in 1955 collectively titled "Le Celluloïd et le marbre (Celluloid and Marble)," which compare the cinema to other art forms and constitute a broad statement of Rohmer's ideas on the cinema as an art. In 1957 Chabrol and Rohmer coauthored a major book on Hitchcock. After Bazin's untimely death in 1958, Rohmer himself assumed the coeditorship of *Cahiers,* which he held until 1963, when demands for an increasingly political emphasis led to a change in the journal's editorial structure and Rohmer was eased out.

Rohmer was associated with the Bazin/*Cahiers*/New Wave circle from the very beginning, and, as one of the older members of the group, he figured as something of a leader. Moreover, he started trying to direct his own films very early, in 1950. Ironically, however, he was one of the last to achieve success and recognition with the general public. His first effort was *Journal d'un scélérat (Journal of a Rascal),* a brief 16mm film undertaken in 1950, apparently never completed and now lost. The next year, he made *Présentation,* with Jean-Luc Godard in the cast and supplying a good part of the funding; in 1961 this little film was given dubbed dialogue by Anna Karina and Stéphane Audran, retitled *Charlotte et son steak (Charlotte and Her Steak),* and combined with three other shorts by Rohmer and Godard under the collective title *Charlotte et Véronique.* In 1952, *Les Petites Filles modèles (Model Girls)* was left uncompleted because of lack of funds. In

1954, he acted in and directed a fifteen-minute version of a tale by Edgar Allan Poe, *Bérénice,* with Rivette as the photographer; it was never released. In 1956 Godard produced a longer work, *La Sonate à Kreutzer (The Kreutzer Sonata),* based on a Tolstoy story, which Rohmer again acted in and directed, but never edited. The following year Rohmer wrote and Godard directed a twenty-one-minute film, *Tous les garçons s'appellent Patrick (All the Boys Are Called Patrick),* which was the first of the *Charlotte et Véronique* series. Rohmer's next work was *Véronique et son cancre (Véronique and Her Dunce,* 1958), again produced by Godard; but Godard's *Charlotte et son Jules* differed so completely from Rohmer's approach that the collaboration went no further. Finally in 1959, with Chabrol as producer, Rohmer made a feature-length film, *Le Signe du lion (The Sign of Leo);* but it found no distributor until 1962, when it flopped and disappeared after a short run.

Thus 1959, the *annus mirabilis* of the French New Wave cinema—when Godard's *Breathless,* Truffaut's *The 400 Blows,* and Alain Resnais's *Hiroshima, mon amour* all opened and dazzled an international public—came and went with Rohmer still in the background. Chabrol had also achieved success with *Le beau Serge (Bitter Reunion)* in 1958, as had Louis Malle with *Les Amants (The Lovers).* By 1962 these directors had all made at least one more successful feature, and Agnès Varda joined their ranks with *Cléo de 5 à 7 (Cléo from 5 to 7)* in 1961. Despite differences that became more pronounced as time passed, in the beginning these filmmakers seemed to share several principles. They emphasized the director's personal contribution, location shooting, self-conscious structure, nonnarrative editing, and spontaneity. Unlike the Hollywood style of editing, which sought to be as unobtrusive as possible and to make the story as easy to follow as possible, New Wave style intruded frequently, reminding the spectator of the artificiality of the medium. New Wave films often quoted other films, partly as a tribute, partly to stress the fact that films were part of an artistic discourse. New Wave directors often sought to communicate something other than a story; gaps, loose ends, discontinuities, and unexplained lapses abound.

Already by 1962, however, some of the early idealism and optimism had faded, and the New Wave revolution seemed to be waning. Until he quit to become coeditor of *Cahiers,* Rohmer had continued to derive his principal income from teaching. After the failure of *The Sign of Leo,* his chances of obtaining government subsidies for other films were diminished. Therefore, when he left the staff of *Cahiers* in 1963, he took a part-time job with the educational television section of the ORTF, the state broadcasting network, and made a substantial number of documentary and educational films for television in the 1960s.

Rohmer's departure from the *Cahiers* editorial board signaled an increasing difference of artistic opinion from his former colleagues and collaborators. It was at about this time that the idea for *Six Moral Tales* came to him: "I had the idea of putting on the screen six moral tales. Instead of going along with the tide (crime, sex, violence), I wanted to keep my freedom as an author—I am an author before

I am a director—by proposing variations on a theme: a man looking for one woman meets another who does not resemble in the least the first one. . . . The idea came to me independently but I had plots for all six before I started making the first."[13] As an outsider, however, he faced exceptional problems: "I decided to go on filming no matter what, and instead of looking for a subject that might be attractive to the public or a producer, I decided that I would find a subject that *I* liked and that a producer would refuse. So here you have someone doing exactly what he wants to. And as you can't do this on 35mm, I made the films on 16mm. That way it didn't cost very much, just the price of the film stock. I found people willing to work for me out of friendship, either as technicians or as actors."[14] The first two moral tales were *La Boulangère de Monceau* (*The Baker's Girl from Monceau,* 1962), a twenty-six-minute film, and *La Carrière de Suzanne* (*Suzanne's Career,* 1963), which lasted fifty-two minutes; except for a festival showing in 1974, neither has been released and Rohmer regards them as too amateurish to merit regular distribution.[15] Because the narrative versions of all six moral tales were published in 1974, however, the stories are well known. One of the cast members of the first was a young German, Barbet Schroeder; he founded a production company called Les Films du Losange soon afterward, and it has produced or co-produced all of Rohmer's films since then.

My Night at Maud's was supposed to be the third of the tales, but the actor Jean-Louis Trintignant, whom Rohmer wanted for the lead, was unavailable when filming should have begun, so Rohmer did the fourth tale, *La Collectionneuse* (*The Collector,* 1967) instead. Filmed on a borrowed shoestring and set on the Riviera, it focuses on a week in the life an amoral gamine named Haydée, who collects men; it proved to be an unexpected critical success, winning a Silver Bear award at the Berlin Film Festival. Even so, Rohmer had difficulty finding money to film *My Night at Maud's;* according to Melton Davis, Truffaut twisted the arms of other directors at the Cannes Film Festival to get them to chip in, so that filming could begin on Christmas Eve 1968. As always, and only partly because of the tight budget, Rohmer shot only one take of each scene, and had the film ready for presentation at the Cannes Festival in May 1969; it fared poorly at the festival, but delighted Paris audiences a few weeks later, and met with similar unexpectedly warm receptions in London and New York. Two successes in a row, *The Collector* and *My Night at Maud's,* finally brought Rohmer recognition as a major director.

Since 1969 he has turned out a steady stream of successful films. *Le Genou de Claire* (*Claire's Knee,* 1970) and *L'Amour l'après-midi* (*Chloe in the Afternoon,* 1972) completed the six moral tales. Next he did two adaptations from literary

13. Davis, "Boy Talks with Girl," p. 86.
14. Petrie, "An Interview," p. 36.
15. Ibid., p. 37.

works, *La Marquise d'O. . .* (*The Marquise of O. . .,* 1975), from a novella by Heinrich von Kleist, and *Perceval le gallois* (*Perceval,* 1979), from a medieval romance by Chrétien de Troyes. Despite his growing reputation he continued many of his habitual practices, such as using little-known and even amateur actors and actresses, and keeping production costs to a bare minimum. Since he has also remained faithful to his conservative religious, moral, and esthetic beliefs, he has usually been regarded as an austere director, in the tradition of Ingmar Bergman, whose works Rohmer greatly admired in the late 1950s.

In 1981 Rohmer began a new series of films, *Comedies and Proverbs,* with *La Femme de l'aviateur, ou on ne saurait penser à rien* (*The Aviator's Wife*). *Le Beau Mariage* (*A Good Marriage*) followed in 1982, as did *Pauline à la plage* (*Pauline at the Beach*) in 1983, *Les Nuits de la pleine lune* (*Full Moon in Paris*) in 1984, *Le Rayon vert* (*Summer*) in 1986, and finally *L'Ami de mon amie* (*Boyfriends and Girlfriends*) in 1987. Like "contes moraux," "comédies et proverbes" suggests an archaic genre, popular in the eighteenth century. Rohmer has not claimed the same sort of repeated structure for the second series as for the first; rather, he says only that the comedies and proverbs have more open endings. In many respects they resemble the moral tales: there is still little or no crime, sex, or violence; the characters belong to a comfortable middle-class world of professionals, intellectuals, and students; their problems relate primarily to reconciling their principles and their desires, especially in affairs of the heart; the events of their stories take place in their minds rather than in the outside world; and, although they typically conclude with a certain melancholy and sense of disenchantment, no tragic or dramatic consequences ensue and the characters give an impression of perpetual resiliency. The same year he completed the final film in the series, he also directed a film composed of short vignettes, *Quatre Aventures de Reinette et Mirabelle* (*Four Adventures of Reinette and Mirabelle,* 1987). In 1990 he began a new series, *Tales of the Seasons,* with the release of *Conte de printemps* (*A Tale of Spring*), followed in 1992 by *Conte d'hiver* (*A Winter's Tale*), which is his last film as of this writing.

My Night at Maud's

My Night at Maud's

The continuity script was prepared from the text published in *L'Avant-Scène* in December 1969 and then corrected by reference to the print of the film at the Museum of Modern Art in New York and a video release. There appear to be no significant differences.

As with any film containing so much dialogue, the subtitles miss a great deal, although the general level of accuracy is acceptable. In the original release, the subtitles were in white letters, which were sometimes difficult to read against light backgrounds. The video release has yellow subtitles, which are much more readable, but their synchronization with the speeches is so poor that the written text is often matched to the wrong speaker.

Camera distance is represented by the following conventional abbreviations:

E L S   extreme long shot (landscape or other large space; human figures are subordinate to the total field)

L S   long shot (ranging from the totality of a unified room-sized decor to the whole human figure)

M S   medium shot (human figure from the knees or waist up)

M C U   medium close-up (head and shoulders)

C U   close-up (the whole of a face, other part of the body, or object)

E C U   extreme close-up (section of the face, other part of the body or object)

P O V   point of view

Credits

Director
Eric Rohmer

Producers
Barbet Schroeder and Pierre Cottrell
  for Les Films du Losange

Production Companies
FFP, Les Films du Carrosse, Les
  Films des Deux Mondes, Les Films
  de la Pléiade, Les Productions de la
  Gueville, Renn Productions, Simar
  Films

Screenplay
Eric Rohmer

Director of Photography
Nestor Almendros

Assistant Cameramen
Emmanuel Machuel, Philippe
  Rousselot

Assistant Directors
Alfred de Graaff, Pierre Grimberg

Chief Electrician
Jean-Claude Gasché

Sound
Jean-Pierre Ruh

Sound Mixing
Jacques Maumont

Sound Assistant
Alain Sempé

Art Direction
Nicole Rachline

Editor
Cécile Decugis

Assistant Editor
Christine Lecouvette

Process
Black and white; 1:1.33

Length
110 minutes

Release Date
May 16, 1969 (France, at the Cannes
  Film Festival); June 13, 1969
  (Paris); September 23, 1969 (New
  York Film Festival); March 22,
  1970 (New York)

Cast

**Narrator (also called "I" and
Jean-Louis)**
Jean-Louis Trintignant

Maud
Françoise Fabian

Françoise
Marie-Christine Barrault

Vidal
Antoine Vitez

Concert Violinist
Léonide Kogan

Blond Woman
Anne Dubot

Priest
Father Guy Léger

Factory Mechanics
Themselves

Marie, Maud's daughter
Marie Becker

The Continuity Script

The Countryside at Ceyrat, in the suburbs of Clermont-Ferrand,[1] early dawn, mid-December

1. ELS: *the winter sun rising on the Forez mountains.[2] The next two shots reveal that this is the POV of the narrator from the balcony of his chalet.*
2. *Reverse low-angle LS: the narrator, a man about thirty-five years old, wearing an overcoat, is leaning on the railing of the balcony of his chalet and contemplating the landscape we have just seen.*

The Chalet, interior, day

3. MLS: *a room, facing the window; on the balcony outside, the narrator is leaning on the railing and admiring the sunrise; then he stands up, turns and enters the room, closes and latches the door behind him, and crosses and exits the frame to the right.*

The Chalet, exterior, day

4. MLS: *the door of the chalet. Close by, an automobile is parked. The narrator comes out, slams the door behind him, gets into the car, starts off, and exits the frame to the right.*
5. LS: *the highway in a forward tracking shot. The car is moving rather fast in spite of many turns.*
6. LS: *the roadside in a tracking shot through the side window. Below in the distance one can see the city.*
7. LS: *as in 6. The Gothic spires of the cathedral are visible.[3]*

A Street, exterior, day

8. MLS: *the white car, which parks in a street near the church of Notre Dame du Port.[4] The narrator gets out of the car and walks alongside the church while buttoning his overcoat. He exits the frame as the camera tilts upward to frame the bell tower. The bells ring.*

The Church, interior, day

9. ELS: *the church interior, the narrator in the foreground, standing near a pillar, his back to the camera. The priest is officiating at the altar in the background, facing the congregation.*

    PRIEST: For us all, finally, we implore thy goodness. Grant that, with the Virgin Mary, the Blessed Mother of God, the Apostles and Saints of all times, who have lived in thy fellowship, we may share in the life everlasting and that we sing thy praise, through Jesus Christ, thy beloved son.

10. ELS: *the choir, with romanesque stained glass windows and pillars. The priest, behind the altar, raises his arms toward heaven.*

    PRIEST: Through him, with him and in him, to thee God the Father Almighty, in the unity of the Holy Spirit, all honor and all glory for ever and ever.

THE CONGREGATION (*partly off*): Amen!
The priest genuflects before the ciborium, which he has placed on the altar.
PRIEST: Let us pray.

11. MCU: *the narrator, standing, reading his missal. In the background, in soft focus, a man is praying.*

    PRIEST (*off*): Prompted by the precepts of salvation, and instructed by the divine command, we make bold to say, Our Father, who art in heaven, hallowed be thy name . . .
    The narrator closes his missal, raises his eyes and recites, with the priest and the other worshipers, the Lord's Prayer.
    PRIEST (*off*), THE CONGREGATION (*off*), NARRATOR: . . . thy kingdom come, thy will be done, on earth as it is in heaven. Give us this day our daily bread . . .

12. MS: *a blond woman (Françoise) in profile and others in the congregation in soft focus, POV of the narrator. They are reciting the Lord's Prayer.*

    PRIEST and CONGREGATION: Forgive us our trespasses, as we forgive those who trespass against us, and lead us not into temptation, but deliver us from evil.

13. MCU: *as in 11. The narrator glances left toward the blond woman.*

    PRIEST (*off*): Deliver us, O Lord, from every evil past, present, and to come.

14. MS: *as in 12. Feeling someone staring at her, the woman glances in the direction of the narrator.*

    PRIEST and CONGREGATION: And by the intercession of the blessed and glorious ever-virgin Mary, Mother of God, of the blessed apostles Peter and Paul, of Andrew and of all the saints, grant us peace in our days.

15. MCU: *as in 13. The narrator, who has opened his missal again, is looking left toward the woman, then glances down at the missal, then looks up toward the priest.*

16. MS: *the priest behind the altar; he continues to officiate and prepares the communion.*

    PRIEST: That by your compassionate aid we may be free of sin and sheltered from all turmoil. Through Jesus Christ, who lives and reigns with You in the unity of the Holy Spirit, for He is God, for ever and ever . . .
    CONGREGATION (*off*): Amen!
    The priest takes the Host and breaks it.
    PRIEST: May the peace of the Lord be always with you . . .
    CONGREGATION (*off*): . . . and with your spirit.

17. MS: *the congregation in profile.*

    PRIEST (*off*): Lamb of God . . . (*with the congregation*) . . . who takes away the sins of the world, have mercy on us (*repeated twice*). Lamb of God, who takes away the sins of the world, grant us your peace.

Pan among the worshipers, from a short dark woman to the blonde to a bearded man.

PRIEST (*off*): This is the Lamb of God who takes away the sins of the world.

18. MS: *as in 16. The priest, about to take communion; first he kisses the chalice.*

19. CU: *as in 14. Profile of the blond woman, praying aloud with the worshipers around her.*

   CONGREGATION and WOMAN: Lord, I am not worthy that you should come under my roof; say but the word and my soul shall be healed (*repeated three times*).

   The woman again glances toward the narrator and then turns away.

   Port Street, exterior, day

20. LS: *people leaving mass, coming up stairs from the churchyard and passing through an open ironwork gate in the foreground; in the background, the doors of the church. In the crowd, the narrator follows the woman at a distance.*

21. LS: *the woman crossing the street and exiting the frame to the right. The narrator walks toward us on the sidewalk, glancing occasionally toward the woman. He turns a corner onto another street to the left, while in the background the woman gets on her motorbike and starts off.*

22. L S :   *the narrator, who quickly gets into his car and starts off, as the woman rides by on her motorbike from left to right on the cross street ahead of him. He turns right, following her.*
23. *Forward tracking* L S , P O V *of the narrator through the windshield as he drives the car; the woman makes a left turn and he follows, getting closer. Track continues through narrow streets.*
24. *Forward tracking* L S :   *as in 23, but with the narrator's hands and the steering wheel now in the frame. The woman passes a car that is wait- ing to enter a gate on the left, but the narrator cannot pass; he gets im- patient, and blows his horn. The car finally pulls out of the way and he starts up again promptly. His head now enters the frame as he looks from right to left driving into and across a square; but the woman has disappeared.*
   The Chalet, interior, dusk
25. M C U :   *the narrator sitting at his worktable, a pencil in his hand, a teapot and cup set in front of him, as well as folders and books. He seems ab- sorbed in thought. He takes a drink of tea, and looks at the book again.*
26. E C U :   *a page of the book, a mathematics book on the calculus of probabilities.*
27. *Screen dark. The sound of an alarm clock.* M C U :   *the narrator, in bed, who has waked up and turned on the bedside lamp. He then turns off the alarm clock and turns on the radio. Station identification for France-Inter[5]*

*and the voice of an announcer giving the time: 6:30 A.M. The narrator, in
pajamas, gets up and exits the frame to the right.*

A Street, exterior, early morning

28. LS: *cars arriving in a parking area, still in darkness.*
29. LS: *the entrance to the Michelin factory.*[6] The employees hurry toward
    the doors of the brightly lit plant.

The Michelin Factory Cafeteria, interior, midday

30. MS: *the narrator, from behind at a three-quarter angle, eating lunch at a
    table with three of his colleagues. In the background in soft focus one sees
    other employees eating.*
31. MCU: *the narrator and the second colleague, sitting side by side, eating
    and listening to the first colleague.*

    FIRST COLLEAGUE (*off*): I got to the curve, toward the bridge, . . .
    where the speed limit is forty miles an hour because of the curve. We
    were doing a hundred going into the curve, . . . we took it with a double
    zigzag, . . . I don't know how . . . anyway we made it.

    SECOND COLLEAGUE: See what you're up against? By the way, where
    do you live?
32. CU: *the first colleague.*

    FIRST COLLEAGUE: In the Chanturgue hills.[7] Well, say the Clermont
    hills, . . . and I was lucky enough to find a place to build myself a little
    house. . . . (*He eats.*)

    SECOND COLLEAGUE (*off*): In the vineyards?[8]
33. CU: *the second colleague.*

    FIRST COLLEAGUE (*off*): In the vineyards, above Chanturgue. And, . . .
    whereabouts do you live?

    SECOND COLLEAGUE: We're almost neighbors, since I live on the
    south slope, . . . no, northwest, . . . I'm sorry, of the Chanturgue hills.
    Well, it's not a villa, obviously, but at least we're lucky enough to have
    some peace, because up until now, we were living in town; it was un-
    bearable.

    The second colleague turns toward the narrator.

    SECOND COLLEAGUE: And you. . . .
34. CU: *the narrator.*

    SECOND COLLEAGUE (*continues off*): . . . where do you live?
    NARRATOR: I live in Ceyrat.
35. CU: *the second colleague.*

    SECOND COLLEAGUE (*smiling*): Ceyrat? Don't you find that's a bit too
    far?
36. CU: *the third colleague.*

    NARRATOR (*off*): No, it's not far.
    THIRD COLLEAGUE: It's nice, Ceyrat.
    FIRST COLLEAGUE (*off*): You risk having a lot of icy roads.

37. C U :   *the narrator.*

NARRATOR: No, up to now, I haven't had any since I've been there. But it's not mine. I'm staying at a colleague's place while he's away.

A Street, exterior, evening

38. L S :   *people leaving the factory at 6:00 P.M.*

39. L S :   *as in 38. Among the crowd coming out, one can see the narrator.*

40. *Forward tracking* L S :   *another street at night,* P O V *of the narrator at the steering wheel, going slowly. Through the windshield, one can make out the many lanterns decorating the streets for the holiday season.*

41. *Forward tracking* L S :   *as in 40.*

42. *Forward tracking* L S :   *as in 41, another street, slight angle to the right toward shops and passersby.*

NARRATOR (*interior monologue*): That day, Monday the 21st of December, the idea came to me, sudden, precise, definitive, that Françoise would be my wife.

Suddenly, a woman—the blonde—on a motorbike pulls alongside and passes the narrator's car, entering the frame from the right. Slight pan to follow her. The narrator honks his horn. She turns around, smiles . . . then pulls away, getting lost in the traffic ahead, while the narrator has to stop.

Outside a Bookstore, exterior, evening

43. L S :   *the narrator entering the bookstore. A woman customer comes out. The narrator is visible through the glass doors, looking at book displays.*

The Bookstore, interior, evening

44. *High-angle* C U :   *several works displayed on a table. One can make out two titles clearly:* Modern Course on the Calculus of Probabilities *and* Mathematics, Probabilities, and Statistics. *The narrator's hand leafs through the second work.*

Outside Another Bookstore, exterior, evening

45. L S :   *the Central Paperback Bookstore from across the street. The narrator goes into the shop.*

The Bookstore, interior, evening

46. L S :   *the narrator passing among the bookshelves (off, sounds of a busy shop and voices of the clerks). He looks distractedly at the titles, then takes up a volume and pages through it.*

47. E C U :   *the book he is reading:* Pascal. Les Pensées. Texte établi et annoté par Jacques Chevalier. Préface de Jean Guitton. (Pascal. Thoughts. Text edited and annotated by Jacques Chevalier. Preface by Jean Guitton.)[9]

48. E C U :   *a page of the book: "commencé: c'est en faisant tout comme s'ils croyaient, en prenant de l'eau bénite, en faisant dire des messes, etc. Naturellement, même cela vous fera croire et vous abêtira.   —Mais c'est ce que je crains.   —Et pourquoi? Qu'avez-vous à perdre? Mais pour vous montrer que cela y mène, c'est que cela diminue les passions qui sont vos grands obstacles." ([Follow the way by which they] began: that is by*

*making believe that they believed, by taking holy water, by hearing mass,
etc. This will quite naturally bring you to believe, and will calm you, . . .
will stupefy you.* — *But that is just what I fear.* — *Pray why? What
have you to lose? But to show you that this is the way, this is what will less-
en your passions, which are your great stumbling block.)*[10]

An Office in the Factory, interior, day

49. M C U : *the narrator in discussion with two colleagues, in an office, near a
large window through which one can see a gray and dull factory courtyard.*

    T H I R D C O L L E A G U E : Are you staying here for Christmas?

    N A R R A T O R : Yes, definitely. I was supposed to go to my family's, but
    that will be for New Year's Day.

    T H I R D C O L L E A G U E : Come skiing with me, they're forecasting snow.

    N A R R A T O R : There's never snow at Christmas!

    T H I R D C O L L E A G U E : Oh, yes, yes. I have friends who've just been
    skiing.

50. C U : *the narrator.*

    N A R R A T O R : No, I was joking. (*Laughing.*) I've just come from British
    Canada.

    T H E P R O T E S T A N T (*off*): Ah yes, in Protestant countries, Christmas Day
    is very important, . . . people don't even go out of the house. They don't
    even know whether it's snowing or not!

    N A R R A T O R : You're Protestant?

    T H E P R O T E S T A N T (*off*): Yes, . . . and you?

    N A R R A T O R : I'm Catholic. My family was Catholic, and I've stayed
    Catholic.

A Street, exterior, night

51. L S : *the brightly lit window of a downtown café: The Suffren.*[11] *Seen from
behind, the narrator crosses the street and goes inside the café.*

The Café, interior, night

52. M S : *the café interior, looking toward the door. Pan following the narrator
as he enters and bumps into a girl with books in her arms, accompanied
by a somewhat older man, on their way out. Reframe as* M C U : *the
threesome in the café, the girl between the two men. The narrator excuses
himself with a gesture to the student and looks astonished at the man with
her.*

    N A R R A T O R : What, Vidal, . . . you're in Clermont?

    V I D A L : Well, yes, . . . and you?

    N A R R A T O R : Let's get together one of these days.

    V I D A L : Fine, . . . right now, if you like. Will you excuse me?

    The girl, having understood, smiles and shakes Vidal's hand.

    T H E S T U D E N T : Okay, . . . good-bye, sir, and happy holiday.

    V I D A L : Good-bye, happy holiday.

Vidal smiles at her. She exits the frame to the left, while the two men go to the right toward a staircase. Pan following them as they go up, their backs toward us.

NARRATOR: You're a professor at the university?

The Upper Floor of the Café, interior, night

53.   MS: *the two friends emerging from the stairs and heading for a table, while taking off their coats, which they put on an empty chair, apologizing to people nearby.*

VIDAL: Instructor in philosophy. And you, what are you doing?

NARRATOR: I've been at Michelin since October. I've just come back from South America.

They have moved closer to the camera; the shot continues as a MCU: *the narrator sitting down, then Vidal, ending with an over-the-shoulder two-shot of the narrator.*

VIDAL: That makes almost three months already. It's funny we haven't run into each other before.

NARRATOR: Well, you know, I live in Ceyrat and at night I go straight home. Sometimes I go to a restaurant, but I prefer to cook. Abroad I used to see too many people. I want to be alone for a while.

54.   *Reverse-angle* MCU   *of Vidal, smiling but very attentive.*

VIDAL: I can leave! . . .

NARRATOR (*off*): No, no, I mean, I don't want to try to meet new people.

VIDAL: Oh, . . . people here, they're neither better nor worse than elsewhere.

NARRATOR (*off*): But I'm delighted to meet by chance . . .

VIDAL (*cutting him off*): You're not married?

NARRATOR (*off*): No. You?

VIDAL: Oh no. Well, no, I'm in no hurry. However, in the provinces, the bachelor life is not a great deal of fun. (*A pause.*) What are you doing this evening?

NARRATOR (*off*): Nothing. Let's have dinner together.

VIDAL: I'm going to the Léonide Kogan concert.[12] Come along, I have a seat.

55. *Reverse-angle* MCU: *the narrator.*

VIDAL (*off*): I was supposed to go with someone who isn't free.

NARRATOR: No, I'm not at all in the mood to listen to music tonight.

VIDAL (*off*): The cream of Clermont society will be there. Lots of good-looking girls.

NARRATOR: Your students?

VIDAL (*off*): There are very pretty girls in Clermont. Unfortunately, one doesn't see much of them. I'm sure you're going to wreak havoc.

NARRATOR: I've never wreaked any havoc. (*He laughs.*) All right, I'll go, just to prove you're wrong.

The waiter's arm appears in the frame, carrying a tray. The narrator turns and looks up.

NARRATOR: A Vittel.[13]

VIDAL (*off*): An orangeade.

The waiter clears the table and leaves. A series of reverse-angle shots follows.

NARRATOR: You come here often?

VIDAL (*off*): Just about never, and you?

NARRATOR: This is the first time I ever set foot here.

56. *As in 54,* CU: *Vidal.*

VIDAL: And it is precisely here that we ran into each other. It's strange.

57. *As in 55,* CU: *the narrator.*

NARRATOR: No, on the contrary, it's completely normal. Our ordinary paths never cross, . . . so it's in the extraordinary that our points of inter-section are situated. Inevitably! (*Smiling.*) At the moment I do mathe-matics endlessly. It would amuse me to calculate the chances we had of meeting, say, in less than two months.

VIDAL (*off*): You think it's possible?

NARRATOR: It's a question of data and data processing. Of course the data must exist. The probability that I have of meeting a person about whom I know neither the home address nor the place of work is obviously impossible to determine. Are you interested in mathematics?

VIDAL (*off*): A philosopher has more and more need to know mathematics.

58. *As in 56,* CU: *Vidal.*

VIDAL (*continues*): For example, in linguistics, . . . but for the simplest things, the arithmetical triangle of Pascal[14] is tied to the whole story of the wager.[15] And in fact that's what makes Pascal prodigiously modern.

59. *As in 57,* CU: *the narrator.*

VIDAL (*continues, off*): The mathematician and the metaphysician are but one person.

NARRATOR (*interested*): Ah, . . . well, Pascal.

VIDAL (*off*): That surprises you?

NARRATOR: It's funny. I'm right in the middle of rereading him at the moment.

The waiter's arm appears, places drinks on the table, and leaves again.

VIDAL (*off*): Well, then?

NARRATOR: I'm very disappointed.

VIDAL (*off*): Go on, tell me, that interests me.

NARRATOR: Well, I don't know, first, I have the impression of knowing it almost by heart, and then it has nothing to say to me. (*A pause.*) And then I find it rather empty. To the degree that I am Catholic, or at least I try to be, it doesn't go at all in the direction of my present Catholicism. It's precisely because I am Christian that I object to this rigidity. Or else if this is Christianity, then I'm an atheist. (*A pause.*) Are you still a Marxist?

The narrator smiles.

60. *As in 58,* CU: *Vidal, who returns the smile.*

VIDAL: Particularly for a communist, the text on the wager is extremely current.

Vidal leans forward on his elbows on the table.

VIDAL: At bottom, I myself doubt profoundly that history has a meaning. However, I wager on the meaning of history, and I find myself in the Pascalian situation. Hypothesis A: life in society and all political action are totally devoid of meaning. Hypothesis B: history has a meaning. I am not absolutely sure that hypothesis B has more likelihood of being true than hypothesis A. I'll even say it has less. Let's concede that hypothesis B has only ten chances in a hundred and hypothesis A ninety in a hundred. Nevertheless, I can't not wager on hypothesis B, because it is the only one, . . . the one, I mean, that history has a meaning, . . . because it is the only one that allows me to live. Let's suppose that I wagered on hypothesis A and that hypothesis B proves true, despite its only 10 percent chance, . . . then I have absolutely wasted my life, therefore I *must* choose hypothesis B because it is the only one that justifies my life and my action.

61. *As in 59,* CU: *the narrator listening with great attention.*

VIDAL (*off*): Naturally, there are ninety chances in a hundred that I am wrong, but that doesn't matter.

NARRATOR: That's what's called mathematical expectation. That is to say, the product of the gain times the probability. In the case of your hypothesis B, the probability may be low, but the gain is infinite, since it is for you the meaning of your life, and for Pascal eternal salvation.

62. *As in 60,* CU: *Vidal.*

VIDAL: It was Gorky, or Lenin, or Mayakovsky,[16] I've forgotten who, who used to say, about the Russian Revolution, about the seizure of power, that the situation was such at that moment that it was necessary to choose the one chance in a thousand, because hope, in choosing this one chance in a thousand, was infinitely greater than in not choosing it.

A Street, exterior, night

63. LS *of the brightly lit façade of the Municipal Theater,*[17] where the concert is taking place. In the foreground, the crowd going in, cars passing.

The Theater, interior, night

64. MS: *the theater audience from the* POV *of the stage. In one row of the orchestra an usher, with programs in her hands, shows Vidal and the narrator to their places. Vidal gives her a tip. The two friends sit down facing us in the crowded hall. The narrator looks to the left, to the right, and upward.*

65. *Low-angle* LS: *the crowded balconies; pan around the theater, then tilt upward. Reframe on the domed ceiling of the hall; the chandelier is alight.*

66. *Low-angle* LS: *as in 65. The chandelier goes out as applause is heard.*

67. MS: *the stage, a violinist (Léonide Kogan) standing before a music stand, near a pianist seated at a piano. The frame remains fixed throughout the duration of the music (Mozart's Sonata for Violin and Piano, K. 358).*

Restaurant, interior, night

68. MS: *the narrator and Vidal, sitting side by side in a brasserie, eating. Behind them a large mirror reflects the rather spacious room with few other customers.*

VIDAL: We can get together tomorrow.

NARRATOR: It's the 24th. I'm going to midnight mass, but if you want to come with me....

VIDAL: Why not? ... To tell the truth, I ought to go to a party at a friend's place, but it's not certain she will be there. She has family problems.

NARRATOR: You know, I just said it on the spur of the moment.

VIDAL: But yes, I want to. In any case, if I go, I won't be there before midnight, she has to go get her daughter. She's divorced. But if you want, we can go there together afterward.

The Church, interior, night

69. *High-angle* ELS: *the inside of the jam-packed cathedral, during the sermon.*

   PRIEST: The joy that I wish you on the feast of Christmas, . . . the joy that I ask for you during this mass . . .

70. ELS: *the priest in the background, Vidal and the narrator, from behind, sitting near a pillar in the foreground.*

   PRIEST (*continues*): . . . that we celebrate together, is a profound and new joy. Not a joy of childhood memories and habits, of Christian customs piously maintained, but a living joy, a joy of today.

   Pan across the worshipers present, POV *of the narrator in search of a face.*

   PRIEST (*continues off*): This birth, at which we rejoice, is not above all the birth of the infant Jesus, it is our own. Something must be born in each of us this night. Each man and each woman is called this evening to believe that an unknown joy can invade them, for at the heart of this night is given unto us the pledge of our hope.

   Pan back to Vidal and the narrator.

71. LS: *the congregation, standing,* POV *of the narrator; the canticle, "The Entire Earth," is being sung.*

72. MS: *Vidal and the narrator at another moment of the mass, communion. They are seen from behind, standing by the pillar. The narrator's gaze follows the worshipers who go to the holy table and return. Pan across the congregation.*

A Bar, interior, night

73. *Slightly low-angle* MS: *the narrator, sitting on a barstool. Vidal comes back from the telephone and sits down.*

   VIDAL: No, . . . tonight, it's not possible, her ex-husband is passing through Clermont. They had some money questions to settle. (*Shrugging his shoulders.*) It seems that's exhausted her. She's going to bed. But come tomorrow. . . .

74. MCU: *the narrator.*

   NARRATOR: No, I don't know her.

   VIDAL (*off*): You'll get acquainted. She's a remarkable woman. You'll see. One of the few really great girls. You'll be delighted to know her, . . . and she will be, too.

   NARRATOR: Don't go too far.

75. MCU: *Vidal, a glass in his hand, leaning on the bar.*

   VIDAL: You know, she leads rather a quiet life since her divorce. She doesn't feel at ease in her milieu. She is a doctor, specializing in pediatrics. Her husband is also a doctor. He was a professor here, at the medical school. I knew him very slightly. He's at Montpellier University[18] now. (*He drinks.*) She's a woman . . . of great beauty.

   NARRATOR (*off*): Marry her!

VIDAL: No. (*Pause.*) If I say no, it's because the problem has been raised and resolved. We don't get along well together on . . . everyday matters. Which doesn't stop us from being the best friends in the world. You see, if I told you to come, it's because I know very well what we would do if you didn't come. . . . We'd make love.

NARRATOR (*off*): Then I'm not coming.

VIDAL: Yes, . . . yes, you are. We would make love casually, . . . out of boredom. That's not a good solution for either of us, for her or for me. Besides, you know me, I'm very puritanical.

76. MCU: *the narrator, smiling.*

NARRATOR: More than I am?

VIDAL (*off*): Oh, so much more!

Maud's Living Room, interior, night

77. MCU: *Vidal and the narrator, from behind, in the entryway. A maid takes their coats. Then they go into the living room. On the right, a table is already set for dinner.*

78. MS: *the two men in the room; in the background, center, a door, through which Maud enters and goes toward Vidal on the right. Slight pan following her.*

MAUD: Hello.

Vidal embraces her and kisses her on the neck. Reframe the two embracing, so that the narrator is out of the frame to the left.

MAUD: Ah! . . . Such affection! . . . You seem to be in good form.

VIDAL: We haven't seen each other for an eternity.

MAUD: Oh! . . . right, . . . for a week. (*Turning away and speaking to the narrator, still off.*) Sit down.

Pan and reframe as a MLS of all three: Maud sits on a sofa bed covered with a white fur blanket, Vidal in an armchair, the narrator in another armchair facing Maud.

MAUD: So, the way it is, you hadn't seen each other for fifteen years.

NARRATOR: Right, . . . well, let's say fourteen.

MAUD: And you recognized each other right away?

VIDAL: Without hesitation. (*To the narrator.*) You haven't changed at all.

79. MS: *Vidal.*

NARRATOR (*off*): You either.

MAUD (*off*): You look like arrested adolescents, both of you.

VIDAL: Is that to be taken as a criticism or a compliment?

80. MS: *Maud, sitting on the bed.*

MAUD: Neither, it's just an observation.

NARRATOR (*off*): And yet we've had very different lives.

VIDAL (*off*): He's had many adventures.

MAUD: Oh! . . . Tell me about them.

Pan to frame the narrator, in profile.

NARRATOR: No! . . . No, I mean I lived abroad for a long time.

MAUD (*off*): In the bush?

NARRATOR: No, no, . . . in cities, as bourgeois as can be: Vancouver in Canada, and Valparaiso.[19]

81. MCU: *Maud.*

MAUD: Even Valparaiso!

NARRATOR (*off*): Yes, . . . well, at least in my milieu, the people I was with were bourgeois, . . . as one might be in Lyons or Marseilles.[20]

VIDAL (*off*): Or here?

Maud leans forward and picks up a packet of Marlboros, while still talking.

MAUD: Wherever you go, you're condemned to the provinces. . . . Anyway, condemned. . . . Me, personally, I prefer to live in the provinces.

VIDAL (*off*): And you want to leave Clermont?

MAUD (*lighting a cigarette*): Not the city, but the people. I've had enough of seeing the same faces.

Pan to frame Vidal in CU; *he leans toward her.*

VIDAL: Even me?

MAUD (*off*): You know, I've thought it over: I'm leaving. (*Pause.*) If you love me, follow me.

Pan following Vidal, who jumps onto the sofa bed. Reframe as a MLS *of the two of them, tussling playfully with each other.*

VIDAL: And what if I did?

MAUD: I'd be very annoyed.

Vidal grabs Maud and holds her close to him.

MAUD (*pretending outrage*): Oh! . . . what a way for a professor to be-have, . . . and a university professor to boot.

Vidal goes back to sit on the chair and exits the frame; the camera remains on Maud.

VIDAL (*off*): Okay, let's be serious. Did you have a good Christmas?

MAUD: Excellent. Marie was in paradise. She's my daughter. (*She has turned toward the narrator, also off.*) She's eight. She's buried in presents. (*Once again to Vidal.*) And you, what did you do?

82. MCU: *Vidal, sitting.*

VIDAL: I went to midnight mass.

MAUD (*off*): I'm not surprised. You'll end up being a priest.

Vidal points toward the narrator, still off.

VIDAL: He's the one who dragged me there.

83. MCU: *the narrator.*

NARRATOR: Well, not exactly.

VIDAL (*off*): Anyway, I wanted to go with you.

MAUD (*off*): You're Catholic?

NARRATOR: Yes.

MAUD (*off*): But . . . a practicing Catholic?

NARRATOR: Well, yes.

VIDAL (*off*): You wouldn't know to look at him.

MAUD (*off*): Yes, you would; I see you very well as a boy scout.

NARRATOR: I was never a boy scout.

VIDAL (*off*): Whereas I was a choirboy.

84. MS: *Maud, sitting; in the foreground, three-quarter angle shot of the narrator's back.*

MAUD (*to Vidal*): I told you, you'll be a priest. Well, my friends, I think you both stink strangely of holy water. Would you like a drink?

Pan following her as she gets up.

NARRATOR: No, thanks.

MAUD: Really, no?

NARRATOR: No, thanks, really.

MAUD (*to Vidal*): And you?

VIDAL (*off*): A little Scotch. . . .

Pan following Maud to the liquor cabinet; the movement brings Vidal into the frame.

MAUD: Me, not only am I not baptized. . . .

VIDAL: You know she belongs to one of the greatest families of freethinkers in central France. But you see, Maud, irreligion the way it was practiced in your family was still a religion.

Pan following Maud, who has filled a glass and comes toward Vidal.

MAUD: I know very well, but I have the right to prefer that religion to the others. If my parents were Catholics, maybe I would have done like you, . . . I wouldn't be one any more.

Maud sits on the arm of Vidal's chair and holds out the glass of whiskey she poured for him.

VIDAL: Thanks.

MAUD: Whereas I, at least, remain faithful.

VIDAL: One can always be faithful to nothing.

MAUD: It's not nothing, but it's a different way of looking at problems. With many principles, furthermore, . . . even very strict ones a lot of the time, but no preconceptions come into it, . . . no trace of. . . .

VIDAL: Okay, we've heard the sales pitch before.

MAUD: Don't be crude, it doesn't become you.

VIDAL: Girls like you would make me a papist. I don't like people without problems.

MAUD: Because you're not normal. You should get psychoanalyzed.

VIDAL (*laughing*): Idiot!

MAUD: Besides, I have problems. But real problems.

85. MCU: *Maud, sitting at the table, and the narrator in profile, sitting near her. They are eating. Maud pours the narrator some wine.*

V I D A L (*off*): Anyway, I understand very well how one can be an atheist, . . . I am myself, but there is something fascinating in Christianity that's impossible not to recognize, and that's its contradictions.

M A U D : Oh, you know, I'm very impervious to dialectics. . . .

V I D A L : That's what makes the strength of somebody like Pascal. You've at least read Pascal?

Pan to the right, reframe on Vidal and Maud.

M A U D : Yes, "Man is a thinking reed," . . . "the two infinites" . . . uh, I dunno.

V I D A L : Cleopatra's nose.[21]

M A U D : He's certainly not one of my favorite authors.

V I D A L : Okay, . . . I'll be alone against the two of you.

M A U D (*reacting and looking toward the narrator*): Why haven't you read Pascal? . . . (*A pause with no response; she turns back to Vidal.*) You see?

N A R R A T O R (*off*): Yes, I have.

V I D A L : He hates Pascal, because Pascal is his bad conscience, . . . because Pascal takes aim at him, the false Christian.

M A U D : Is that true?

V I D A L : He's jesuitical hairsplitting incarnate.[22]

M A U D : Let him defend himself.

86. M C U : *the narrator.*

N A R R A T O R : No, . . . I said that I didn't like Pascal, because Pascal has a very . . . particular conception of Christianity. Which, moreover, was condemned by the Church.

V I D A L (*off*): Pascal was not condemned, . . . at least not the *Pensées.*

N A R R A T O R : But Jansenism was![23] And then, Pascal is not a saint.

M A U D (*off*): Well answered.

V I D A L (*off*): Then, . . . okay . . . watch out. I won't talk about the man.

M A U D (*off*): Stop talking. . . . You're all we hear around here. You're a crashing bore.

The narrator eats and listens, very attentive, ready to speak. A silent pause.

M A U D (*off*): So, you were saying?

N A R R A T O R : Nothing. No, . . . I think there is another way of conceiving Christianity. As a scientist, I have an immense respect for Pascal. But as a scientist, it shocks me that he condemns science.

V I D A L (*off*): He doesn't condemn it.

N A R R A T O R : At the end of his life, he does.

V I D A L (*off*): It's not exactly a condemnation.

N A R R A T O R : No, I'm expressing myself badly. Let's take an example. . . . Okay . . . for example, at this moment we are eating and we . . . we, while talking we forget what we are eating. We forget this excellent

Chanturgue wine. This is the first time I ever drank any of it. (*He shows the bottle.*)

VIDAL (*off*): It's only drunk by old families of Clermont.

MAUD (*off*): Look, if you don't mind. . . .

VIDAL (*off*): Old Catholic and Masonic[24] families.

MAUD (*off*): Really, do shut up.

NARRATOR: This excellent Chanturgue, Pascal no doubt drank some, since he was from Clermont. What I reproach him for, is not for having deprived himself of it. I'm rather for depriving oneself, for Lent. (*He laughs and drinks. Laughter off.*) I'm against the suppression of Lent. No, it's that when he drank it, he didn't notice it. Since he was sick, he had to follow a diet and could only eat good things. But he never remembered what he had eaten.

VIDAL (*off*): Right, it's his sister Gilberte who tells that story, he never said, "This is good."[25]

NARRATOR: Well, I say, "This is good."

MAUD (*off*): Bravo!

NARRATOR: Not to recognize what is good, that's an evil. Speaking as a Christian, I say it is an evil.

MAUD (*off*): Yes, . . . yes, that's right.

VIDAL (*off*): Really, however, your argument is a little thin.

NARRATOR: Ah! . . . not thin at all, it's very . . . very important. And there's something else, also, that profoundly shocked me in Pascal. He says that marriage . . .

87. *As in 85,* MCU: *Maud and Vidal, very attentive.*

NARRATOR (*off*): . . . is the lowest state of Christendom.

MAUD: Yes, I find marriage is a very low state . . . but no, . . . it's not for the same reasons.

VIDAL: Yes, but Pascal is right. Maybe you want to get married, me too, but that doesn't prevent marriage from being lower than priesthood in the order of sacraments.

NARRATOR (*off*): It happens I was thinking about that sentence the other day when I was at mass. There was a girl in front of me.

VIDAL: That makes me think I should go to mass to look for girls.

MAUD: They are surely not as dowdy as the ones at the Communist Party meetings.

VIDAL: Your vocabulary betrays your nature, little daughter of the bourgeoisie! . . .

With one finger, Vidal strokes Maud's face.

MAUD: Little daughter of the bourgeoisie! . . . Exactly. . . . (*To the narrator, off-camera.*) So? . . . That pretty girl?

88. *As in 86,* CU: *the narrator.*

NARRATOR: I didn't say she was pretty. She was, though. (*He smiles.*) Anyway, enough. (*He laughs.*) No, and then, I shouldn't say "a girl," . . . a woman, . . . a young woman, with her husband.

VIDAL (*off, interrupting*): Or her lover.

MAUD (*off, annoyed*): Stop it!

NARRATOR: They had wedding rings.

MAUD (*off*): Unhuh, you took a close look.

NARRATOR: Well, it's a . . . a difficult impression to communicate.

VIDAL (*off*): Yeah! . . .

89. *As in 87,* MCU: *Maud and Vidal laughing; he is making a pair of binoculars with his hands.*

NARRATOR (*off*): No, I'm going to stop, you're making fun of me.

MAUD (*sincere*): No, we're not, not at all.

VIDAL: In any case, I think it's a very, very, very good thing to be obsessed by the idea of marriage. It's entirely right for your age . . . that is, for our age. That Christian couple was sublime.

NARRATOR (*off*): Yes.

VIDAL: That's what you mean: religion adds a lot to women.

NARRATOR (*off*): Yes, it's true, and I don't see what's wrong with that: . . .

90. MS: *the room, toward the living room side. It is empty. At this moment, the door at the rear opens halfway, pushed by Maud's daughter, Marie, eight years old.*

NARRATOR (*continuing, off*): . . . religion adds to love, but love in turn adds to religion.

MAUD (*off, to Marie*): Hey, what are you doing in here?

Marie, in her nightgown, stays in the doorway, shy.

MAUD (*off*): Come on, come on in.

Marie moves forward.

91. MS: *the table where the three adults are still eating. Marie goes toward her mother.*

MAUD: This is Marie.

The narrator rises and shakes the little girl's hand.

MARIE: Sir.

VIDAL (*from his seat*): Hello, Marie.

MARIE: Hello.

Marie goes to her mother and puts her arms around her neck. The narrator sits down again.

MAUD: What do you want?

MARIE (*in a whisper*): I would like you to show me the Christmas tree lights.

MAUD (*surprised*): Now?

Marie nods "yes." Maud kisses her and gets up with a little sigh.

MAUD: Okay!

She exits the frame to the right, while Vidal holds out his arms to Marie, who goes toward him.

VIDAL (*to Marie*): Give me a kiss?

He kisses her. Pan to frame, behind them, Maud crouching to turn on the flashing lights of the fir tree.

MAUD: Do you see? . . . Isn't it beautiful? (*Pause.*) Okay, that's enough. (*She turns it off and gets up.*) Is that what you wanted?

Marie nods "yes." Maud leads her daughter away.

MAUD: Okay, . . . Let's go, off to bed now. Come on, darling. Good night, everybody!

Maud and Marie exit the frame to the left.

VIDAL: Good night, Marie.

92. MS: *Vidal, who has gotten up and is at the bookcase, looking at the titles.*

VIDAL: There must be a Pascal here. Even in a Freemason's house.

Vidal crouches, while the narrator's legs appear on the left.

VIDAL: What were you saying? Is there . . . a precise reference . . . to mathematics . . . (*he leafs through a book.*) in the text on the wager? (*He reads.*) "Wherever there is infinity, and not an infinity of chances of loss against the chance of gain, there can be no hesitation, you must stake all. . . . (*He gets up, and keeps on reading; the narrator is seen from behind at a three-quarter angle, facing him.*) And thus, when you are forced to play, you must renounce reason in order to keep life, etc."[26]

Vidal gives the narrator the book.

NARRATOR: It's precisely that, mathematical expectation. In Pascal's case, it's always infinite. Unless the probability of salvation is zero, since infinity multiplied by zero equals zero. Therefore the argument is worthless for someone who is an absolute nonbeliever.

The narrator puts the book down.

VIDAL: But if you believe, no matter how little, it becomes infinite again.

93. LS: *the two men in the room; the narrator crosses to the left away from Vidal.*

VIDAL: Then you must wager.

NARRATOR: Yes, if I believe that there is probability, if I believe in addition that the gain is infinite.

They both walk around in the room. In the background, the maid is clearing the table.

VIDAL: Is that what you believe? . . . And yet, you don't wager, you don't risk anything, you don't give up anything.

Vidal sits in an armchair.

NARRATOR: Oh yes, there are things I give up.

VIDAL (*ironic*): Not the Chanturgue.

The narrator smiles and goes to sit in an armchair facing Vidal.

94. MS: *the narrator, sitting.*

NARRATOR: But the Chanturgue isn't at stake.

VIDAL (*off*): Yes it is.

NARRATOR: Why give it up? In the name of what? No, what I don't like in the wager is the idea of giving in exchange, of buying a ticket like in a lottery.

VIDAL (*off*): Let's say of choosing, you've got to choose between the finite and the infinite.

NARRATOR: When I choose the Chanturgue, I don't choose it over God, . . . that's not what the choice is.

VIDAL (*off*): And girls?

Pan toward the door, through which Maud enters and goes toward the table, while listening to the conversation. Reframe as a MCU of Maud.

NARRATOR (*off*): Girls, maybe, but not women, . . . at least not where I'm concerned.

VIDAL (*off*): Do you chase girls?

NARRATOR (*off*): No.

VIDAL (*off*): You used to chase them.

NARRATOR (*off*): No I didn't!

VIDAL (*off, speaking to Maud, who approaches him*): You know, when I knew him, he was a remarkable skirt-chaser. A specialist.

NARRATOR (*off*): You knew me when I was ten years old.

Pan following Maud, who passes near Vidal and goes to pick up a pack of cigarettes from the table behind him, where the maid is still clearing.

95. MS: *Vidal; Maud approaches and stands behind his chair.*

VIDAL: I mean rather when I lost track of you. After you left school.

NARRATOR (*off*): You're talking nonsense!

VIDAL: Nonsense? . . . What about Marie-Hélène?

NARRATOR (*off*): What a memory! I have no idea what has become of her.

Still standing by Vidal, Maud lights a cigarette. In the background, the maid finishes clearing.

VIDAL: She went into a convent.

NARRATOR (*off*): No!

MAUD: Who is this Marie-Hélène?

NARRATOR (*off*): She was a girlfriend of mine.

VIDAL: His mistress, to be more accurate.

Maud moves from behind the chair and exits the frame.

MAUD (*off*): Is that so?

NARRATOR (*off*): I don't deny having had "mistresses," to use his terminology.

Pan and reframe as a MS of Maud and Vidal, as before, the maid in the background.

MAUD: Ah! . . . then there were several of them?

NARRATOR (*off*): I'm not going to tell you my life story. He's not my confessor. I'm thirty-four, I've known a lot of girls. I don't claim to offer myself as a model, not at all, not at all. . . . And then besides, that doesn't prove anything.

Maud goes into the kitchen, exiting the frame to the right.

96. MCU: *the narrator, sitting.*

VIDAL (*off*): I don't want to prove anything, my friend.

NARRATOR (*slight zoom in*): Oh yes, I know: I shock you. I've had affairs with girls I loved and that I was thinking about marrying, but I have never slept with a girl just for the hell of it. . . . If I haven't done it, it's not for moral reasons, it's because I just don't see the point of it.

VIDAL (*off*): Yes, . . . but let's suppose you found yourself on a trip with a gorgeous girl you knew you would never see again. . . . There are circumstances in which it is hard to resist.

NARRATOR: Fate, I don't want to say God, has always spared me that kind of circumstance. I have never had any luck with flings. In fact, incredibly bad luck.

97. MCU: *Vidal, sitting.*

VIDAL: Well I, who never have any luck in general, I've had lots of luck with those sorts of things. Once in Italy with a Swedish girl, another time in Poland with an English girl. . . .

Pan to frame Maud, who brings in coffee on a tray; then pan following her.

VIDAL (*off*): Those two nights are perhaps the most beautiful memories that life has left me with. I am very much for shipboard romances, love affairs on convention trips.

Maud puts the tray down on a low table, near Vidal, and leaves again; pan following her briefly.

VIDAL (*off*): There, at least, you don't have the sticky, bourgeois side.

98. MS: *the two men sitting face to face, Vidal from behind.*

NARRATOR: In principle, I'm against them. But nevertheless, to the degree that it's never happened to me. . . .

VIDAL: But it could happen to you.

NARRATOR: No.

VIDAL: Come on, be serious. . . . If it happens to you, if I understand you correctly, you'll go along with it!

Maud returns with the coffeepot in her hand. While the narrator talks, she pours the coffee into the cups.

NARRATOR: No! . . . I was talking about how it used to be. You're crazy, . . . you make me think about things that have completely gone out of my mind. Maybe I have chased girls, but what's past is past.

Maud holds out a cup and the sugar bowl to the narrator.

NARRATOR: Thanks.

VIDAL: But if tomorrow, if tonight, a woman as beautiful as Maud . . .

Maud holds out a cup and the sugar bowl to Vidal.

VIDAL: . . . Thanks . . . and as full of spirit, proposed to you, . . . or at least made you feel. . . .

MAUD: Stop! . . . You're not funny.

VIDAL: But let me finish. . . . If Maud, for example. . . .

NARRATOR: He's completely drunk! . . . It's the Chanturgue, don't you think?

Pan following Maud, who goes and sits on the sofa facing the narrator, her knees almost touching his and looking intently into his eyes.

MAUD: Go ahead and answer.

Long look between them.

NARRATOR (*after a hesitation*): Let's say that once upon a time, . . . yes. Now, no.

VIDAL (*off*): Why?

NARRATOR: I told you. I have converted.

99. MCU: *Vidal, sitting.*

VIDAL: Oh! . . .

NARRATOR (*off*): Ah, conversion, . . . it happens. Look at Pascal.[27]

A silence. The camera stays on Vidal, who drinks his coffee, then speaks.

VIDAL: Maybe I'm indiscreet, but I flatter myself that I have quite a bit of intuition. This conversion seems to me very, very, very, very fishy.

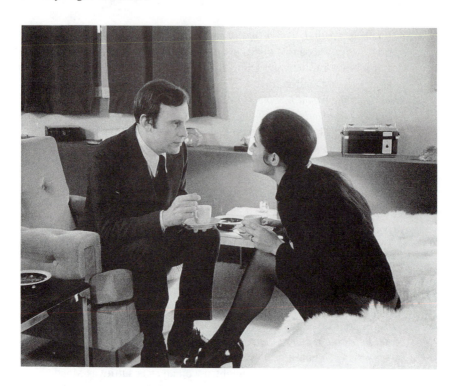

(*To Maud.*) I thought there was something strange about his behavior. He has moments when his mind wanders, when he
daydreams. . . .

100. MCU: *the narrator, in the foreground, and Maud, sitting face to face, she
on the sofa bed, he in an armchair.*
      VIDAL (*off*): . . . As if he were thinking about somebody. Not some thing,
      some body. If he were in love, I wouldn't be surprised.
      Maud smiles at the narrator, who never stops looking at her.
      NARRATOR: News to me!
      MAUD: Is she blond or brunette?
      VIDAL (*off*): I think he likes them blond.
      MAUD: Tell us, . . . C'mon! . . . That doesn't commit you to anything.
      NARRATOR: No, I tell you.
      *The narrator leans back, against the back of the armchair, and moves out
      of the frame. The camera stays on Maud, as she puts her coffee cup on the
      little table near her and draws back on the sofa.*
      MAUD: Tell us. In exchange, I'll tell you my life story.
      VIDAL (*off*): That could take a long time!
      MAUD: We'll have several sessions.

NARRATOR (*off*): I don't know anybody, I don't love anybody, period, end of story.

MAUD: Is she in Clermont?

NARRATOR (*off*): No.

VIDAL (*off*): He said no. If she's not here, she must exist somewhere.

NARRATOR (*off*): No, I said no, she doesn't exist. And furthermore even if she existed, I have the right not to tell you anything about her.

MAUD (*looking toward Vidal*): We're being mean, you know?

NARRATOR (*off*): No, ... no, it amuses me, ... in fact, it amuses me a lot more than you think.

101. MS: *Vidal, who gets up and goes to the liquor cabinet.*

MAUD (*off*): Stop drinking. I don't want to drive you home.

Vidal pours himself a glass of cognac.

VIDAL: Anyway, you wouldn't drive me home, he would. (*He drinks.*)

102. MS: *Maud on the sofa bed.*

MAUD: My friends, I'm going to make you a proposition. Since I've been feeling rather tired recently, the doctor told me to stay in bed as much as possible.

VIDAL (*off*): The doctor ... is that you?

She arranges the cushions on the sofa.

MAUD: Obviously. (*She makes a gesture in their direction, to keep them from leaving.*) Ah! ... I'm not throwing you out. Stay, ... yes, stay, I want you to, ... I order you to. I'm not at all sleepy, ... and I adore having people around my bed.

VIDAL (*off*): And in it?

She shrugs her shoulders.

MAUD (*to Vidal*): In any case, not you. (*To both of them.*) You'll see, we'll be very comfortable, like in the days of the salons of the Precious Ladies.[28] That's why I sleep here. I can't stand bedrooms!

Pan following her as she stands, and goes toward the bathroom; as she passes by the narrator, the camera stops and reframes him in a MCU, then pans following him as he starts to stand up and goes toward Vidal, who enters the frame from the right.

NARRATOR: In any case, I'm leaving. I'm sleepy.

Reframe the two men standing, in MCU. Vidal still has his glass in his hand. The narrator is holding a pack of Gitanes cigarettes.[29]

VIDAL: Don't do this to me.

NARRATOR: Let's leave, ... what the hell. She wants to sleep.

VIDAL: That's what you say! ... It's just part of her little act! (*He drinks.*) You'll see; I think she's up to something.

The narrator lights a cigarette.

NARRATOR: I'll see what?

VIDAL: You'll see. Stay.

NARRATOR: You're drunk. I hate being impolite. As soon as she comes back, I'm leaving.

103. MS: *the door of the bathroom, which opens as Maud enters, wearing a mid-thigh-length middy, with her hair down.*

MAUD: For the moment I admit I don't look much like the marquise de Rambouillet.[30]

VIDAL (*off*): I get it. You wanted to show us your legs.

She closes the bathroom door and advances; pan following her to her bed.

MAUD: Exactly! Since that's my only seductive feature! ...

VIDAL (*off*): Only! ... Don't exaggerate. Let's say the main one.

Reframe as a MS *Maud pulling the covers off the sofa cushions, which also serve as her bed pillows. She remains standing on the bed.*

MAUD: I am a great exhibitionist. It comes on me in fits. You can look: I'm not exposing anything improper.

VIDAL (*off*): I would laugh if you fell and broke your neck. (*Pause.*) That's a sailor whatsis?

MAUD (*slipping between the sheets*): Yes, a real one, ... as real as they come.

VIDAL (*off*): That's practical. It keeps you warm.

MAUD: Anyway, I take it off to go to sleep. I always sleep naked. ... (*She smokes.*) I don't understand how one can wear something that ... wrinkles and climbs up when you turn over.

VIDAL (*off*): You need to sleep peacefully. Take sedatives.

Vidal enters the frame in the foreground, from a three-quarter rear angle, and sits on the bed.

MAUD: They're bad for the health. I prescribe them only in desperate cases. Move over a little, let me stretch out my legs.

VIDAL (*stretched out full length*): I adore feeling your toes under the covers. (*He plays with her feet and moves the covers around them.*) That's in your way. Now you must feel more comfortable.

MAUD (*to the narrator*): Sit down.

104. MS: *the narrator, standing in the middle of the room. Pan following him as he goes and sits in a chair; reframe as a slightly high-angle* MCU.

MAUD (*off*): Ah! ... good. What were we talking about?

VIDAL (*off*): About girls ...

105. *As at the end of 103,* MCU: *Maud and Vidal.*

VIDAL: ... about his girls!

MAUD: Ah, yes ... that's right. He was supposed to tell us his adventures.

Vidal drinks.

NARRATOR (*off*): No, you were!

MAUD: You know you really shock me a lot.

NARRATOR (*off*): Me! It's him! He never stops saying terrible things about me.

VIDAL (*laughing*): Tell me I'm lying.

NARRATOR (*off*): No, you're not lying, but. . . .

MAUD (*interrupting him gently*): I thought a true Christian was supposed to remain chaste until marriage.

NARRATOR (*off*): I don't at all set myself up as an example, I told you.

VIDAL: And then, anyway, between the theory and the practice. . . .

MAUD: . . . I know guys who have never slept with girls.

NARRATOR (*off, insisting*): I do not set myself up, . . . I don't. . . .

VIDAL: Bald guys, hunchbacks!

MAUD (*to Vidal*): No, not necessarily.

NARRATOR (*off*): No, . . . I don't set myself up as an example. To begin with, it was in the past. And furthermore I draw no. . . .

MAUD: Don't get mad! . . . On the contrary, I find you very attractive.

Vidal, almost lying on Maud's shoulder, gives a curious and rather tipsy smile.

MAUD: No, it's true, I like your frankness.

She pushes Vidal away and exits the frame to the left.

VIDAL: Very, very, very relative.

106. *As in 104,* MCU: *the narrator, sitting in the armchair.*

NARRATOR: Is it true that I shocked you?

MAUD (*off*): Well, . . . yes.

NARRATOR: I'm sorry if I did. My Christianity and my adventures with women are two very different things, . . . even opposite things, which are in conflict.

VIDAL (*off*): But that coexist in the same individual.

NARRATOR: A rather quarrelsome coexistence. . . .

107. MCU: *Vidal, lying on the sofa.*

NARRATOR (*off*): . . . Although, maybe I'm going to shock you again, too bad. Chasing girls doesn't take you away from God any more than . . . I don't know . . . doing mathematics. (*Vidal drinks; the narrator pauses, then continues, still off.*) Right, precisely, than doing mathematics. No, Pascal, to come back to him, condemned not only good eating, . . . but also, at the end of his life, mathematics, which he had practiced, as you know.

VIDAL: As for me, deep down, I'm very. . . . No, you're very much more Pascalian than I am.

NARRATOR (*off*): Maybe so, after all! . . . Mathematics takes one away from God, mathematics is useless . . . mathematics is an intellectual pastime . . . a distraction like any other . . . worse than another.

MAUD (*off*): Why worse?

NARRATOR (*off*): Because it's purely abstract and has nothing human in it.

VIDAL: Whereas women. . . . I want to write an article on "Pascal and Women." Pascal was very much interested in women, although, in fact, we still don't really know whether the "Discourse on the Passions of Love"[31] . . .

MAUD (*off*): Couldn't you open the window a little, please? It's smoky in here!

She gives Vidal a little push with her foot under the covers.

VIDAL (*continuing*): . . . is apocryphal, or whether. . . . And even whether . . . even whether Pascal "knew" any women . . .

Vidal, glass in hand, gets up; pan as he exits the frame to reframe on Maud, sitting in the bed.

VIDAL (*off*): . . . I mean "knew" in the Biblical sense of the word, . . . although really, I think it's crap, that expression, "to know in the Biblical sense of the term."

108. MS: *the Christmas tree and the window, with the curtains drawn; Vidal enters from the left, pulls back the curtains, and opens the window.*

109. LS: *a building outside, Vidal's POV looking out the window; it is night but there is light from several windows, and snow is falling.*

VIDAL (*off*): It's snowing. . . .

110. *As in 108,* MS: *Vidal at the window; the narrator comes to join him, then Maud.*

VIDAL: It looks phony! . . . I don't much like snow. It looks fake. It's kid's stuff. I hate everything that brings back childhood.

MAUD: Because you have a thoroughly twisted mind.

VIDAL (*tapping her bare thigh*): Hey, go to bed, . . . you'll catch cold.

She leaves promptly, toward the bed, exiting the frame. The camera stays on the two men.

MAUD (*as she leaves*): Go to bed yourself, you bully!

NARRATOR: Look, it's late, I'm going home.

Vidal closes the window again and pushes the curtains, while the narrator turns around and exits from the frame.

111. MS: *Maud, who is getting into bed; the narrator enters from the right and crosses to the left.*

MAUD (*to the narrator*): Where do you live?

NARRATOR: In Ceyrat. But I have my car.

MAUD: You'll kill yourself in that snow.

The narrator is near the bed, in profile. Vidal also enters from the right, seen from behind, and remains standing in the foreground.

NARRATOR: No . . . a little bit of snow doesn't scare me.

MAUD: Yes, . . . it's dangerous when it's falling. I have a friend who was killed that way. That accident was very traumatic for me. You can sleep in the other room. Go on, accept, it would keep me from sleeping.

VIDAL (*after a pause*): I just remembered! . . . I left my window open. The snow will get inside. I've got to go.

He comes around the sofa and bends to kiss Maud.

NARRATOR: Okay, I'll go with you.

Vidal, after kissing Maud, straightens up, turns to the narrator on the left, and as he speaks the next lines pushes him so that he loses his balance and plops down into the armchair.

VIDAL: But you can stay here. . . . No, no, no. . . . Good-bye, Maud.

MAUD: Good-bye.

Reframe as a MLS *of Maud, lying in the bed on the right side of the frame, and the narrator, sitting in the chair on the left side, as Vidal exits the frame in the left foreground.*

VIDAL (*off*): We'll keep in touch?

MAUD: Hey, . . . are you forgetting about tomorrow?

VIDAL (*off*): Hey, that's right. What time?

MAUD: Noon on the dot.

VIDAL (*off*): And what are you doing with your daughter?

112. MS: *Vidal near the door, putting on his coat.*

MAUD (*off*): She's seeing her father. (*To the narrator.*) You should come, too.

NARRATOR (*off*): What's going on?

MAUD (*off*): A walk, with some friends, over toward the peaks. We'll have supper at an inn. If it's snowing, it will be even better.

Vidal opens the door, ready to go out.

VIDAL: Good-bye!

MAUD (*off*): Good-bye!

VIDAL: Good-bye, see you tomorrow!

NARRATOR (*off*): Good-bye.

Vidal closes the door behind him.

113. *As in 111,* MLS: *the room, facing the bed, the narrator sitting in a chair, near Maud in her bed.*

NARRATOR: Honestly, I'm used to snow, I'm used to mountains. There's really no danger.

MAUD: That soft snow is very nasty, you know.

NARRATOR: Okay, well, I'll let you get some sleep. I'm leaving.

The narrator gets up and comes toward her.

MAUD: Stay a minute, please.

NARRATOR: You really insist on it?

MAUD: Okay, . . . well, leave then! . . . Go back home. . . . Leave, good-bye!

He shakes her hand. Pan following him as he backs away from the bed.

NARRATOR: Good-bye, . . . I'm embarrassed. I was told, . . . uh, . . . no, excuse me, . . . don't get mad, . . . I had been told that people, . . . in these parts liked to play hard to get. . . .

114. MCU: *Maud, in the bed, laughing.*
     MAUD: Well, there's some truth in that. But for the moment, you're the country boy. As for me, when I say yes, I mean yes. And when I say no, I mean no. If I want someone to leave, I say leave.
115. *Slightly low-angle* MCU: *the narrator, standing.*
     NARRATOR: You said "Leave!" (*He smiles.*) I'll stay a minute.
     He sits back down in a chair.
116. *As in 114,* MCU: *Maud.*
     MAUD: You definitely shock me a lot.
     NARRATOR (*off*): Right, you already said so.
     MAUD: No, it's true, I never met anyone who shocks me as much as you do. Religion has always left me completely unmoved. I'm neither for it nor against it, but what would keep me from taking it seriously is . . . it's people like you. Deep down, all that matters to you is respectability. Staying in a woman's bedroom after midnight, that's awful. But the possibility that you might please me somehow . . . by staying with me because I feel a little lonely . . . or that you might get to know someone a little less conventional, even if we were never to see each other again, that would never cross your mind. Which I find . . . pretty stupid and not very Christian.
     NARRATOR (*off*): Religion has nothing to do with it. . . . Uh, . . . I just thought you were sleepy.
     MAUD: Do you still think so?
     NARRATOR (*off*): Obviously not, since I'm still here.
     MAUD: You know, what bugs me the most about you is that you sidestep. You don't live up to your responsibilities. You are a shamefaced Christian . . . on top of a shamefaced Don Juan.[32] That really takes the cake!
117. *Reverse-angle* MCU: *the narrator, sitting in the chair.*
     NARRATOR: No, hold on, that's wrong. I have loved, that's very different. I have loved two or three women in my life, . . . well, let's say three or four. I've lived with them for very long periods, lasting several years. Maybe I didn't love them madly. (*He smiles.*) Yes, I did, . . . pretty madly, all the same. And it was reciprocated.
     The narrator stands up, and walks toward a wall of the room, where there is a chest of drawers.
     NARRATOR: I'm not saying that to be bragging.
     MAUD (*off*): No false modesty. . . .
     He turns around, having reached the chest of drawers, and puts his hands in his trouser pockets.
     NARRATOR: No, I say that because I don't think there truly is love unless it's shared. Besides, that's what would make me believe in a certain predestination. It's very good that it happened and it's very good that it didn't work out.

MAUD (*off*): Did you break it off?

NARRATOR: No. They didn't either. It was the circumstances.

He takes his hands out of his pockets and crosses his arms.

MAUD (*off*): You should have overcome the circumstances.

NARRATOR: Circumstances that couldn't be overcome. Okay, yeah, I know, you always can. But it would have been contrary to all reason, completely crazy, idiotic. . . . No, no, it was impossible. It was necessary for it not to be possible, it was better that it be that way. . . .

118. *Reverse-angle* MCU: *Maud, lying down.*

NARRATOR (*continues, off*): Do you see?

MAUD: Oh, sure, I understand very well. It seems very human, but not very Christian.

119. *As in 117,* MS: *the narrator, standing, arms crossed.*

NARRATOR: In any case, to return to what I was saying, Christian or not, it doesn't matter. . . . Let's put religion in brackets, I don't place myself at all in that perspective. Women have done a lot for me. Done a lot morally. When I say "women," it's a little. . . .

He uncrosses his arms and leans back against the chest of drawers.

MAUD (*off*): Yeah, it's a little vulgar.

NARRATOR: Yeah. Each time I have known a girl, anyway, it has always been an individual case, it would be stupid to talk in general terms . . . it has revealed to me a moral problem I was unaware of, that I had never had to face concretely. I've had to assume an attitude that . . . for me has been beneficial, that has drawn me out of my moral lethargy.

MAUD (*off*): But you could very well assume the moral side and leave the physical alone.

NARRATOR: Yes, but the moral only appeared, . . . even only existed. . . . (*Short pause.*) Oh, yes, of course, I know, you can always do everything! . . . But physical and moral are inseparable. All the same you've got to see things as they are.

The narrator moves forward toward the bed.

MAUD (*off*): Maybe it was only a trap set by the devil?

The narrator stops, now in a slightly low-angle MCU, *and puts his hands in his jacket pockets.*

NARRATOR: Well, then, I must have fallen into it! Yeah, . . . in a certain way, I fell into it. If I hadn't fallen into it, I would have been a saint.

MAUD (*off*): Don't you want to be a saint?

NARRATOR: No, not at all.

MAUD (*off*): Oh, the things one hears! . . . I thought all Christians were supposed to aspire to sainthood.

NARRATOR: When I say I don't want to, I mean I can't.

MAUD (*off*): What a defeatist! What about grace?

NARRATOR: I ask for grace to help me glimpse the possibility of being
   saintly.
He walks out of the frame to the left.

120. MCU: *the narrator walking in the room as he talks; he goes into the*
   corner where the window and Christmas tree are, turns around, comes
   back toward us, and repeats the trip.

   NARRATOR (*continuing*): Whether I'm wrong or right, I think that . . .
   since not everyone can be a saint, there must be some who are not . . .
   and that it's plausible I'm one of them. With my nature, my aspirations,
   my possibilities . . . but that in my mediocrity, in my happy medium, in
   my tepidness, which God abhors, I know, I've been able to attain, if not
   plenitude, at least a certain righteousness, in the sense that the Gospel
   says, the Righteous. I am in the world, the world exists within religion.
   Contrary to what you may think, I'm not at all Jansenist.

121. MS: *Maud, still lying down.*

   MAUD: I never thought that.

   NARRATOR (*off*): You . . . or Vidal?

   MAUD (*shrugging her shoulders*): Oh well! . . . He'll say anything.

   NARRATOR (*off*): To get me going. I don't know what was the matter
   with him tonight. . . . He was completely drunk. It's the first time I've
   ever seen him like that.

Maud extends her arm toward him.

MAUD: Do you want to pass me my cigarettes, please?

Pan following her gesture to the table: the narrator's hand takes the package of cigarettes. Pan following the hand, reframe as a MS: *Maud and the narrator; he lights her cigarette.*

MAUD: Thanks. (*Pause; she takes a drag.*) Do you know each other well?

NARRATOR: We hadn't seen each other for fourteen years.

The narrator sits on the bed in the foreground, seen from behind, leaning back on his elbows.

NARRATOR: But we were close friends once, even after school.

MAUD: You were not very nice tonight.

NARRATOR: Not nice?

122. CU: *Maud, over his shoulder.*

MAUD: Me either, I'm bad, . . . I'm very bad. The poor boy won't be able to sleep tonight from knowing we're together.

NARRATOR: But he's the one who wanted to go.

MAUD: Yeah, out of bravado. (*She leans toward him a little.*) You can be a little thick sometimes, you know? Didn't he tell you he was in love with me?

NARRATOR: No, he told me he had a very high regard for you. And that he had an enormous friendship for you.

MAUD: He's a very discreet fellow. A really nice guy, too. Although . . . he doesn't have much sense of humor. Well, humor about his life, I mean. I know perfectly well I make him suffer, but . . . I can't help it. He's not at all my type. I was stupid enough to sleep with him one night, just out of boredom. I'm very . . . hard to please, you know, where men are concerned. It's not just a physical thing, . . . besides, he is smart enough to understand that. I know very well why he brought you this evening. (*Brief pause.*) To test me. No, I don't believe that. No, it's rather to have an excuse to despise me, . . . to hate me. He's one of those people who want to believe the worst. (*Pause.*) Now where were we?

123. *Reverse-angle* MS: *both of them, almost in profile. The narrator leans toward her on the bed.*

NARRATOR: You're really not sleepy?

MAUD: No, not at all. And you?

NARRATOR: No. (*They stare at each other and whisper.*) But you, really?

MAUD: Yes. If I were sleepy, I'd tell you. It's been a long time since I've talked to someone like this. It's good for me. (*Pause.*) But, even so, you seem to be terribly complicated.

NARRATOR: Complicated?

MAUD: Yes. I thought that, for a Christian, you were judged by your actions, . . . and you don't seem to attach much importance to them.

NARRATOR: To actions? . . . Oh, yes, I do. A tremendous amount. But for me, it's not a particular act that counts, it's life in its entirety.

Pan on the narrator backing to the foot of the bed; Maud is thus out of the frame.

NARRATOR (*continuing*): Life is a unit. It makes a whole. I mean by that that . . . the choice is never offered like that, . . . exactly. I have never said to myself, "Should I sleep with a girl, or should I not sleep with her?"

124. *Reverse-angle* MCU: *Maud, lying down, smoking, very attentive.*

NARRATOR (*off*): I've just made one choice, in advance, a global choice about a certain way of living.

MAUD: Please, would you get me a glass of water?

NARRATOR (*off*): Yes. If there is one thing I don't like in the Church, . . . and that, moreover, is tending to disappear, it's the accounting for actions, sins, . . . or good deeds.

The sound, off, of the narrator pouring water into a glass.

NARRATOR (*off*): What's necessary is a pure heart. When you really love a girl, you don't want to sleep with any other.

He enters the frame in the foreground, moving right to left, gives her the glass of water; she smiles and murmurs "Thanks"; he goes to sit back down in the armchair, near the bed, exiting the frame. She laughs.

NARRATOR (*off*): There's no problem. Why are you laughing?

MAUD: No reason. Then it's true?

NARRATOR (*off*): What?

MAUD: You're in love. (*She drinks.*)

NARRATOR (*off*): In love? With whom?

MAUD: I don't know, . . . with the blonde, . . . with the one and only. . . . (*She puts the glass down near her.*) Have you found her?

NARRATOR: No. I told you no.

MAUD (*with an ironic smile*): Aw, . . . don't hold back any secrets. Do you want to get married?

125. MCU: *the narrator in the chair.*

NARRATOR: Yeah, like everybody.

MAUD (*off*): A little bit more than everybody? . . . Come on, admit it!

NARRATOR: No, but I don't see what idea has gotten into you to want to marry me off at any cost.

MAUD (*off*): Perhaps I have the soul of a matchmaker. Such women exist.

NARRATOR: Yes, I avoid them.

MAUD (*off*): How will you get married then?

NARRATOR: I don't know. With a personal ad. . . . (*Pause.*) Yes. Engineer, thirty-four, Catholic, five nine . . .

MAUD (*off*): . . . good-looking, with car, seeks blond, practicing Catholic.

NARRATOR: You know, you've given me an idea. Lots of people get married that way. (*Pause.*) No, . . . I'm kidding! I'm in no hurry.

MAUD (*off*): Obviously, so you can play around. . . .

NARRATOR (*interrupting her*): Oh, no, anything but that!

MAUD (*off*): Then, if today you found the one you were looking for, . . . you'd get married right away and you would swear to be faithful to her for the rest of your life.

NARRATOR (*serious*): Absolutely.

MAUD (*off*): You're sure you'll be faithful to your wife?

NARRATOR: Well, of course.

MAUD (*off*): And what if she cheats on you?

NARRATOR: Well, . . . she won't . . . if she loves me, she won't cheat on me.

MAUD (*off*): Love doesn't last forever.

NARRATOR: Yes, it does, at least the way I conceive it.

126. *Reverse-angle* MCU: *Maud, sitting in her bed, smoking. The narrator enters the frame from the left and sits on the bed near her. Reframe on him alone.*

NARRATOR: If there's one thing I don't understand, it's infidelity. If only out of self-esteem. I don't want to say white, after I said black.

127. CU: *Maud, sitting in her bed, smoking.*

NARRATOR (*off*): If I choose a woman for my wife, it's because I love her with a love that resists time. If I stopped loving her, I would despise myself.

MAUD: Hunh . . . I do see a lot of self-esteem in that.

NARRATOR (*off*): I said, "if only out of self-esteem."

MAUD: But it's mostly self-esteem. Then you don't approve of divorce?

NARRATOR (*off*): No.

MAUD (*she smokes*): So you damn me with no hope of remission.

NARRATOR (*off*): No, not at all. You're not Catholic, . . . and I respect all religions, even those of people without one. No, what I say is valid for me, that's all. . . . Excuse me if I offended you.

MAUD: No, you didn't offend me.

Silent pause.

NARRATOR (*off*): Why were you divorced?

MAUD: I don't know. Yes, I know very well. We didn't get along. . . . We realized it very quickly. Just a question of temperament.

NARRATOR (*off*): Maybe it was something you could have overcome, I don't know. . . .

MAUD: Oh, . . . my husband was a very nice man, in all respects. . . . Moreover he's the man I will always have the most regard for. But he got on my nerves. Profoundly. . . .

NARRATOR (*off*): How did he get on your nerves? Somebody like me?

MAUD: Ha, ha, ha! No! . . . Not at all! . . . You, . . . you don't get on my nerves. With you, the idea of marrying you would never have entered my mind. (*Pause.*) Even in the days of my wildest youth.

NARRATOR (*off*): But you lived together. . . . You had a daughter.

MAUD: So, then, you think it's fun, for a kid, to have parents who don't get along? . . . Then there was another thing. . . . You really want me to tell you my life story? (*Pause.*) Well, I had a lover. And my husband, a mistress. What's amusing is that she was a girl a little bit of your type . . . very moral, very Catholic, . . . not hypocritical or calculating, very sincere. (*Speaking as if for herself.*) That didn't stop me from detesting her like you wouldn't think possible. I think she was crazy about him. Anyway he's a fellow who makes girls crazy. I was crazy, too. Besides, I did everything to make him break it off. . . . That was my only good deed. But I don't think she would have gone as far as marrying him. That's why you amused me a while ago when you talked about insurmountable circumstances. For her, too, I think.

NARRATOR (*off*): And your lover? . . .

She leans forward, in the bed, her head upright at first, then bent forward, her knees against her chest. She holds her neck, almost painfully.

MAUD (*forcing herself to speak*): Well, as for that! . . . That's what proves that I'm an unlucky person . . . (*thoughtful*) . . . and when I want to accomplish something good, it fails! I'm sure I had found the man of my life. Someone . . . who liked me, someone I liked in all respects. . . . A doctor, like me, . . . very brilliant, but even more in love with life, . . . insanely cheerful! I've never known anyone whom . . . it was more pleasant, more joyful, to be with. (*Silence.*) Then, he died, . . . just like that, stupidly, in an auto accident. His car skidded on an icy road. That's fate.

She lowers her eyes, then looks up again. A faint shadow crosses her face and one can hear the narrator getting to his feet. A rather long pause.

MAUD: Is it still falling?

128. MS: *the room. The narrator is standing near the window and raises the curtain.*

NARRATOR: Yes.

He turns from the window and moves forward, slowly, taking a Gitane from his pack of cigarettes. Reframe as a slightly low-angle MCU.

MAUD (*off*): Well, there it is, it's in the past! . . . What's done is done! . . . That was a year ago. (*Pause.*) Does that disturb you?

NARRATOR: No. Forgive me if I spoke a bit lightly. I have the detestable habit of seeing things only from my own petty point of view.

MAUD (*off*): No. Your point of view interests me. (*He lights a cigarette.*) Otherwise, I would already have said good night to you.

NARRATOR: Well, it's late. Where is the other bedroom?

MAUD (*off*): Nowhere!

NARRATOR (*stupefied*): What? There aren't any other rooms?

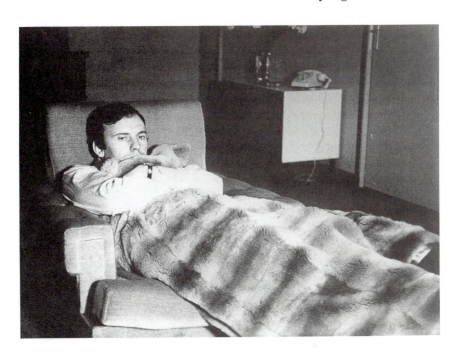

MAUD (*off*): Oh, yes: my office, the waiting room, my daughter's room, and the maid's room; she's Spanish and very prudish.

NARRATOR (*looking around*): But . . . Vidal knew that?

129. MCU: *Maud.*

MAUD: Of course! . . . That's why he left in such a bad mood. Don't act like a little boy. Come get into bed with me. On top of the covers, if you want, . . . or under the covers . . . if you don't find me too repulsive.

130. *As in 128,* CU: *the narrator, his hand on his head, smiling, then looking around.*

NARRATOR: I can use the armchair.

MAUD (*off*): You'll be stiff in the morning. Are you afraid? . . . Of yourself? . . . Of me? I swear I won't lay a finger on you. Besides, I thought you were in control of yourself.

He approaches her.

131. MS: *the narrator, from behind, leaning over the bed and taking a blanket, Maud in the background.*

NARRATOR: Can I take a blanket?

MAUD: Do you want to turn off the lights, please?

Pan following the narrator as he turns off a lamp by the bed, then goes to the chest of drawers to turn off a lamp and finally to the door, where the

switch for the ceiling light is. Then he comes back to the armchair. The room is lit only by Maud's bedside lamp.

132. MS: *Maud, who has taken off her middy blouse and is slipping completely under the covers, up to her neck.*

133. *Reverse-angle* MS: *the narrator, blowing out a large candle on the low table by the chair; then he takes off his jacket and his tie. Finally, he takes up the blanket; wraps it around himself; sits on the chair; pushes off his shoes; stretches out, putting his feet on the little table; and looks toward her.*

134. CU: *Maud, in bed, looking back at him; she smiles.*
    MAUD (*very softly*): Idiot! . . .

135. *As in 133,* MS: *the narrator, getting up from the chair.*

136. CU *and pan: the narrator crossing left to right and lying down beside her, but on top of the bed, still wrapped up in the blanket; reframe as a* MS *of the two, stretched out side by side. Maud has turned over, to face the narrator, and with a finger she caresses his shoulder. She is still smiling.*
    MAUD: You'll be cold.
    NARRATOR: I'll see about that. (*Pause.*) Good night.
    MAUD: Good night.

She turns off the light, leaving the screen almost dark.
...

137. ms: *the window; in the gap between the incompletely closed curtains one sees the light of dawn.*

138. ms: *the two, sleeping side by side. The narrator wakes up, tugs on his blanket, then slips under Maud's fur cover. Maud stirs. She turns around, and clings to him. She wraps her arms around him. His hand is caressing her back. He turns toward her and they embrace. . . . Suddenly he pulls away, pushing her back, and he sits up. Maud also pulls back, flings the cover off, and springs out of bed, exiting the frame. The narrator jumps up and goes after her, also exiting the frame. The camera lingers on the empty bed.*

139. ms: *the bathroom door; Maud, naked, seen from behind, arrives very quickly at the door. Reframe as a* mcu *as the narrator also arrives, as she opens the door; this causes her to turn slightly toward him. She is clutching her blouse in front of her. He tries to put his arms around her; she draws back stiffly.*

maud: No! . . . (*Harshly.*) I like people who know what they want.
She goes into the bathroom and slams the door behind her. The camera stays on the narrator, facing the closed door, embarrassed, sheepish. He turns around and starts to walk away from the door.

140. M S : *the room. The narrator enters the frame and goes to the chair, puts on
      and ties his tie, puts on his shoes, puts on his jacket, and exits the frame. One
      can hear a shower running. The camera holds a* M S *of the door of the
      bathroom, which opens to show Maud, wearing a terrycloth bathrobe.*
      M A U D : Were you leaving without saying good-bye?
      *Pan following her as she crosses to the left and comes close to him.
      Reframe as a* M C U *of the two, face to face.*
      N A R R A T O R : I was going to get my overcoat. (*Pause.*) No, . . . don't see
      me out. You'll catch cold.
      They advance toward the entryway.

141. *Over-the-shoulder* M C U : *Maud.*
      M A U D : Will you come this afternoon?
      N A R R A T O R : Uh, well. . . .
      The narrator puts on his coat without answering.
      M A U D : Aw, . . . come. Vidal would gossip if you didn't. . . . Come on, be
      a good sport.
      N A R R A T O R : Do you really want me to?
      M A U D : Besides, we won't be alone. There will be a girl you might like
      . . . a blonde!
      He opens the door.
      M A U D : So, you'll come? It's settled? . . . Noon sharp.
      N A R R A T O R : Well, okay, I'll try. Good-bye.
      He leaves. The camera stays on her.
      A Street, exterior, day

142. L S : *the street covered with a blanket of snow. The narrator has just left
      Maud's and heads toward his car, parked in the foreground, a general
      view of the square in the background. Other cars go by, slowly because of
      the snow. The narrator clears the piles of snow from the windshield of his
      car, then gets behind the wheel, turns on the wipers, warms up the engine,
      and starts off. The camera lingers briefly on the empty parking space.*
      The Narrator's Bedroom in the Chalet, interior, day

143. M S : *the narrator passing in front of the window, pulling on a sweater.
      Pan following him as he passes by another window, picks up a sheepskin
      jacket, puts it on, and exits the frame to the right.*
      The Highway, exterior, day

144. *Tracking* E L S : *the snow-covered countryside, the narrator's* P O V *from
      his car looking out the side window, toward Clermont visible in the
      distance.*

145. ̠C U : *the big clock of the Municipal Theater, showing 11:45.*
      A Café, interior, day

146. M S : *the narrator, his back to us, going into the café, to a table, taking off
      his jacket, giving an order to a waiter as he enters.*
      N A R R A T O R : Waiter—a coffee, please.

He sits down and remains silent and thoughtful, his head on his hand. The third colleague, seen from behind in a fur-lined coat, enters the frame coming into the café, crosses left to right, stops near the narrator (who appears not to see him), and taps him on the shoulder. The narrator reacts with a start and stands up.

THIRD COLLEAGUE: Did I wake you up?

The two men shake hands.

THIRD COLLEAGUE: You coming skiing with me?

NARRATOR: Uhhh! . . . No.

THIRD COLLEAGUE *(looking at his wristwatch)*: I'm going up to the Mont-Dore in half an hour.[33]

NARRATOR: No. I have a date with. . . .

He is looking into the distance, and gives a start.

147. LS: *the street, seen through the café windows. The blond woman goes by, right to left, on her motorbike.*

148. As in 146, MS *of the two men in the café.*

NARRATOR *(excited)*: Excuse me. . . .

149. MS: *the narrator, from behind; he dashes out of the café, without taking his coat, as another client enters.*

In the Street, exterior, day

150. LS: *the narrator from behind, as he leaves the café and runs along the sidewalk. He tries to cross amid fairly heavy traffic; among the cars,*

Françoise is on her motorbike, on the other side of the street, heading toward the nearby Place de Jaude. The narrator zigzags across between the cars.

151. *Reverse-angle* L S : *Françoise approaching on her bike, stopping at the curb, getting off, and bringing the bike toward us, onto the sidewalk near a tree. The narrator enters the frame in the background, slows down a few feet behind her and approaches, no longer running, but walking. She turns to leave and stops short, as she sees him in front of her.*

152. *Reverse-angle* M C U : *Françoise,* P O V *of the narrator; she watches him approach, until he enters the frame.*

153. *As in 151,* M S : *the two as he approaches.*

    N A R R A T O R : Ahem. . . . I realize I should find some clever line, . . . but a clever line is always silly! . . . How should I go about getting to know you?

    They turn and take a few steps forward.

    F R A N Ç O I S E : You seem to know that better than I do.

    N A R R A T O R : No. . . . Or else I wouldn't have followed you like that, . . . in spite of all my principles.

    F R A N Ç O I S E : It's very bad to violate one's principles.

    Slight tracking shot following her; he is out of the frame.

    N A R R A T O R (*off*): I do it sometimes. How about you?

    F R A N Ç O I S E : Yes, but I regret it.

    N A R R A T O R (*off, slight zoom in on her smiling*): Not me. . . . And besides, if I violate my principles, it's because sometimes it's really worth doing it. Anyway, I don't have any principles. . . . Well, at least, not about. . . .

    F R A N Ç O I S E : Ways of getting to know people?

    N A R R A T O R (*off*): Yes. . . . No. . . . I mean, I think it would be stupid to miss knowing someone because of a matter of principles.

    F R A N Ç O I S E : Remains to be seen whether it's worth doing.

    N A R R A T O R (*off*): We'll certainly find out.

    He laughs. A pause.

    F R A N Ç O I S E : You don't look like somebody who likes to rely on chance.

    N A R R A T O R (*off*): On the contrary, my life is only made up of chance events.

    F R A N Ç O I S E : That's not my impression.

    Slight backward tracking shot, bringing him into the frame. In the background, the traffic in the street, moving slowly because of the weather. The narrator looks at Françoise's motorbike.

    N A R R A T O R : That thing must be pretty dangerous in this weather.

    F R A N Ç O I S E : I'm used to it, and anyway, I only use it in town. To go home I take the bus.

    N A R R A T O R : Where do you live?

FRANÇOISE: In Sauzet,[34] out past Ceyrat.

NARRATOR: When do we see each other?

FRANÇOISE: When we meet again.

NARRATOR: Well, we never meet.

FRANÇOISE: Oh, yes, we do, come on. (*She laughs.*)

NARRATOR: Tomorrow, okay? . . . I didn't see you last Sunday.

FRANÇOISE: I had work to do, so I stayed home. It was an exception.

NARRATOR: Okay. . . . Afterward we'll have lunch together.

FRANÇOISE: Okay, maybe, we'll see. . . . Good-bye. Hurry up, you're going to catch cold.

She backs off, crosses behind him, and exits the frame to the left; he stands a moment, then runs off away from us, crossing the street toward the café.

In the Mountains, exterior, day

154. ELS: *the snow-covered crater of the Puy de Pariou.*[35] *In the distant foreground, a couple—Maud and the narrator—advances, sliding sometimes; far behind them is another couple—Vidal and a young blond woman.*

155. MS: *Maud and the narrator, from behind; they have already reached the summit, and turn back toward the other couple.*

MAUD (*shouting*): We're leaving!

NARRATOR (*also shouting*): We'll see you back at the car.

156. MS: *Vidal and the blonde, who have just heard the shouts. They stop.*

VIDAL (*shouting*): Okay!

Vidal helps the blonde adjust her shawl.

VIDAL: It's incredible how much you look like a Ukrainian.

Another Part of the Mountain, exterior, day

157. MS: *Maud, from behind, wearing a big white fur hat. She turns around toward the narrator, who enters the frame from the left and follows her.*

MAUD: I hope they're not going to take too long.

NARRATOR: There's no way to know, is there?

MAUD: It's a good thing you came. I'd have been a sorry sight, all by myself, . . . with the two of them.

NARRATOR: Did you think I would come?

MAUD: Why not?

158. MCU: *the narrator.*

NARRATOR: I almost didn't come. But I keep my promises.

159. *Reverse-angle* MCU: *Maud.*

MAUD: And now you're sorry you came?

NARRATOR (*off*): No, . . . not at all. . . .

Pan as she approaches the narrator, reframe as a CU *of the two in profile.*

NARRATOR: I've never had such a good time.

As they talk, he takes her by the shoulders and draws her to him.

MAUD: Is that true?

NARRATOR: Yes. I'm sure you can tell. (*He kisses her.*) It's amazing how happy I am with you.

MAUD: You'd be happier with the blonde.

NARRATOR: Who? . . . Vidal's girl? No. No way.

MAUD: Of two evils, choose the lesser. (*They kiss again.*) Your lips are cold.

NARRATOR: Yours too. I like that.

MAUD: It's in the tone of your feelings.

NARRATOR: Right! . . . I mean, this was just a friendly kiss.

MAUD: If it were. . . .

NARRATOR: You don't believe in my friendship?

MAUD: I don't know you.

NARRATOR: That's true, we've been together for less than twenty-four hours, and even then there were interruptions, . . . and yet it seems to me I've known you for an eternity. (*Pause.*) Not to you?

MAUD: It's possible. We confided in each other on very short acquaintance.

NARRATOR: I don't know what's happening to me, for the past few days I haven't stopped talking. I need to get things off my chest.

MAUD: You have to get married!

She pulls away from him and exits the frame to the right, moving forward.

NARRATOR: To whom?

MAUD (*off*): To your blonde. . . . Yours, I mean!

160. MCU: *Maud.*

NARRATOR (*off*): She doesn't exist!

MAUD: Really?

Backward tracking shot as he enters the frame and the two walk toward us, side by side.

NARRATOR: What if I married you? . . . Do you want to?

MAUD: Anyway, I don't meet the conditions.

NARRATOR: What conditions?

MAUD: Blond, Catholic. . . .

They stop.

NARRATOR: Who said blond?

MAUD: Vidal, I think.

NARRATOR: Oh, he doesn't know anything about it.

MAUD: Well, Catholic, anyway.

NARRATOR: That, yes!

MAUD: So there you are.

They begin walking again; resume backward tracking shot.

NARRATOR: I can convert you.

MAUD: Ha! . . . You'd have a hard time. You, especially!

He stops her, and presses close against her from behind. They remain facing the camera.

NARRATOR: Then you accept? Look how well matched we are. We're completely at ease with each other.

MAUD: Why not. . . . you're certainly as good as Vidal!

NARRATOR: But you won't marry him.

MAUD: God forbid! . . . However, it wouldn't be the first stupid thing I ever did.

NARRATOR: I think he's resigned to it.

MAUD: He'd better be! . . . I wonder what was eating him yesterday. At bottom, it was to . . . keep away from me that he threw you into my arms.

NARRATOR: But I'm not in your arms!

He kisses her ear, her neck.

MAUD: You've cured him. You've done a good deed, so your conscience is clear.

NARRATOR: It is, anyway.

VIDAL (*shouting, off*): Hello-o-o, ho-o-o! . . .

MAUD (*with a start, smiling*): Well, here they are.

A Street, exterior, night

161. MS: *the narrator's car, seen from a three-quarter front angle, has just stopped. Maud is sitting beside the narrator. In the back are Vidal and the blonde. Pan following Maud, who gets out of the car at the same time as Vidal.*

VIDAL: Shall we go have a drink?

MAUD: No, . . . I don't have time. I have some errands to do. . . . It's the maid's day off. In fact I'm very late.

While Maud is talking, the blonde gets out the far side of the car and comes around behind it to join Vidal and Maud on the sidewalk. Pan following Maud, who leans on the front door of the car, the narrator having stayed inside, leaning over from the driver's seat.

MAUD: Do you want to go to the market with me? . . . And then we can have dinner together, if you're not in too big a hurry.

NARRATOR: Fine, but I'll have to leave at 10:00. . . . I've got to get some sleep.

MAUD: No, at 9:30. I need some sleep.

The narrator opens the door for Maud to get back into the car. Maud turns for a second toward Vidal and the blonde off-camera.

VIDAL (*off*): I'll give you a call.

MAUD (*sitting in the car*): See you soon!

Maud pulls the door shut. The car backs up, then pulls away and exits the frame to the right. Pan to reframe Vidal and his girlfriend in a MCU.

VIDAL: Shall we go have that drink anyway?

BLONDE: Okay.

VIDAL (*taking her arm*): Are you in a hurry?

The Market, exterior, night

162. LS: *the row of brightly lit shops on the Rue de la Boucherie. In the crowd, Maud and the narrator are shopping.*

Maud's Kitchen, interior, night

163. MS: *the narrator busy in the kitchen, while Maud, off-camera, talks on the telephone in the next room.*

MAUD (*off*): No, that's very nice of you. You're leaving tonight? . . . (*Pause.*) You know I've still got some of your things here, . . . some pajamas.

Pan following the narrator, who goes to the open door. One can then see Maud, standing, at the telephone. He smiles to her.

MAUD: Fine, I'll keep them. They may come in handy. Good-bye.

He exits the frame to the left. She hangs up; pan following her as she goes into the kitchen.

MAUD: You know who that was?

Reframe as a MS *of the two: his back is to her and he seems to be working on a dish.*

MAUD: My husband.

NARRATOR: Hmmm! . . .

She pours a drink and drinks.

MAUD: He's really very nice. He has just gotten me a practice in Toulouse, . . .[36] a very profitable position.

He seasons the dish he has prepared. She empties the contents of a can into a saucepan.

MAUD: You knew I was going to leave Clermont?

NARRATOR: Yeah. I believe . . . you had already told me. When will it be?

MAUD: Sooner than I thought. In a month, maybe. (*She exits the frame and continues speaking off.*) Don't you think that was nice of him?

He turns toward her.

NARRATOR: Nice of your husband?

MAUD (*off*): Of my ex-husband. He's a very nice man. (*She reenters the frame and puts out the cigarette she was smoking.*) It's too bad we didn't get along. (*Pause.*) He was in Clermont on business and to see our daughter.

NARRATOR: Is he remarried?

She takes his place at the counter, and he moves over to the stove.

MAUD: No. . . . Why do you ask me that?

NARRATOR: Just because! . . . (*He turns on the gas and lights the stove.*) So, you're going to leave me.

MAUD: Well, . . . yes!

He stands up straight and gets very close to her.

NARRATOR: That makes twenty-four hours we've been together, . . . a whole day. . . . That's a long time, and not much time. (*He grazes her hair with the tip of his finger.*)

MAUD: Not even a day! . . . You were unfaithful to me this morning.

NARRATOR (*after a silence*): It's funny how I don't like to leave people. . . . I'm faithful, even to you. That's why, ideally, one should never have to forget. I should love only one girl . . . and not another one. Even platonically.

MAUD: Especially not platonically.

Maud leaves the kitchen, exiting the frame to the right; the camera stays briefly on the narrator.

164. MCU: *Maud, in the living room a few hours later, sitting in an armchair and holding her cup of coffee on the armrest. She smiles.*

165. *Reverse-angle* MCU: *the narrator, sitting on the armrest of the other armchair. He has an unlit cigarette in his hand and, behind him in soft focus, the Christmas tree is twinkling. He smiles.*

NARRATOR: Thanks to you, I have taken a step along the road to sainthood. I told you: women have always contributed to my moral progress.

MAUD (*off*): Even in the brothels of Vera Cruz?[37]

NARRATOR: I have never been to a brothel, neither here, nor in Vera Cruz, nor in Valparaiso.

MAUD (*off*): I meant Valparaiso.

He shows his empty box of matches.

NARRATOR: Do you have a light, please?

Maud's hand enters the frame, holding out a lighter. He leans forward and takes it.

NARRATOR: Thanks.

MAUD (*off*): Well, . . . no matter. . . . It would have done you good, physically and morally.

NARRATOR: You think?

He lights his cigarette and puts the lighter on the table.

MAUD (*off*): You idiot! . . . No, you see, what I think is wrong with you is . . . your lack of spontaneity.

NARRATOR (*crossing his arms*): But I've poured out my heart to you, . . . what more do you want?

MAUD (*off*): I don't have much faith in your way of loving with conditions.

NARRATOR: But I didn't say you had to love with conditions. I said you had to love just one woman. I don't see any condition there.

MAUD (*off*): Well, I don't mean that. I'm talking about your manner of calculating, anticipating, classifying: the condition sine qua non is, my wife must be Catholic. Love comes afterward.

NARRATOR: Not at all. . . . I only think it's easier to love when there's a sharing of ideas. You, for example, I could marry you, what's missing for me is love.

MAUD (*laughing, off*): Well, thanks a lot!

NARRATOR: Love on your side as well as on mine.

166. *As in 164,* MCU: *Maud.*

MAUD: So you would really marry me, then?

NARRATOR (*off*): Were you married in a religious ceremony?

MAUD: No. . . .

NARRATOR (*off*): You see, for the Church, that doesn't count. I could even marry you with full ceremony. Personally, that would shock me a little, but . . . I see no reason to be more Catholic than the Pope.

MAUD: Your Jesuitism amuses me.

167. *Slightly high-angle* MS: *the narrator in the background, sitting on the arm of the chair, and Maud's head in the foreground, from behind.*

NARRATOR: Then I'm not a Jansenist.

MAUD: No, I don't think so.

NARRATOR: So much the better. Jansenists are gloomy people.

MAUD: At heart, you have a very happy character.

He puts out his cigarette and goes to get his fur-lined jacket, which is lying on the bed; pan following him.

MAUD: You'd never know it to look at you.

NARRATOR: Yes, it's true, with you I'm very happy.

She gets up and goes toward him.

MAUD: And with the others?

NARRATOR: Gloomy! It's true. (*Pause.*) If I'm happy with you, it's because I know we're not going to see each other again.

MAUD: Well, I'll be . . . that beats all!

NARRATOR: Yes. The idea of a future doesn't arise, and in general, that's what's sad.

He buttons his coat.

MAUD: I see, I see, but all the same, we will see each other again, won't we?

NARRATOR: Maybe not. Or anyway very little.

MAUD: What makes you say that? A premonition?

NARRATOR: No. A deduction as logical as can possibly be. You're going away.

MAUD: Not immediately.

NARRATOR: But I'm going to have a lot to do these days. I'm going to be very busy.

MAUD: What kind of business—professional affairs or affairs of the heart?

He walks to the door; she follows him. Pan following them.

NARRATOR: Of the heart, of course!

168. CU: *the two, face to face, close to the door. He takes her head in his hands. In the background, the out-of-focus lights of the Christmas tree, blinking occasionally.*

MAUD: Then it's true?

NARRATOR: I love to tease you. In any case, you'll never know anything about it.

MAUD: Therefore there's something to know.

NARRATOR: Yes, if it pleases you to think so.

He draws her toward him; she holds out her lips for a kiss, but he avoids them and plants a kiss on each of her cheeks. She laughs.

NARRATOR: Then, . . . shall we keep in touch?

MAUD: Hmmm, . . . it's up to you to call first.

NARRATOR: Okay. Good-bye.

They exit the frame to the right; the camera stays on the Christmas tree, in soft focus. Its lights blink off.

Entrance Hall of the Apartment Building, interior, night

169. LS: *the narrator, seen from behind, walking toward the glass door of Maud's apartment building. He goes out into the street, turns left; the camera lingers on the empty hallway.*

The Street, exterior, night

170. CU: *the narrator in his car, from behind, driving. He is driving toward the square, looking to both sides. The wipers swing back and forth on the windshield.*

171. *Reverse-angle* LS: *the square, with the narrator's car advancing, flashing its headlights.*

172. *As in 170,* CU: *the interior of the car. Through the windshield on the right one can see Françoise pushing her motorbike. The narrator stops and gets out of the car.*

173. MS: *the two, in profile, as he appears in front of her and startles her. He is wearing glasses.*

   NARRATOR: You see, . . . this morning, we were talking about chance.

   FRANÇOISE: Did you recognize me from so far away?

   NARRATOR: Even if there had been only ten chances in a hundred that it was you, I would have stopped.

   FRANÇOISE (*laughing*): Well, as you see, . . . it's me.

   NARRATOR: Are you going home on your motorbike?

   FRANÇOISE: Yes, I missed my bus.

   NARRATOR (*He takes the motorbike*): I'll take you home.

   FRANÇOISE: No, don't bother.

NARRATOR: Yes, yes, . . . it's dangerous in this weather. And besides, it's on my way. I'll take you back.

He goes to park the motorbike, and exits the frame to the left.

NARRATOR (*off*): Get in!

She turns toward the car.

174. CU: *Françoise inside the car, from behind at a three-quarter angle. He, at the wheel, is out of the frame. Glimpses of scenery as they drive along.*

NARRATOR (*off*): What are you studying?

FRANÇOISE: Biology. I'm also working in a lab. That's why I didn't go away for the holidays.

NARRATOR (*off*): Does it interest you?

FRANÇOISE: I was especially good at math, but I couldn't see myself as an engineer or a professor.

NARRATOR (*off*): And as a doctor?

FRANÇOISE: No, that's not a profession for me.

175. *Forward tracking* LS: *the road, seen through the windshield, lit up by the headlights and streetlamps.*

176. CU: *the narrator inside the car, from behind, still driving; Françoise is partly in the frame.*

NARRATOR: You live a long way out. It's out in the country.

FRANÇOISE: No, it's in a village. It's a house that's rented to students. (*Pause.*) It's there, on the right. Be careful, because there's surely ice on the road. Whoa! Watch out! . . .

NARRATOR: Yeah, sure enough! . . .

The car is on a little road packed with ice and snow. The car skids. Françoise, worried, looks out the back occasionally.

FRANÇOISE: Oh! . . . we won't make it.

The car skids again, then starts off again.

NARRATOR: No, it's adventurous. . . . It's not dangerous. . . . Don't be afraid.

She looks back again.

FRANÇOISE: Look out! . . . There's a wall.

The headlights reveal a wall a few feet ahead of the car, which stops.

NARRATOR: Uh-oh. I'm afraid I'm stuck.

He tries to get started again, in vain.

NARRATOR: I'm stuck. I can't go forward or backward any more.

FRANÇOISE: That doesn't matter. Stop the car. We can just walk from here. . . . And then you can just as well sleep there. (*He tries to start again.*) Everybody's away on vacation. There's bound to be a free room.

NARRATOR (*talking about the car*): Damn! . . . Damn, damn, I can't do anything!

FRANÇOISE: You coming?

NARRATOR: It's not far?

FRANÇOISE: No, it's right there.
The Road in the Country, exterior, night
177.   LS: *the two getting out of the car. In the darkness, the vague shape of a large villa can be seen in the distance.*
NARRATOR: You think it's all right to leave the car like that?
FRANÇOISE: Well, . . . in any case, no one else can get through. We'll ask someone to come help you tomorrow.
Their backs to us, they set off toward the villa.
NARRATOR: It's slippery. Be careful!
FRANÇOISE: No, . . . no, it's okay.
The House, interior, night
178.   *High-angle* LS *from the top of a narrow staircase. Françoise is coming up, followed by the narrator.*
179.   CU: *the two in the corridor. She leads the way into a room.*
Françoise's Room, interior, night
180.   MCU: *the two as they enter the room. The camera stays on him as she exits the frame to the right to close the door and put her handbag on a chair, then she reenters the frame and crosses right to left to a table, opens a drawer, takes out a key (which she holds out for him), and then takes off her gloves.*
FRANÇOISE: Here it is! . . . This is home for me! Okay, . . . well, then. . . .
He takes out a pack of cigarettes.
NARRATOR: Do you smoke?
FRANÇOISE: No, but go ahead.
He puts a cigarette in his mouth and rummages in his pockets.
NARRATOR: I don't have a light.
She goes toward a shelf, comes back, and gives him a box of matches.
NARRATOR: Thanks.
FRANÇOISE: You want some tea?
Françoise takes off her coat while he lights his cigarette.
NARRATOR: Yes, I'd like some.
Pan following her to the washbasin, where she fills an electric kettle with water. The narrator, because of the camera movement, is out of the frame.
NARRATOR (*off*):   Can I help?
FRANÇOISE: No, there's no need.
Pan in reverse as Françoise goes to plug in the kettle. The narrator comes back into the frame.
FRANÇOISE: I don't see very well what you could do.
NARRATOR: I'm an expert at making tea. It's one of my rare talents.
She holds out the cord to the kettle for him; he plugs it in, as she comes around the table.
FRANÇOISE: Well, okay, then, you make it.
Then she opens a cupboard to take out a box of tea and a teapot.

NARRATOR: Hand me the box.

She hands it to him. Pan following her as she advances to the left.

181. CU: *Françoise, sitting, watching him at work.*

FRANÇOISE: Hey, you don't put it in right away!

182. MCU: *the narrator, standing, awkward, with the box of tea in his hands.*

NARRATOR: Oh, is that right? ... I thought ... you boiled it.

183. MCU: *Françoise, breaking out in a laugh.*

NARRATOR (*off*): It's nice in your place. ... You feel at home. (*Pause; still off.*) Me, I've got a furnished apartment. I have a kitchen but I practically never use it. ... Is there room here for me?

FRANÇOISE: Everything is taken. And besides they only take students.

NARRATOR (*off*): Boys?

FRANÇOISE: Boys and girls. It's not a boarding school. (*She smiles.*)

184. *As in 182,* MCU: *the narrator, still standing, with the box of tea in his hand.*

NARRATOR: Then I'm going to register at the university next year. Save me a room.

185. *As in 183,* CU: *Françoise, sitting and laughing.*

FRANÇOISE: Have you been in Clermont a long time?

186. *As in 184,* MCU: *the narrator.*

NARRATOR: Three months. I work for Michelin. Before, I was in America, Canada, and Chile. I was a little afraid of coming here, but in the end I like it.

187. *As in 185,* MCU: *Françoise, very attentive.*

NARRATOR (*off*): Clermont is not a bad city.

FRANÇOISE: Are you talking about the place or the people?

NARRATOR (*off*): The place. I don't know the people. Are they okay?

FRANÇOISE: Yes, the ones I know. Otherwise I wouldn't know them.

NARRATOR (*off*): Do you see them often?

FRANÇOISE: Yes. Actually, at the moment, I'm a little bit lonely, ... but it's because of the circumstances.

NARRATOR (*off*): Why?

FRANÇOISE: No reason. Purely external circumstances. I had some friends who went away. It's of no interest.

NARRATOR (*off*): No interest for you or for me?

FRANÇOISE: For you. But you, do you have colleagues?

NARRATOR (*off*): Yes. I'm kind of choosy about making friends. Yes, I think it's stupid to be friends with someone just because he sits at the table next to you ... or because his office is next to yours. Don't you agree?

FRANÇOISE: Yes, in a sense.

NARRATOR (*off*): But?

FRANÇOISE: No, nothing. In fact, yes, you're right.

NARRATOR (*off*): You think I was wrong to run after you?

FRANÇOISE: No, but I could have told you to get lost.

NARRATOR (*off*): I've always been lucky. The proof is that you didn't do that.

FRANÇOISE: Maybe I was wrong. It's the first time I ever let myself be picked up by somebody in the street like that.

NARRATOR (*off*): For me, it's the first time I ever picked up someone I didn't know. Luckily, I didn't think about it, . . . otherwise, I would never have had the courage to do it.

FRANÇOISE: The water's boiling.

She gets up.

188. MS: *the narrator, standing, his back against the wall, the box of tea in his hand.*

NARRATOR: No, . . . no, let me. I'll take care of everything. I enjoy it.

He puts the box on the table, unplugs the kettle, and pours the hot water into the teapot. He shakes the pot to warm it. She laughs, off. He smiles and glances at her repeatedly.

NARRATOR: Are you laughing at me?

FRANÇOISE (*off*): No, I'm educating myself. (*He pours some tea into the pot.*) Hey, you're not putting very much in!

NARRATOR (*looking up*): You like it strong?

FRANÇOISE (*off*): Not too strong.

He adds a pinch of tea to the pot.

NARRATOR: People always put in too much. The important thing is to let it steep for seven minutes.

FRANÇOISE (*off*): As long as that?

She enters the frame from the left, opens a cupboard, and takes out two bowls and a box of sugar cubes.

NARRATOR: Yes, it's right on the box. Don't you ever read what's on the box? . . . You'll end up poisoning yourself one of these days.

189. CU: *the narrator as he takes off his fur-lined jacket; pan following him as he goes and sits down.*

NARRATOR: It doesn't shock you that I talk all the time about my good luck?

She comes and sits facing him, her back to us in the foreground.

190. *Reverse-angle* MCU: *Françoise, sitting.*

FRANÇOISE: No. And anyway, you don't talk about it.

191. *Reverse-angle* MCU: *the narrator.*

NARRATOR: Yes, I do! . . . I like to try my chances. But I only have luck for good causes. Even if I wanted to commit a crime, I don't think I could do it.

FRANÇOISE (*off*): That way you have no problems with your conscience.

NARRATOR: No, very few. Do you have any?

192. *As in 190,* MCU: *Françoise.*

   FRANÇOISE: With me, it's really the opposite. Success always seems a little bit suspect to me.

   NARRATOR (*off*): That's what's called to sin against hope, which is very serious. Don't you believe in grace?

   FRANÇOISE: Of course. But really, grace, that's not what it is at all. It has nothing to do with material success.

   NARRATOR (*off*): But I'm not necessarily talking about material things.

   FRANÇOISE: If grace were just given to us, to nourish our good conscience, if it weren't earned, . . . if it were just a pretext for justifying everything. . . .

   NARRATOR (*off*): You're very Jansenist.

   FRANÇOISE (*playing with the key*): Me? Not at all. Unlike you, I don't believe in predestination. I think that at every moment of our lives we're free to choose. God can help us choose, . . . but there is a choice.

193. *As in 191,* MCU: *the narrator.*

   NARRATOR: But I choose, too. It just happens that my choice is always easy. . . . That's the way it is, I realize afterward.

194. *As in 192,* MCU: *Françoise, who pours some tea into a bowl and holds it out to him.*

   FRANÇOISE: Sugar?

   NARRATOR (*off*): Yes, please.

   FRANÇOISE: Not all choices are necessarily heartbreaking. But they can be.

   She pours some tea into a second bowl.

   NARRATOR (*off*): No, you misunderstand me. I don't mean I choose what pleases me, but it happens that it's for my good, for my moral good.

195. *As in 193,* MCU: *the narrator.*

   NARRATOR (*continues*): For example, I had some bad luck. I was in love with a girl, she didn't love me, she left me for another guy. And in the end it's good that she married him, him and not me.

   FRANÇOISE (*off*): Yes, if she loved him.

   NARRATOR: No, I mean, it's very good for me. In fact, I didn't really love her. The other man left his wife and children for her. Me, I didn't have any wife or children to leave. But she knew very well that, even if I'd had them . . .

196. *As in 194,* MCU: *Françoise, stirring her tea.*

   NARRATOR (*off*): . . . I wouldn't have left them for her; therefore that bad luck was really good luck.

   FRANÇOISE: Yes, because you have principles . . . and these principles come before love. And she knew very well that, for you, the choice was already made.

NARRATOR (*off*): I didn't have to choose, because she left me.

FRANÇOISE: Yes, . . . because she knew your principles. But if it had been her with a husband and children . . . (*she puts down her bowl*) . . . and if she had wanted to leave them for you; then you would have had to choose.

197. *As in 195,* MCU: *the narrator.*

NARRATOR: No, because I was lucky.

198. *As in 196,* MCU: *Françoise. She picks up her bowl, puts it down again.*

FRANÇOISE: Don't you think it's getting late? . . . I'm going to show you to your room.

She picks up the key and stands up; pan following her as she heads to the door and opens it. She goes out. He follows her.

Another Room, interior, night

199. *Slightly high-angle* MS: *the narrator sitting on a sofa bed, taking off his shoes. He turns on a lamp. Next he looks at a little bookshelf on the wall above the bed. After looking over the titles, he reaches up and takes out a book, pages through it, and puts it down open beside him.*

200. ECU: *the title page of the book:*

DE LA VRAIE	OF TRUE
ET DE LA FAUSSE CONVERSION	AND FALSE CONVERSION
ou la fausse querelle de l'athéisme	or atheism's false quarrel
par	by
Léon Brunschvicg	Léon Brunschvicg
Éditions	Editions of the
Presses Universitaires de France	French University Presses[38]

201. *As in 199,* CU: *the narrator, seated. He picks up the book again, stretches out on the sofa bed, and begins to read. A pause. He puts the book down, looks in his coat pocket for his pack of cigarettes, takes one, feels the pockets of his trousers.*

202. MCU: *the narrator; pan as he gets up and, his back toward us, goes to the mantelpiece, beneath a huge mirror, in which his face is reflected. He grabs a big matchbox and shakes it. It is empty. The camera stays on the mirror, in which one sees him turn away and cross the room to a desk.*

203. CU: *the narrator as he bends over the desk and opens a drawer; he rummages around in vain: nothing but papers and photos. He opens another drawer: papers and more photos, one of which, for a second, draws his attention: it's a wedding picture. He closes the drawer again. Another drawer, still in vain. A fourth, full of postcards. On the table, he lifts up a notepad with sketches and looks under it, then exits the frame as the camera lingers on the desktop.*

204. *As in 202,* MS: *the room in the mirror: the narrator comes back to the mantelpiece, where he pauses thoughtfully; then pan following him as he heads to the door, which he opens very gently.*

205. MCU: *the narrator, in the semidark hallway, coming out of his room.*

206. MS: *Françoise's door,* POV *of the narrator, with light showing through the cracks.*

207. *As in 205,* MCU: *the narrator, the unlit cigarette in his mouth; he waits for a long moment, listening or thinking, before advancing down the hallway.*

208. CU: *Françoise's door; the narrator's head appears, seen from behind, then his hand, which knocks lightly at the door.*
    FRANÇOISE (*off*): Yes? . . . Come in.
    He goes in.
    NARRATOR: Excuse me.

209. *Slight high-angle* MS: *Françoise,* POV *of the narrator. She is in her bed, reading.*
    NARRATOR (*off*): I still don't have any matches.
    FRANÇOISE: They're on the mantelpiece.
    She is looking in his direction, out of the frame. A pause.
    FRANÇOISE: No, keep them.
    NARRATOR (*off*): Thanks. Good night. Excuse me.
    FRANÇOISE: Good night.
    The camera lingers on her as he leaves; one hears the sound of a door closing.

210. LS: *the corridor, with the narrator's room in the background, the door open, partly lighting the hallway. He goes in, his back to us, while lighting his cigarette, and closes the door, darkening the screen. . . .*

211. MS: *the window in the narrator's room, where the curtains let in daylight. A cock crows. A knock is heard at the door.*

212. MS: *the narrator, stretched out on his back on the sofa bed, fully dressed, with a blanket over him. On the floor, near the bed, an open book.*
    NARRATOR (*waking up*): Yes? . . .
    FRANÇOISE (*off*): It's nine thirty!
    NARRATOR (*raising his head*): Come in!

213. MS: *the door, which opens to reveal Françoise, who remains on the threshold, smiling.*
    FRANÇOISE: Did you sleep well?

214. *As in 212,* MS: *the narrator, in bed, rousing himself, adjusting his turtleneck.*
    NARRATOR: It was hard at first.
    FRANÇOISE (*off*): I'm sorry, but it's late. You're forgetting your appointment.
    NARRATOR (*surprised*): What appointment?

215. *As in 213,* MS: *Françoise.*
    FRANÇOISE: With a girl, at mass.
    NARRATOR (*off*): Oh, that's right, it's Sunday! . . . And then I have to do something about my car.

FRANÇOISE: We'll ask someone to help you.

NARRATOR (*off*): I have to go by my place to shave and dress.

FRANÇOISE: You're fine just as you are. . . . Come have a cup of tea, . . .
it's ready.

She leaves and closes the door.

Françoise's Room, interior, day

216. MCU: *the narrator, standing, drinking his tea from a bowl.*

217. MCU: *Françoise, combing her hair by the door.*

NARRATOR (*off*): You see, I was right to give you a ride home.

She picks up her coat, and, while putting it on, answers.

FRANÇOISE: In spite of the bad night?

NARRATOR: Oh, yes! . . . Do I look half asleep?

*He comes forward and enters the frame in the left foreground, seen from
behind. Slight pan following her movements getting ready to go out.*

NARRATOR: Why are you laughing?

FRANÇOISE: Just because!

NARRATOR: You seem to be rather a cheerful sort.

FRANÇOISE: Very. Aren't you?

NARRATOR: No, not really! . . . Well, it depends who's with me.

*At the point of opening the door, she turns back to face him. He moves
right up against her, surrounding her with his two arms against the
wall.*

NARRATOR: With you, I feel very good.

He tries to kiss her. She turns away. A pause.

NARRATOR: Françoise, do you know that I love you?

FRANÇOISE: Don't say that!

NARRATOR: Why not?

FRANÇOISE: You don't know me.

NARRATOR: I never make mistakes about people.

FRANÇOISE: I may disappoint you.

NARRATOR: Don't say that.

FRANÇOISE: Come on, . . . let's go.

She frees herself. They go out. The camera stays on the door, which closes.

The Church, interior, day

218. MCU: *a Dominican[39] priest.*

PRIEST: Christian life is not a moral code. It is a life. And this life is an adventure, the most glorious of all adventures, the adventure of saintliness. I am not overlooking the fact one must be mad to be a saint and that many of those who have been canonized were afraid of that involvement, of that progression that led them to saintliness.

219. *Slightly high-angle* MS: *Françoise and the narrator sitting side by side in the congregation, visible in soft focus behind them. The priest continues, off.*

PRIEST (*off*): But beyond our fears, we must have a faith rooted in the God of Jesus Christ, a faith that goes beyond the most fantastic hopes of men, . . . and that reminds us, simply, that God loves us, . . . and that always, this man, this saint, whom we are called to be . . . this man is a man . . .

They are sitting almost motionless, but each glances briefly at the other, then looks away again.

PRIEST (*off*): . . . who on the one hand is dominated by a certain difficulty in living, in being, . . . in living with his existence as a man, with his passions, his weaknesses, his affections . . . (*brief glance by the narrator toward Françoise*) . . . but also in living insofar as he *wants* to be a disciple of Jesus Christ.

A Street, exterior, noon

220. LS: *people leaving the Michelin factory. In the crowd coming out toward us, one sees the narrator, who exits the frame at the lower right.*

The Café, interior, day

221. MCU: *the narrator, seen behind the bar, a telephone in his hand.*

NARRATOR: Hello, . . . is the doctor there, please? (*Pause.*) Has she gone out, or has she left? (*Pause.*) Very well. She'll be there Friday? Thank you.

He hangs up, takes some coins from his pocket, sorts through them, and pays for the call.

The Street, exterior, evening

222. M L S : *the narrator and Françoise: they are walking toward us, along a row of illuminated shop windows. Pan as they turn down another street and walk away.*

223. M L S : *resuming the front view of the narrator and Françoise, slowing down by the window of a bookstore. There Vidal is looking at the books on display. He turns around, his back to us, and sees them.*

    V I D A L :   Hello, how are you?

    He shakes Françoise's hand. The narrator seems quite surprised.

    N A R R A T O R :   You know each other?

224. C U : *Vidal.*

    V I D A L :   Yes.

225. C U : *Françoise.*

    V I D A L (*off*):   Clermont is a small town, you know. Anyway, you're a dirty bastard! . . . You haven't called me.

    N A R R A T O R (*off*):   I phoned you yesterday, you weren't there.

    Pan from Françoise to frame the narrator.

    V I D A L (*off*):   I was in Toulouse yesterday and the day before. Hey, I have a message for you. Our friend is leaving.

    N A R R A T O R :   She's left? (*He looks toward Françoise.*)

    V I D A L (*off*):   No, not yet. I went with her to have a look.

    Pan in reverse to frame Françoise again, who is looking at the narrator, then at Vidal.

226. C U : *Vidal.*

    V I D A L :   We just got back. She's going to leave soon, . . . this time without me!

    N A R R A T O R (*off*):   When?

227. C U : *Françoise, who is staring fixedly at Vidal, then at the narrator.*

    V I D A L (*off*):   Tomorrow, I think. The deal was settled very quickly.

    N A R R A T O R (*off*):   Is she home tonight?

    V I D A L (*off*):   Yes, . . . I suppose so!

    N A R R A T O R (*off*):   I'll phone her. Good-bye.

228. *As in 226,* C U : *Vidal.*

    V I D A L :   And happy new year!

229. *As in 227,* C U : *Françoise, who exits the frame to the left.*

The Bookstore, interior, evening

230. M S *over a shelf of books in the foreground. Françoise enters and passes behind it, right to left, followed by the narrator. She takes a book and leafs through it.*

    N A R R A T O R :   Did you[40] know him?

    F R A N Ç O I S E :   Slightly. . . . He teaches philosophy at the university.

NARRATOR: You're not studying philosophy.

FRANÇOISE: You know, Clermont is a small town. Anyway, we hardly know each other. (*She looks at him.*) Is he a friend of yours?

NARRATOR: A friend from high school. What do you have against him?

FRANÇOISE: Oh ... nothing! We barely know each other, that's all.

The Snow-Covered Countryside, exterior, day

231. LS: *Françoise and the narrator, on the heights overlooking the city. It is snowing. They are in each other's arms. She pulls free. He seems annoyed, holding back his irritation. He hugs her from behind.*

NARRATOR: What would you really like?

FRANÇOISE: Well, ... that we had always known each other.

NARRATOR: Me, too, I'd really like that! ... (*Pause.*) And besides, it's true, I have always known you. I have the impression that you have always been part of my life.

Slight zoom in.

FRANÇOISE: There are sometimes false impressions.

NARRATOR: Too bad if I've made a mistake. (*Smiling.*) Anyway, I never make mistakes. Kiss me.

He tries to kiss her, but she pulls free and exits the frame to the left. Slight zoom in on him.

NARRATOR: You don't want to kiss me? What's the matter?

232. MCU: *Françoise, lowering her eyes, ill at ease, twisting her scarf, unhappy. Zoom in to a CU of her.*

FRANÇOISE: Nothing. ...

NARRATOR (*off*): Well, ... I don't know ... I think you're acting strangely.

FRANÇOISE: No, I'm being sensible.

NARRATOR (*off*): Oh, listen, Françoise, ...

233. *As in 231,* MCU: *the narrator.*

NARRATOR: ... I'm thirty-four years old. You're twenty-two, and we're acting like fifteen-year-old kids. Don't you trust me any more? ... Don't you think I'm serious?

234. *As in 232,* CU: *Françoise, chewing her scarf.*

FRANÇOISE: You are, yes.

NARRATOR (*off*): Well, then?

Before answering, she looks away, looks at him, looks down; the camera follows her agitation with slight movements.

FRANÇOISE: I have a lover.

235. *As in 233,* MCU: *the narrator, thunderstruck. A silence.*

NARRATOR (*awkward*): You have ... now?

FRANÇOISE (*off*): Well, I had one. Not so long ago.

Pan as he goes toward her. Reframe as a MCU *of the two.*

NARRATOR: But, ... do you love him?

FRANÇOISE: I loved him!

NARRATOR: Who is it?

FRANÇOISE: You don't know him. Don't worry, it's not Vidal. (*She gives a dry laugh.*)

NARRATOR: Did he leave you?

FRANÇOISE: No, it's more complicated than that. He's married.

NARRATOR: Listen, Françoise, you know how much I respect you, and I respect your freedom. . . . (*Pause.*) . . . If you don't love me. . . .

FRANÇOISE (*interrupting him*): No . . . are you crazy?

NARRATOR: No, I mean, if you're not sure about loving me. . . .

FRANÇOISE: Yes, I love you, it's you I love.

NARRATOR: And him?

FRANÇOISE: I loved him. I was madly in love. I could tell you I've forgotten him, but you can't completely forget someone you've loved. . . . I had seen him just before I met you.

NARRATOR: Do you see him often?

FRANÇOISE: No. He's left Clermont. It's over, you know! . . . (*Sad.*) We won't see each other any more, it's over.

He takes her gently by the neck, and toys with the fasteners of her loden coat during the next speech.

NARRATOR: Listen, Françoise, if you want, we can wait as long as you want. But now, if you think I love you less, that I respect you less because of all that, you're wrong. First of all, because I have no right to. And besides, I can admit it to you, I'm glad. Yes, it's true, I felt embarrassed next to you. I've had affairs and some of them lasted a very long time. Well, this way we're even.

She turns to him.

FRANÇOISE: Yes, but they weren't married.

NARRATOR: So what?

FRANÇOISE: And besides, it was far away, in America.

NARRATOR: I'm going to tell you a secret. The very morning we met . . . I was coming from a girl's house. I had slept with her.

FRANÇOISE: What if we never talked about all that? Do you agree, never talk about it?

Fade to dark as she turns away, before she finishes speaking.

A Beach in Summer, exterior, day, five years later

236. *High-angle* ELS: *the beach from atop the dunes: in the far background, coming up from the beach, a woman; somewhat nearer, going down the slope, a couple and a child: the narrator, his wife Françoise, and their four-year-old son Arnaud. The narrator is walking in front, carrying a beach bag.*

237. *Reverse low-angle* MS: *the family approaching. The narrator exits the frame to the left as Françoise and Arnaud come nearer.*

238. MS: *the narrator from behind. The woman climbing up from the beach advances toward him and passes by him. He stops in surprise, recognizing Maud. She stops, too.*

MAUD: Well, it's you!

239. *Low-angle* MLS: *Françoise and Arnaud approaching slowly.*

MAUD (*off*): Have you been here long?

NARRATOR (*off*): We just got here.

MAUD (*off*): You're the last person I expected to meet.

NARRATOR (*off*): We come here every year, though.

Françoise and Arnaud stop, seeing the narrator talking to someone.

MAUD (*off*): You haven't changed.

NARRATOR (*off*): You either.

240. MCU: *Maud.*

NARRATOR (*off*): You know my wife?

Pan to a CU *of Françoise in profile.*

Françoise shakes Maud's hand, while Maud is still out of the frame; then she crosses in front of Maud to be closer to the narrator. Pan following her, stopping to reframe Maud in a CU.

MAUD: Yes, yes . . . we know each other, . . . by sight, anyway. Congratulations. Why didn't you send me an announcement?

241. MCU: *the narrator and Françoise.*

NARRATOR: I didn't know your address.

MAUD (*off*): You could've telephoned before I left.

NARRATOR: I did, I think.

MAUD (*off*): No need to lie. I have a good memory. You dropped me shamelessly.

Tilt down to Arnaud. He is holding his parents' hands.

MAUD (*off*): Well, you had your reasons. . . .

Françoise takes Arnaud and goes away with him toward the beach. Pan briefly following them.

FRANÇOISE: Excuse me.

NARRATOR (*off, to Françoise*): I'll catch up with you.

242. *As in 240,* MCU: *Maud, watching Françoise and Arnaud leave. A pause.*

MAUD (*with a little sigh*): It was her! . . . How odd, I should have thought of it.

NARRATOR (*off*): Her?

MAUD: Yes, your wife, Françoise.

NARRATOR (*off*): But I never talked to you about her.

MAUD: And how! About your blond Catholic fiancée. . . .

243. MCU: *the narrator.*

MAUD (*continues, off*): . . . I have a good memory, you know.

NARRATOR: How could I have talked to you about her, since I didn't know her?

MAUD (*off*): But why lie?

NARRATOR: I met her the very next day after . . . the evening I went to your place.

244. *As in 242,* MCU: *Maud.*

MAUD: The evening? The night, you mean. Our night. I haven't forgotten a thing, you never stopped talking to me about her.

245. *As in 243,* MCU: *the narrator, playing with the cord of the beach bag, ill at ease.*

MAUD (*continues, off*): Has she talked to you about me?

NARRATOR: No.

246. *As in 244,* MCU: *Maud.*

MAUD: You're still secretive. . . . Okay, let's not stir up old ashes, . . . cold ashes. It's long ago, all that!

NARRATOR (*off*): Still, it's amazing how little you've changed.

MAUD (*with a little smile*): You too.

NARRATOR (*off*): And at the same time, it seems terribly distant to me.

MAUD: No more distant than anything else, no more than . . . in the final analysis. (*Pause.*) By the way, you know I've remarried. . . .

NARRATOR (*off*): My compliments.

MAUD: Oh, . . . there's no call for them! . . . It's going badly. Yes, it's going badly right now. I don't know how I manage, but I've never had

any luck with men. (*She smiles.*) I'm glad to see you again, . . . even if
it's to find out that. . . . Okay, I see that I upset you by talking about that.
She moves forward, toward him.

247. *Over-the-shoulder* M C U : *the narrator, facing her, as they shake hands.
The camera stays on him as she backs out of the frame to the left, and he
starts to edge backward down the dune.*

  N A R R A T O R : Will you be in the area a long time?

  M A U D (*off*): No, . . . no. We're leaving again this evening.

  N A R R A T O R : Do you ever come to Clermont?

  M A U D (*off*): No, never. And you to Toulouse?

  N A R R A T O R : Never. Oh, well . . . maybe in another five years.

248. M S : *Maud, backing slowly up the dune.*

  M A U D : Yes, . . . that's right, in another five years. . . . Run along now,
  your wife is going to think I'm telling you horrible things.
  She turns and walks away up the dune, her back to us.

249. L S : *Françoise and Arnaud, sitting alone on the sand on the beach. In the
background the narrator comes down off the dune and runs up to them.*

  N A R R A T O R : She sends you greetings.

250. *Slight pan and zoom in on Françoise, to frame her in a slightly high-angle*
M C U . *Her eyes are downcast.*

  N A R R A T O R (*off*): She's taking the boat back again this evening with her
  husband. It's strange, I didn't know you knew each other. When she left
  Clermont, I didn't know you. . . . Oh! . . . I had just met you. She said
  we haven't changed. (*Pause.*) She hasn't either.

251. C U : *the narrator, standing, in profile.*

  N A R R A T O R : It's strange, I hadn't seen her for five years. . . . It's amazing how little people change. I couldn't pretend not to know her, . . . and
  besides, since she's a very likable girl. . . . (*Pause.*) You know, when I
  met you, I was coming from her place, but. . . .

  *As the narrator stops speaking, the camera stays on his motionless face,
  almost in a freeze frame, and then his voice continues as an interior
  monologue.*

  N A R R A T O R ' S I N T E R I O R M O N O L O G U E : I was about to say: "Nothing
  happened," when, all at once, I understood that Françoise's uneasiness
  wasn't coming from what she was hearing about me . . .

252. *As in 250,* C U : *Françoise, who looks up and then back down. Pan to an*
E C U *of her hands, which are nervously twisting her wedding band.*

  N A R R A T O R ' S I N T E R I O R M O N O L O G U E (*continues*): . . . but from
  what she guessed I was hearing about her, and which I discovered at
  that moment, and only at that moment. . . . And I said, quite to the
  contrary:

253. *As in 251,* C U : *the narrator, who crouches in front of Françoise; end of
the interior monologue.*

NARRATOR: Yes, that was my last fling! . . . It's odd that I should run across her, of all people, don't you think?

254. MS: *Françoise, who looks up and smiles.*

FRANÇOISE: I find it rather funny! . . . Anyway, it's long ago . . . it's very long ago . . . and besides we said we'd never talk about it again.

She straightens up and begins to unfasten her dress.

NARRATOR: Yes, that's right. . . . It has absolutely no importance. Ready for a swim?

She stands and pulls her dress off over her head. She is wearing a dark swimsuit underneath.

FRANÇOISE (*to Arnaud*): You coming for a swim?

Pan following Françoise, as she advances toward the sea. The narrator and Arnaud are glimpsed as she passes.

255. CU: *Françoise, from behind, walking toward the water. When she reaches middle range, she turns back and holds out a hand to Arnaud, who runs up to her. The narrator then follows and takes his son's other hand, and all three run toward the sea. The film ends as an* ELS *of all three running into the distant sea.*

The word "FIN" is superimposed at the end of the scene. Then cut to a dark screen, on which appear the date 1969 and the name of the production company, Les Films du Losange.

Notes on the
Continuity Script

1. Clermont-Ferrand is a city with a population of about 150,000 in central France; Ceyrat is a village with a population of about 2,000 located a few miles to the south.
2. The Forez mountains are part of the chain known as the Massif Central.
3. The cathedral was built in the thirteenth century in Gothic style.
4. The basilica of Notre-Dame-du-Port was built in the eleventh and twelfth centuries and is an excellent example of Auvergne romanesque architecture.
5. A French radio network.
6. A French tire manufacturer, founded by the two Michelin brothers, André (1853–1931) and Édouard (1859–1940); the latter was born in Clermont-Ferrand, and the original factory was located there. The company has since become equally famous for its guidebooks.
7. The Puy de Chanturgue is a small peak on the north side of Clermont-Ferrand.
8. Chanturgue is also the name of a highly regarded local wine, which will play a certain role in the film.
9. This is the Livre de Poche edition of Pascal's *Pensées,* published in 1962; on Blaise Pascal and his *Pensées,* which play an important role in this film, see the Introduction.
10. This passage occurs near the end of the passage on the wager. Blaise Pascal, *Pensées,* trans. and ed. M. F. Stewart (New York: Pantheon, 1965), p. 121.
11. Pierre André de Suffren (1729–1788) was a noted naval commander. Presumably the café takes its name from the street where it is located.
12. A noted violinist, born in the Ukraine in 1924.
13. Vittel is a spa town in the Vosges and the source of a popular bottled water.
14. The arithmetical triangle was the subject of a treatise by Pascal, written around 1654 and published in 1665.
15. The wager is discussed in the *Pensées;* see the Introduction.

16. Maxim Gorky (1868–1936) was a Soviet novelist. Vladimir Ilyich Lenin (1870–1924) was a Marxist theorist and political leader during and after the Revolution of 1917, and a founder of the first Soviet state. Vladimir Mayakovsky (1893–1930) was a Soviet writer who became disenchanted with the new regime and died by his own hand.

17. The theater is located on the Place de Jaude, a large square in Clermont-- Ferrand.

18. Montpellier is a city with a population of about 200,000 in the south of France; its famous medical school was founded in 1221.

19. Vancouver is a Canadian Pacific port city in southwestern British Columbia, with a metropolitan area population of over one million; Valparaiso is a port city in central Chile, with a population of about 280,000.

20. Lyons is a city in southeastern France with a metropolitan area population of about 1.2 million; Marseilles is a Mediterranean port city in southwestern France with a population of about 875,000.

21. Allusions to famous passages in Pascal; see the Introduction.

22. The Jesuits were members of the Society of Jesus, founded by Saint Ignatius Loyola in the sixteenth century. They were adversaries of Pascal and the Jansenists, who accused them of hypocrisy and moral laxity. They were skilled teachers and intellectuals, and noted for their casuistry, a form of subtle argument. In France, the term "Jesuit" is still used as a synonym for "hypocrite."

23. On Jansenism, a puritanical form of Catholicism to which Pascal subscribed, see the Introduction.

24. The Freemasons were a secret society that spread in Europe in the seventeenth and eighteenth centuries, favoring liberal ideals and opposing religious dogmatism.

25. Gilberte Pascal Périer (1620–1687) wrote a life of her brother in which she relates this trait of character as a sign of his humility and detachment from the world.

26. Pascal, p. 119.

27. Pascal underwent a mystical experience after a close brush with death and converted to an extremely strict form of religious belief; see the Introduction.

28. "Précieuses" was the name given to women in seventeenth-century Paris who, as members of salon society, sought to purify language and manners.

29. A popular French brand of cigarette; the name means "gypsies."

30. The marquise de Rambouillet (1588–1665) was the most famous of the salon hostesses.

31. An essay sometimes attributed to Pascal.

32. A legendary seducer first portrayed in a play by Tirso de Molina, but best known in France from Molière's play *Don Juan* (1665).

33. The Mont-Dore is a famous resort, with hot springs and winter sports, about thirty miles southwest of Clermont-Ferrand.

34. Sauzet, or Saulzet, is a village near Ceyrat.

35. The Puy de Pariou is an extinct volcanic peak a few miles west of Clermont-Ferrand.
36. Toulouse is a city with a population of about 350,000 in south-central France.
37. Vera Cruz is a Mexican port city, on the Gulf of Mexico, with a population of about 265,000; like many ports, it has the reputation of being a wide-open city.
38. Léon Brunschvicg (1869–1944) was a distinguished French philosopher who wrote on the relationships between philosophy and mathematics and between religion and science; the articles in this book were first written and published in 1930–1932 but collected in book form after his death. He also produced a famous edition of Pascal's *Pensées*.
39. The Dominicans are a religious order founded by Saint Dominic in the thirteenth century.
40. He uses the intimate pronoun *tu;* he always used the formal *vous* with Maud.

Contexts

Interviews

Rohmer has given many interviews. He began his career as a critic and spent almost fifteen years closely involved in editing film journals, especially *Cahiers du cinéma,* so talking about his work came naturally to him. By the time he made *My Night at Maud's,* however, his relations with his former colleagues at *Cahiers* had deteriorated. They were political activists of the left, he was politically uninvolved and unashamed of his bourgeois Catholic origins. They regarded certain avant-garde cinema theories as politically significant; he clung to an old-fashioned classicism and realism. The interview he gave to *Cahiers* in 1970 resembles a debate, in which Rohmer patiently sticks to his ideas and relies on his experience as a filmmaker, while his interrogators try to expose his theoretical errors. The interview is too long to reprint in full; the passages dealing specifically with *My Night at Maud's* have been retained.

The shorter interview with Graham Petrie came after *Claire's Knee* and covers a number of subjects not germane to *My Night at Maud's*. Petrie's more sympathetic and respectful questions, however, elicit some very informative answers on Rohmer's broad purposes in making the *Six Moral Tales.*

A New Conversation with Eric Rohmer

Pascal Bonitzer, Jean-Louis Comolli,
Serge Daney, and Jean Narboni

Interviewer: Let's begin with a point that may seem secondary to you: since our last conversation (1965), your two films *The Collector* and *My Night at Maud's* have met with a certain success, both public and critical. Has this success led you to rethink the principle of the "moral tale" or your relation to the public or to the cinema?

Eric Rohmer: One tells oneself that success will come at one time or another. Has it changed my intentions in any way? No. I have always known that I would make the last moral tales with more resources that the first ones, because the subjects required it. They required older characters: and it is easier to find twenty-year-old amateurs than thirty- or forty-year-olds. However, if neither *The Collector* nor *My Night at Maud's* had succeeded, that would no doubt have been the death knell for the *Moral Tales*.

Interviewer: You say that this success changes nothing in the overall plan of the *Moral Tales;* had you built success into the program too? For it is a new objective factor that is going to interfere objectively with your plan.

Rohmer: No, I hadn't programmed it; I'd hoped for it, in the sense that, financially, it would allow me to continue the *Moral Tales*. I believed in the snowball effect, that with the success of the first, I could do the second, then the third, and so on. I played the cards right.

Interviewer: Every success depends on a reading; do you think that, in your case, this reading is adequate to what your films are for you?

Rohmer: Well, I don't know. When you haven't succeeded, you can be proud of it; when you have succeeded, you can be proud of that too. Or conversely, one can complain of succeeding too much or too little. Yes, my success scares me a little: after having been on the margins of the cinema, after having made films almost clandestinely, outside the laws of cinematography and the habits of technicians, all of a sudden now I am accepted, I am welcomed. That could be dangerous, to the extent that a success is always intoxicating. Luckily that isn't the case for the moment, because I have my *Moral Tales* thought out in my mind and my way of filming them is not changing. The proof of that is that, for my next film, I'm not using any more resources than for the previous ones, although I could. When you have a little success, you tend to think you're not against success, and when you have no success, you tend to think that success proves nothing. Both are true, I think. An author agrees more or less with the present time; some are always with

Translated by the editor from Pascal Bonitzer, Jean-Louis Comolli, Serge Daney, and Jean Narboni, "Nouvel Entretien avec Eric Rohmer," *Cahiers du Cinéma* 219 (April 1970): 46–55.

the times, with the flaws that implies, because you can't always be with the times; it isn't normal for a creator to be with the times of the people who receive the work: the creator has to be a little ahead. One is therefore a little ahead with regard to the public, but they catch up in the end. And they go very fast. We are no longer in the age of Stendhal,[1] who was speculating on the next century.

Cahiers: But do you think that the public and critical reception correspond to what these films are?

Rohmer: I think I have been better understood and better received by the public than by the critics. I have the impression that the public was moved in a rather fresh way, whereas the critical reception seems to me more banal.

Interviewer: On what do you base your idea that the public was able to receive your films better than the critics?

Rohmer: On nothing. Except the fact that, if people went to see the film, it's because there was good word of mouth about it. I don't think the critical praise was enough, because it was excessive this year for some films that didn't go over. All the more because there were some a priori forbidding elements in *My Night at Maud's:* the Catholic element, the long conversations, the black and white. The publicity didn't have much effect, either. I had told the distributor to do very little. So the success of this film is pure word of mouth. Now, what are the reactions? I have no idea. I haven't received any letters, except for one or two.

Interviewer: We weren't talking about success as a fact, but about its nature. There is in any case a continuity between the public response and the critical response: the emphasis on "the intelligence of the characters," "the profundity of the themes." . . .

Rohmer: To be sure, but I read it in the press just like you and I can explain it even less than you can.

Interviewer: For example, the film elicited a commentary that could be summarized thus: "in contrast to all these 'modern' films, here is a film that, far from showing us bumbling idiots—as Godard does, for example—presents us intelligent characters, debating extremely high-level problems, and what's more, in the provinces, and all this in a text that is coherent, cultivated, and logically articulated." Which comes down to crediting the film with the intelligence of the characters, to taking as the discourse *of* the film the discourse *in* the film. Now, it seems to us that there is a confusion in this: the interest of the film is located precisely in the connections between the various discourses uttered, more than in these discourses themselves.

Rohmer: Your point of view—and that's to be expected—is more refined and more profound than the point of view of most spectators. But any text, it seems to

---

1. Henri Beyle (1783–1842), a major French novelist, wrote under the name Stendhal. His best-known work is *The Red and the Black* (1830). He was less appreciated by his contemporaries than by posterity, and self-consciously wrote for a small élite readership, "the happy few" capable of understanding him.

me, allows two readings: an immediate reading and a between-the-lines reading, by means of a more thorough analysis with reference to aesthetic theories. But I think that the simplistic interpretation is not worth less than the other. I have always thought, even when I was a critic, that the brutal and simplistic reaction of the spectator has value. I know, in the old days at the *Cahiers* we praised very commercial films while trying to defend them from a point of view that is not shared by the man in the street. But this point of view does not disturb me. If people want to take things in the film literally, things I don't take literally, I don't say that's a misinterpretation, I just say it's an unsophisticated way of taking the film. I accept absolutely all interpretations. Anyway, it's not for me to accept them or not: I make a film, and once it's made, it gets away from me, it closes in on itself, I can no longer get inside it. It's for the public to get in however it chooses. I'm not talking about the critic who, for his part, claims to find the key, the right key, that opens the grand portal. But for me, thank God, the question no longer arises. I'm no longer looking for the keys to Hitchcock the way I used to.

Interviewer: My Night at Maud's is like Hitchcock's films in this respect: the spectator's point of view is not in question, but we do question whether with this point of view one can explain how the films really work.

Rohmer: No, it's a little different. This attitude that consists of looking for the meaning of the film beyond what is most obvious, . . . I think it was valid for American cinema, for a mass audience cinema, but it's not so valid nowadays. I'd like the distance between the interpretations of critics and those of the public to be minimal. (Is the public so naive? I doubt it.) I write films to be, above all, enjoyed, felt, not to provoke an intellectual analysis, but to touch people. A Chaplin film, even if one can think profoundly about it, has to make you laugh, or else it's a failure.

Interviewer: With Chaplin or Hitchcock, to be sure, what's most immediate is in fact enjoyment. Analysis can come later. Whereas in *My Night at Maud's* the philosophical reflections of the characters produce and legitimize the enjoyment of the spectators who are delighted to see the characters do their thinking for them. . . .

Rohmer: Let's say that just now in the history of the cinema, only a film that provokes a certain amount of thought can touch people. There are subjects, like melodrama, that used to touch people and don't any more; and one needs characters with more depth. But I don't understand how the public misinterpreted.

Interviewer: It seems that for *My Night at Maud's,* there was not as much difference between the critics' point of view and the public's, as for Hitchcock's films, for example. For what is the enjoyment factor in a film like *My Night at Maud's* that would be equivalent to the spectacle in Hitchcock, or laughter in Chaplin? It's thought: this is a film whose enjoyment factor was thought.

Rohmer: That's true. But I think there is also thought in a detective novel, in the form of logical and even mathematical deductions, whether explicit or not. And even in a comic film, there is an underlying logical statement.

Interviewer: In *My Night at Maud's* the part given to thought, bearing on elements of intelligence, of discourse, was more important than usual, so that pleasure and the pleasure of thought are more closely tied together than in a comic film, for example.

Rohmer: That's true, but it's a difference of degree and not of nature: in any pleasure there is thought and one must hope that in any thought there is pleasure. I think a work of art is made for pleasure and also for thought. I have always rejected the distinction between art as entertainment and art as thought. One can perfectly well think about Johnny Halliday[2] and take immediate pleasure in Beethoven. For me that distinction is a misconception.

What strikes you is that my characters make long speeches, whereas in most films they don't. Note that in general I've always been prejudiced against films with lots of speeches. But one is often drawn to the things that seem the most difficult and the most dangerous. My purpose was precisely to integrate the speech into the film and to avoid having the film be in the service of the speech, that is, of a thesis. But from the beginning of time, beginning with the Greeks, speech has been important in the theater. The Greek theater was composed of maxims and moral philosophy, which did not prevent it from being real theater.

Interviewer: In *My Night at Maud's,* what allowed people to enjoy the film, more than real or new thinking, was the *idea* of "thinking," with "thinking" in quotation marks. That is, "thinking" filled the role that maxims played in the Greek theater, as a cultural discourse, already well known in advance and labeled as propitious to thinking. In *My Night at Maud's* a material designated by name as intellectual serves to bring pleasure. Whence the risk of misunderstanding we were talking about at the start, a misunderstanding arising from the fact that the spectator had a tendency to consider you, the author of the film, on an equal footing with the speeches proffered in the films, whereas, it seems to us, the film is elsewhere. It is somewhere *between* these speeches, it plays with these speeches, it stages these speeches.

Rohmer: What you are saying is film criticism, and I find it very interesting. I even agree in a way: of all the things that have been said about the film it's one of the most perceptive. But what do you need me here for? My position with respect to the film doesn't matter. Probably because you know I used to be a critic, you're trying to get me to do criticism of my film, which I absolutely refuse to do, and which moreover I am incapable of doing.

Interviewer: Let's say then that there is an ambiguity attached to the notion of "moral tale," that title functioning like a sign saying: "Warning: Thought!"

Rohmer: If there's an ambiguity, it exists in the moral tale. There are subjects, "sentimental" subjects, which can be interpreted only one way, while in my subject there is a fundamental ambiguity to the extent that one does not know who

2. Johnny Halliday was a popular singer in France in the 1960s.

is right or wrong, whether it's happy or sad. That comes from the fact that the cinema has evolved, and that it's more sophisticated, less naive than it used to be. . . .

Interviewer: You told us a while ago that you had bet on success in the 1970s. So you thought your last two films would coincide more precisely with this moment in time. . . .

Rohmer: You want to make a prophet out of me, which I am not at all. I was only hoping. Since, when I began my *Tales*—as Comolli [one of the interviewers] remembers very well—I said "Long live 16mm!" as a provocation and from necessity, more than from real conviction. It was obvious that 16mm presented major technical problems. That was 1962; it's gotten a little better since. Even so I briefly intended to film *The Collector* in 16mm, but Nestor [Almendros, Rohmer's cinematographer] advised against it and convinced me that Eastmancolor was much better and not much more expensive. Likewise for *My Night at Maud's:* I tried to see if it couldn't be done with amateurs and I gave up on finding people capable of playing the parts. The next film will be made "professionally." But the sixth, it's very possible that suddenly I'll find it more interesting to do it in 16mm with amateurs. I don't feel myself imprisoned by success and after the *Moral Tales* I have no idea what I'll do. I don't even regard myself as a career filmmaker yet.

My Night at Maud's is a subject I had been carrying in my mind since 1945. Since then it has undergone enormous modifications. A character locked in a room with a woman by some external circumstance is the primary dramatic idea. But it was a question of the curfew, during the war, and not snow.

Interviewer: Did the fact that it's snow that detains him rather than a wartime curfew bring about any other changes?

Rohmer: Snow is for me the passage from the "tale" to directing. Snow has a great cinematographic importance for me. It makes the situation stronger in the cinema, more universal than the external historical circumstance of the occupation.

Interviewer: Do you think that with respect to the general structure of the "moral tale" snow has a fictional role equivalent to that of the occupation?

Rohmer: Given the subject, yes. Because the subject, as I had imagined it, had no relation to the basis of the occupation, that is, the conflict between French and Germans. You remember Eluard's poem: "It was getting late / Night had fallen / We loved one another, etc."[3] Perhaps that gave me the idea.

Cahiers: Isn't the real problem in the very notion of a "moral tale," between a certain eternity of an abstract schema and its obligatory and precise articulation and insertion into History?

Rohmer: Not into "History," simply into the present-day world, into the world to be filmed, and so there's no problem. Heretofore—and this is related to the

---

3. Eugène Grindel (1895–1952), a French surrealist and resistance poet, wrote under the name Paul Éluard.

realism of my purpose—I've always liked to film in the present era. If I film in Saint-Tropez,[4] it's not the same thing as if I film in the mists of the Baltic. If I film in 1970 the era will affirm itself in a sense, without my looking for it, moreover: I take it because it's there. At the same time, I avoid showing things that go out of fashion too much. Actually, there is a fairly marked "fashion" side to *The Collector,* but I managed not to be its slave, but to dominate it. That goes with my general conception, quasi-documentary; to the degree that I take real characters, who exist outside the film, I take them whole, I don't want to deprive them of their peculiarities, even if these pass with time. In *My Night at Maud's* the discourse is less dated: let's say it's "milieu de siècle."[5] Inserting my characters into time has never been a problem; it's a matter of course.

Cahiers: On the one hand you film the present, on the other the general schema of the *Moral Tales* is ahistorical: now, in *My Night at Maud's* there is also a specific discourse on history and its course and the various wagers one can make about its course: namely, a very coherent Catholic discourse and a less coherent Marxist discourse, which is to say very coherent from a Catholic point of view.

Rohmer: Obviously! The cinema shows real things. If I show a house, it's a real, coherent house, not something made of cardboard. When I show traffic in the streets, it's the traffic in a given city at a given period. Likewise with the discourses in the film, I don't look for schematization. I show *a* Marxist, *a* Catholic, and not the Marxist, the Catholic. . . .

   My Catholic says things that may shock certain Catholics, my Marxist need not be a model Marxist. He's a character who says he's a Marxist, as Trintignant says he's a Catholic. Is he a Marxist from an orthodox Marxist point of view, is Trintignant a Catholic from the orthodox Catholic point of view? I don't know, but that's what my purpose was, for that's what interested me: show men who aren't absolutely sure about the grounds for their adhesion to a doctrine, who question themselves and who wager.

Interviewer: One can say of Trintignant that he is a hesitant Catholic, not model, wavering, but nevertheless a Catholic; whereas for Vitez, what he says in the film makes him not a Marxist.

Rohmer: It's Vitez's text. What gave me the idea for his character was an article on Pascal by Lucien Goldmann.[6] I had written in my scenario several sentences

---

4. A famous resort on the French Riviera, the setting of *The Collector.*

5. A play on the term "fin de siècle" or "end of the century," which designates not only the period of time, but also a decadent style and apocalyptic mood associated with the ends of historical periods; "milieu de siècle" would mean "middle of the century" and thus presumably refer to a less extreme style and mood.

6. Lucien Goldmann (1913–1970), a Romanian-born French Marxist intellectual, is best known for his book *The Hidden God* (1956), about the "tragic universe" of Pascal and Racine.

inspired by this reading, but it needed more work. Now, when I offered the role to Vitez, he told me right off that he liked Pascal and that he had lots to say about him. So we decided to proceed as with *The Collector:* we sat down with a tape recorder, we talked about Pascal, and that's how I drafted the café scene. I took Vitez's words as those of a Marxist—a good or a bad Marxist, who cares? Now, if you don't consider him a Marxist, that's your business. All I can say is that for me the most important thing is the question of loyalty. To a woman, but also to an idea, to a dogma. All the characters are presented as hesitant dogmatists: the Catholic on one side, the Marxist on the other, but also Maud, who clings to her upbringing as a free-thinking radical socialist. Loyalty is one of the major themes of my *Moral Tales,* with betrayal as a counterpart.

Cahiers: There are to be sure in your films a certain number of moral values, to the extent that you play on the ambiguity between the adjective "moral" (attached to "tale" [and suggesting a moral, or lesson to be learned]) and the noun "morals." But these values are always countered by a certain number of elements, which the public and the critics don't seem to have been aware of, elements that relate to repressed desire, to dishonesty, to cowardice, to contempt, and that are always hidden in the readings of your films. There is in fact a sort of dialectic of loyalty and betrayal, which can be expressed at times on an "elevated" plane (*My Night at Maud's*) but just as well in a completely trivial mode (*Suzanne's Career*).

Rohmer: Suzanne's Career is certainly a less accessible film. I've been reproached for the superficiality of the characters. The reproach doesn't bother me. But if I've made *My Night at Maud's,* it's because it pleased me *also* to treat elevation. . . .

Interviewer: Your wish to refer constantly to the "outside" of the film—the "world" existing before and after it—as if to a concrete reality, in the end isn't that something quite different from a search for the "natural," rather instead the quest for a *guarantee?* Is the fundamental realism of the cinematographic image a guarantee of the "presence" of the world? Or rather isn't it the real world itself that would be the guarantee of the "cinematographic realism"?

Rohmer: Since you push me to it, I'll go farther. Not only is there a beauty, an order in the world, but there is no beauty, no order, except in the world. For how could art, a human product, equal nature, a divine work? At best it's only the revelation, in the Universe, of the hand of the Creator. It's true, there's no more teleological, no more theological position than mine. It's the spectator's position. If he hadn't already found beauty in the world, how could he look for it in an image of the world? How could he admire the imitation of life, if he didn't admire life? That's the filmmaker's position. If I film something, it's because I find it beautiful, therefore beautiful things exist in nature. . . .

Interviewer: Let's take the example of the night at Maud's. There is a place, where you filmed: this place preexists. Yet what is striking when one sees the film is that, as the scene advances—by means of editing, the play of looks, the scansion of surfaces—a filmic place is created that has nothing to do with the preexisting place, a much more interesting filmic place, the fruit of real work.

Rohmer: For the first time in my life, I didn't film in an apartment but on a set. Why? Because the subject required a very exact regulation of the actors' places and their movements in relation to the geometry of the place. But once the set was built, according to my instructions, it turned out to be endowed with the same quality of real, autonomous existence as a "natural place." And I wanted to offer it to be seen, as something I was discovering, not that I was inventing. If I had shot in a real apartment, I might have had to fake, move furniture, etc. This constructed set existed much more objectively than a natural setting. So what do you mean when you say this set ends up by becoming "other"?

Interviewer: One can very well reconstruct Maud's apartment at the end of the film and redesign it: the film doesn't consist of that. . . .

Rohmer: But it was very important for my staging because if I had been obliged to cheat, I wouldn't have been sure of my characters' movements. They were guided by the real paths they had to take.

Interviewer: Then we come back to the idea of the preexisting real as a guarantee, not as an object. We fully agree that the "filmic place" couldn't have existed if there hadn't been this filmed place. That doesn't stop the created filmic place from totally replacing the filmed place as the scene unfolds.

Rohmer: I have trouble following you on that. On the contrary, I strongly felt the presence of the filmed place (artificial in this case, natural in others), to the point that its topography dictated the placing of the camera.

Interviewer: What we mean is that the time factor is very important: this set you built is more and more vested in the drama. So then it takes on meanings that are no longer those of its topography. Its filmic function is not equivalent to its function in filming.

Rohmer: Architecture being a functional art, every set is functional, that's obvious. That I built it for dramatic necessities, that's no less obvious. But once again, the set, once created, existed for me as a real being, for the same reason as my actors. My direction was born from the contact between the actors and this set. You should know that in fact that's how things happened. . . .

Interviewer: Instead of conceiving of the cinema as a "window open on the world," one can conceive of it as a "mirror turned toward the spectator." The spectator puts himself in the place of the camera, fills the "absent field"; he is the fourth wall. This is particularly noticeable in *My Night at Maud's,* because of the systematic editing.

Rohmer: The fourth wall is the fourth wall of the room. It bothers me a lot in a film when the fourth wall is not shown. For me, when Trintignant talks, he looks at Françoise Fabian and the spectator feels that this gaze is directed at the woman who is in the bed and not at the audience or anything else.

Interviewer: The spectator is not at all unaware that Trintignant is talking to Fabian, but at the same time he vests himself in the absent field, he is in

Fabian's *place,* without identifying himself with her for all that. And the same thing when there's a countershot: he finds himself back in Trintignant's place, etc.

Rohmer: The essential, what I'm striving for, is to have the camera be forgotten. Add to that the fact, which is very important for me, that it's a first-person film, Trintignant being the narrator. Did you get this feeling?

Interviewer: It's complicated. You know the narrator of the story is Trintignant, but through the conduct of the story, he becomes the subject of the *énoncé* [what is said] and not just of the *énonciation* [the act of saying]. His "I" also becomes part of the film's discourse.

Rohmer: For a film to be taken as a first-person narration, the narrator must be shown. That's a necessary condition. Is it enough? In my next film, there won't be any narration, or commentary, but a character present in all the scenes. Will he be taken for the "narrator"? My tales are all written from the point of view of a character. But when I film, I show him from outside. In any case I do not assume his identification with the spectator. In *The Sign of Leo,* by contrast, where there was no narration, I'm sure the identification was greater. And in *The Collector* the presence of the commentary hinders that identification.

Interviewer: This seems very important to us, because the spectator's investment in a character works strongly when there's no commentary; when there's an "I," far from facilitating the identification, it makes it more difficult. The narrator, although bearer of the discourse, is contained in this discourse.

Rohmer: It's a procedure that has often been used. In American detective films, for example, there is often a first-person narrator, say in *The Lady from Shanghai.* . . .[7]

Cahiers: When the spectator sees a character in a cinematographic fiction, he tends most often to become the *Cause* of this character, the deus ex machina outside the film. If the character already in the film says "I" and claims to be in control of the story, that becomes almost impossible.

Rohmer: That's true. Besides, one of the reasons why I didn't expand Trintignant's commentary was precisely that: the character would have become more distant, antipathetic.

Interviewer: All the more because here there is a *play* among several "I"s, since the characters of the *Moral Tales* can't define themselves, can't come on stage except as "I." We come back then to the beginning of our conversation: to the constant slippages where it seems to us the interest lies. Seeing three characters at once, three "I"s, and being unable to count on one or the other, the spectator ends up thinking of these fictional characters what he thinks of their real-life models.

Rohmer: Yes, but at the same time it's the most ordinary thing there is. Put four people together and they'll talk in the first person.

---

7. *The Lady from Shanghai* (1947, directed by Orson Welles).

Interviewer: In life, but not in the movies. The fact that the characters talk nonstop about themselves in *My Night at Maud's,* that they explain themselves, only makes the film more opaque, however.

Rohmer: That comes no doubt from the fact that *The Sign of Leo* is closer to current cinematographic narration whereas the *Moral Tales* are not at all marked in their origin by a cinematographic influence. My first idea was that they were translatable to the screen only with the aid of a commentary and that traditional means like dialogue, etc., would have been insufficient, artificial. It's about a character who makes a judgment on himself, on his behavior. It's not enough to show his behavior, without the thoughts that the awareness of this behavior arouses in him. That's the main idea. For example, *The Baker's Girl from Monceau,* reduced to its plot alone, without the narrator's musings, entirely changes meaning. In *My Night at Maud's* the fact that the character never stops talking about himself makes the commentary superfluous. All the same I retained two sentences. I don't know if I was right but it seemed to me necessary that one know that my character really intended to marry Françoise, that it wasn't a game. And I find it important also that he didn't guess right away who Françoise's lover was: it had to be said, it had to be said by him.

Eric Rohmer: An Interview

Graham Petrie

Petrie: Where and when were you born?

Rohmer: What I say most often—and I don't want to stake my life that it's true—is that I was born at Nancy on April 4, 1923. Sometimes I give other dates, but if you use that one you'll be in agreement with other biographers. It was certainly 1923.

Petrie: Have you always been interested in the cinema?

Rohmer: No, I couldn't say that. I became interested in cinema very late, when I was a student. Up till then I despised the cinema, I didn't like it, I just liked reading, painting, then music a little later. I didn't take any part in theater, I didn't go to it very much. I liked classical French theatre, Racine, Corneille, Molière, but to read it rather than see it. I discovered the cinema at the Cinémathèque. I came to like cinema because I liked silent films, but I didn't discover film through just going to the movies.

Petrie: Do you think this idea of the man who hesitates between two women is the connecting link between all the Contes Moraux?

Rohmer: He doesn't really hesitate, it just happens that, at the very moment that he's made his choice, made up his mind, another woman turns up. But there isn't really any hesitation. All that happens is that this confirms his choice. In *The Collector,* for example, he just spends a week with her and then leaves her. In *Maud* too it's an adventure for him, but he doesn't hesitate between one girl and the other: if he'd had an affair with Maud it would have lasted a week and then it would have been over. In my latest film the hero's choice is already made, he's going to get married, and if he has an adventure it's nothing more than that.

Petrie: Did you start this series with very precise ideas about the subject matter?

Rohmer: Yes. I had had the stories in my mind for a long time, and when I started the series I knew what the theme of each *Conte* would be. But I hadn't developed them, they were still very vague.

Petrie: You've made some in color and some in black and white. . . .

Rohmer: Three in black and white, two of them in 16mm and *Maud* in 35mm. *The Collector* and *Claire's Knee* are in color and the final one, for which I haven't decided on a title yet, will be too. I haven't written the script for it yet, I'm still thinking about it.

Petrie: Why did you choose black and white for Maud?

Rohmer: Because it suited the nature of the subject matter. Color wouldn't have added anything positive to it; on the contrary, it would only have destroyed the atmosphere of the film and introduced distracting elements that had no useful

From *Film Quarterly* 24, no. 4 (Summer 1971): 34–41.

purpose. It's a film that I *saw* in black and white, I couldn't see any color in it. There is nothing in it that brings colors to mind, and in fact there weren't any colors in what I filmed—for example I filmed a town in which the houses were gray. Certainly there were a few colored hoardings and road signs, but I avoided these; you don't see them because they weren't interesting. There is a stone church and there are no colors in that church. Then there is snow—no color there either. The people are really dressed in black or in gray, they're not wearing anything colored. The apartment too didn't have any color in it, it was decorated in gray already. I was concerned above all with exploiting the contrast between black and white, between light and shadow. It's a film in color in a way, except that the colors are black and white. There's a sheet that is white, it's not colorless, it's *white*. In the same way the snow is white, white in a positive way, whereas if I had shot it in color, it wouldn't have been white any more, it would have been smudged, and I wanted it really *white*.

Petrie: So you don't agree with directors like Antonioni who say it's no longer possible to make films in black and white and that all films should be in color?

Rohmer: I would agree that nowadays the normal thing would be to make films in color, and it might seem a bit archaic to film in black and white. And yet I don't agree really. I think that man has a very strong feeling for black and white; it doesn't just exist in photography, it's there in drawings and engravings too—painters created pictures in color, but they also worked in black and white for drawings and engravings, in order to create a certain effect. As a result I think that black and white is now accepted by the public, and so I think that people are wrong when they say that black and white is impossible nowadays. It's a very curious phenomenon. I think that black and white will always exist, even if it's true that it will be an exception and the use of color will be standard. However, it's quite certain that at the moment filmmakers aren't particularly inspired by color; most films in color have the same banal look about them and might as well be in black and white. Color adds nothing to them. For me color has to contribute something to a film; if it doesn't do this, I prefer black and white for, despite everything, it gives a kind of basis, a unity, that is more useful to a film than color badly used.

Petrie: What would you say color contributes to The Collector *and* Claire's Knee?

Rohmer: I didn't use color as a dramatic element, as some filmmakers have done. For me it's something inherent in the film as a whole. I think that in *The Collector* color above all heightens the sense of reality and increases the immediacy of the settings. In this film color acts in an indirect way; it's not direct and there aren't any color effects, as there are for example in Bergman's most recent film, his second one in color,[1] in which the color is very deliberately worked out and he gets

---

1. *En Passion* (*The Passion of Anna* or *A Passion,* 1969) marked Ingmar Bergman's successful transition to filming in color. An attempt five years earlier had failed and for a time Bergman preferred black and white.

his effects mainly by the way he uses red. I've never tried for dramatic effects of this kind, but, for example, the sense of time—evening, morning, and so on—can be rendered in a much more precise way through color. Color can also give a stronger sense of warmth, of heat, for when the film is in black and white you get less of a feeling of the different moments of the day, and there is less of what you might call a tactile impression about it. In *Claire's Knee* I think it works in the same way: the presence of the lake and the mountains is stronger in color than in black and white. It's a film I couldn't imagine in black and white. The color green seems to me essential in that film; I couldn't imagine it without the green in it. And the blue too—the cold color as a whole. This film would have no value for me in black and white. It's a very difficult thing to explain. It's more a feeling I have that can't be reasoned out logically.

Petrie: What exactly do you mean by the word "moral" in the title of this series of films?

Rohmer: In French there is a word, moraliste, that I don't think has any equivalent in English. It doesn't really have much connection with the word "moral"; a moraliste is someone who is interested in the description of what goes on inside man. He's concerned with states of mind and feelings. For example in the seventeenth century Pascal was a moraliste, and a moraliste is a particularly French kind of writer like La Bruyère or La Rochefoucauld, and you could also call Stendhal a moraliste because he describes what people feel and think. So *Contes Moraux* doesn't really mean that there's a moral contained in them, even though there might be one and all the characters in these films act according to certain moral ideas that are fairly clearly worked out. In *My Night at Maud's* these ideas are very precise; for all the characters in the other films they are rather more vague, and morality is a very personal matter. But they try to justify everything in their behavior and that fits the word "moral" in its narrowest sense. But "moral" can also mean that they are people who like to bring their motives, the reasons for their actions, into the open; they try to analyze; they are not people who act without thinking about what they are doing. What matters is what they think about their behavior, rather than their behavior itself. They aren't films of action, they aren't films in which physical action takes place, they aren't films in which there is anything very dramatic; they are films in which a particular feeling is analyzed and where even the characters themselves analyze their feelings and are very introspective. That's what *Conte Moral* means.

Petrie: In Maud *and* Claire's Knee *in particular you show us some people around thirty-five to forty years old and also some who are very much younger. Do you think there is now a real disparity between these age groups, in the way that people often talk of the new generation having a completely different set of customs and moral values?*

Rohmer: My films are pure works of fiction; I don't claim to be a sociologist. I'm not making investigations or collecting statistics. I simply take particular cases that I have invented myself; they aren't meant to be scientific, they are works of imagination. Personally, I've never believed very much in the idea of a difference between age groups; I don't think it's very strong and it's certainly not an opposition between one group and another, and I don't think it's so very much stronger nowadays than it was before. And even if it is true, it doesn't interest me very much. It's not something I'm concerned with. The fact that the young generation today in 1971 might as a whole have a certain kind of mentality doesn't interest me. What interests me is to show young people as they really are just now, but also as they might be if they were fifty years old or a hundred years old, and the events of the film could have taken place in ancient Greece, for things haven't changed all that much. For me what is interesting in mankind is what is permanent and eternal and doesn't change, rather than what changes, and that's what I'm interested in showing.

Petrie: Have you ever wanted to make a film in the United States?

Rohmer: No. First of all I don't speak English, and I couldn't work in a country where I don't know the language. And I want to show the reality of life in France, I don't want to deal with a way of life I don't understand. In a pinch I could make a documentary about life in a foreign country, but that's a different matter. Also I have a very personal way of working and in France I have a great deal of freedom in this respect. I work with an extremely small crew; I have no assistant director, no scriptgirl, and I take care of the continuity myself. Perhaps I make mistakes and put an ashtray here when it should be there, but that's just too bad. And as usually there are no special clothes for the actors and few objects of special importance, in the long run there are no problems with this way of working. I use very few technicians because there are very few camera movements, but those technicians that I have are excellent, even though there aren't many of them. In other countries you have crews that are quite terrifying. I use five or six people and there you have sixty. That frightens me and I would be quite incapable of working in that way. I don't like to be the big boss who dominates everyone else; I like to be close to everyone, and I don't see how I could work under these conditions in the United States. Certainly that applies to traditional filmmaking; "underground" films would be a different matter. But I can show on the screen only those things I know about, and I think that there's still a lot to deal with in France. There's the question of language too; I place a lot of importance on speech, on style, on voice quality and intonation, and it's very important. The French language counts for a great deal in my films. I'm a writer too. I write my own scripts, and as a writer the French language is important to me. I couldn't write something and give it to someone else to translate, for I'm my own author in my films. So I could only make films in France.

Petrie: What films or directors have most influenced your own, in style or themes?

Rohmer: Silent films above all, though I don't know how direct the influence is. People say that there is a lot of talk in my films, that I express myself through speech rather than images, and yet in actual fact I learned about cinema by seeing the films of Griffith, Stroheim, and Murnau, and even the silent comedies. That's how I learned about cinema. There are two directors after the silent period whom

I like very much and these are Jean Renoir and Roberto Rossellini; they are the people who most influenced me. As for the others, I admire Americans like Hitchcock, but I don't think I've been really influenced by them; if I have, it's quite unconsciously. I can tell you whom I admire, but influence is a different matter, for sometimes you don't even know yourself who has influenced you and I'm perhaps not the right person to talk about it.

Petrie: Do you prefer to work for a small audience that will appreciate what you are doing, rather than for a large public?

Rohmer: Yes, certainly. If it depended only on me, instead of attracting people to my films, I would try to drive them away. I would tell them the films are more difficult than they really are, because I don't like to deceive people. I like to show my films to people who can appreciate them. I'm not interested in the number of spectators. Having said that, it's true that a film is a commercial undertaking and ought to recover its costs. But as my films don't cost much, I don't think I need a very large audience, and I've always thought that they should be shown in theaters that aren't too big. The intimate character of my films doesn't suit a theater or an audience too large for them. And I don't think they are suited to a mass reaction or a collective reaction. It's better if the spectator feels he is experiencing a completely personal reaction to it. Each reaction should be unique, individual, different. I think the film is enjoyed better if the spectators aren't sitting too near one another, if the theater isn't too full, and they don't know each other. Then each has a different reaction. That's better than a theater where there's a uniform reaction. I don't like watching one of my films in public and it distresses me if everyone laughs in the same place, as my film wasn't made with that in mind. I didn't write something just to make everyone laugh at the same time. It's all right if someone smiles, but it shouldn't happen at exactly the same place in the film. Perhaps this is because my films are more like reading than like watching a spectacle, they are made more to be read like a book than seen like something on the stage. So it distresses me to see a collective reaction.

Petrie: Would you agree that the endings of your films tend to be rather sad?

Rohmer: They are not what one is expecting to happen, they are to some extent *against* the person concerned. What happens is against the wishes of the character, it's a kind of disillusionment, a conflict—not exactly a failure on his part but a disillusionment. The character has made a mistake; he realizes he has created an illusion for himself. He had created a kind of world for himself, with himself at the center, and it all seemed perfectly logical that he should be the ruler or the god of this world. Everything seemed very simple and all my characters are a bit obsessed with logic. They have a system and principles, and they build up a world that can be explained by this system. And then the conclusion of the film demolishes their system and their illusions collapse. It's not exactly happy, but that's what the films are all about.

Director's Statements

Besides his interviews and general criticism, Rohmer has written two short pieces concerning the *Moral Tales* as a whole. The first is the preface to the short-story version of the tales, in which the author discusses both the relationship between film and literature and his general purposes in creating the story cycle. The second is called "Letter to a Critic"; it was published in *La Nouvelle Revue Française* in 1971 and discusses the literariness of Rohmer's films, with some comments about the writers who have influenced him.

Preface to *Six Moral Tales*

Eric Rohmer

Why film a story when one can write it? Why write it when one is going to film it? Both these questions may seem trivial, but not to me. The idea for these stories came to me at a point when I did not yet know whether I was going to be a filmmaker. If eventually I did turn them into films, it was because I had not succeeded in writing them. And if, in a certain way, it is true that I did write them—exactly as you are about to read them—it was solely in order to film them.

These texts, therefore, are not "adapted" from my films. Chronologically, the stories precede the films; from the outset I wanted them to be something other than "film scripts." Thus, any reference to camera angles, shots, or any other cinematic or directorial terms is notably lacking in them. From the first draft on, the stories took on a resolutely literary quality. It was as though the stories, and what they were portraying—characters, plot, dialogues—had a need to assert that they did precede the films, even though only the act of making the films gave the stories their full meaning. For one never makes a film out of nothing. To shoot a film is always to shoot *something,* be it fiction or reality, and the more shaky the reality, the more solid the fiction must be. Although I have to confess I was fascinated by the methods of cinéma vérité, I did not close my eyes to the fact that certain forms—the psychodrama and the personal diary, to name but two—were totally foreign to my purpose. These "tales," as the term implies, must stand on their own as works of fiction, even if at times they borrow, or even steal, certain of their elements from reality.

The contemporary filmmaker—and this includes me—dreams of being the sole creator of his work, which implies that he assumes, among other things, the job that traditionally devolved upon the screenwriter. Sometimes that omnipotence, instead of being an advantage and a stimulus, acts as a constraint. To be the absolute master of your subject, to be able to add to it or delete from it whatever you like, depending on the inspiration or exigencies of the moment, without having to account for what you do to anyone, is on one hand intoxicating and, on the other, paralyzing: that facility becomes a trap. What is important is that your own text be foreign to you; otherwise you flounder, and the actors with you. Or, in case you opt to improvise, be it in the plot or the dialogue, you must find a way to create a certain distance between you and what you have shot when you cut the film, so that in place of the tyranny of the written text you have that of the filmed material. And I think it safe to say that it is easier to compose images starting with

From *Six Moral Tales,* trans. Sabine d'Estrée (New York: Viking, 1980), pp. v–x.

a story than it is to make up a story on the basis of a series of images shot more or less at random.

Strangely, it was the latter method that tempted me at first. In these films, in which the written text was of prime importance, I was depriving myself—by the very act of writing the text first—of the pleasure of creation at the time of shooting. That the text was mine rather than someone else's made no difference: I resented that I was but the servant of that script, and decided that if that were the case, I would prefer to devote my time and effort to someone else's creation rather than my own. But little by little I realized that this confidence in the role of chance, which such a method required, did not fit in with what I had in mind, which was premeditated and very clearly defined. I realized, too, that it would have taken a miracle in which, I must confess, I did not believe, for the various elements to come together in a meaningful whole exactly as I had conceived of them. Not to mention the fact that my shoestring budget severely limited the amount of experimentation I could indulge in. And although it is true that in some cases the actors—especially in the fourth and fifth tales—participated in the writing of the dialogue, once a final text was finished, they learned it by heart, just as they would have learned a text by another author, forgetting that parts of it were their creation.

Those portions of the texts that resulted from pure improvisation are few. They affect only the cinematic form of the story, do not really emanate from the texts themselves, and therefore have no place here. For instance, in *The Baker's Girl from Monceau,* as is generally the case in any film, there were times when the actors added, because it seemed natural, such greetings as "good morning," "good-bye," "how are you?"—as distinguished from those same "good mornings" and "good-byes" that were part of the tale and not of the film. There are places, too, where descriptive phrases that on paper are expressed indirectly on the screen become direct descriptions. Finally, I might note a number of improvised expressions or exchanges, the picturesque quality of which, taken out of its cinematic context, would have jarred. I refer, for example, to the table conversation of the engineers in the film *My Night at Maud's* and Jerome's revelations in the film *Claire's Knee.*

Aside from these willful omissions, the attentive reader who has seen the films will doubtless be able to pick out certain discrepancies between dialogues as presented in these pages and those actually spoken by the actors in the films. The fact is that, deeming I had full right to do so, I quite simply corrected occasional errors, omissions, and memory lapses on the part of the actors. My desire that we adhere as closely as possible to the written text was more a principle than an ironclad rule. In no way did I want the quality of the acting to suffer by too rigorously adhering to the text, and I considered myself more than satisfied if my actors, who had to cope with more than their share of restrictions, could, in return for committing these venial errors, breathe a trifle more easily.

There is another factor that obliged me from the start to clothe the tales in literary garb. Here, literature—and this is my principal excuse—belongs less to form than to content. My intent was to film not raw, unvarnished events but rather the account of them as given by one of the characters. The story, the selection and arrangement of the facts, as well as the way they were learned, happened to relate very clearly and specifically to the person relating them, independently of any pressures I might exert on that person. One of the reasons these tales are called "moral" is that they are effectively stripped of physical action: everything takes place in the narrator's mind. The same story, told by someone else, would be quite different, or might well not have been told at all. My heroes, somewhat like Don Quixote, think of themselves as characters in a novel, but perhaps there isn't any novel. The presence of a first-person narrator owes less to the necessity to reveal innermost thoughts—which are impossible to transpose, either visually or through dialogue—than to the necessity to situate with absolute clarity the protagonist's viewpoint, and to make this viewpoint the target at which, as both author and director, I am aiming.

In my early drafts of these tales there was very little direct dialogue, and for a time I seriously considered using a constant voiceover, from the beginning to the final shot. Little by little, however, the text initially intended for the voiceover shifted into the mouth of one character or another. In *Claire's Knee,* the voiceover disappeared completely, the gist of what it revealed being taken over by the various stories contained in the dialogue. Events, instead of being commented on at the time they take place, are only discussed afterward by Jerome, the titular narrator, in the presence of Aurora, the real narrator. In *My Night at Maud's,* the film version contains only two sentences of interior monologue, much less than was in the original shooting script. For ease of reading, however, in the present volume I have restored the balance of the stream of consciousness as it appeared in the script itself. Not that it reveals one iota more about the character than we have seen on the screen; it introduces a flexibility that the image no longer needed but that on the printed page seems once again necessary.

Here, I would like for a moment to broaden the area of discussion. The anxiety of my six characters in search of a story mirrors that of the author faced with his own creative impotence, which the quasimechanical process of invention utilized here—the variation on a theme—conceals but imperfectly. Perhaps it also mirrors the anxiety of the cinema, which throughout its short history has proved a terrifying devourer of subjects, plundering the repertory of the theater, the novel, and the realms of nonfiction. But when you take a close look at the vast spoils that the output of the film industry represents, you realize that what it has evolved out of its own storehouse is slight indeed, both qualitatively and quantitatively. When you scratch the surface a little, you see that there are really very few original scenarios: those that claim originality derive more or less openly from a novel or a dramatic work. There is no film literature, as there is a literature for the theater; nothing vaguely resembling a work, a "play," capable of inspiring and withstanding a thousand possible approaches, a thousand different ways of being staged. In film, the power relationship is reversed: the direction is king, the text subservient.

A film script is in itself of little or no consequence, and mine is no exception to that rule. If it seems to resemble literature, the appearance is deceiving; it is rather a yearning for it. It takes as a model a form of narration already a century old and settles for it with seeming smugness, as though, when it comes to literature, it preferred the hallucinatory to the practical.

It is only on the screen that the form of these tales is fully realized, if only because a new viewpoint is added—that of the camera—that no longer coincides with that of the narrator. Here there is a perspective lacking, which, admittedly, might have been brought into being by the act of writing—by some more or less colorful or vivid description of the characters and their actions, or of the setting in which they live and move. I preferred not to attempt this embellishment; or, to be more precise, I was incapable of doing it. If I had been able to, and if it had been successful, I would have considered these tales sufficient unto themselves in this form and felt no need to turn them into films. For, as I said at the start of this preface, why be a filmmaker if you can be a novelist?

Letter to a Critic

Eric Rohmer

My films, you say, are literary: The things I say could be said in a novel. Yes, but what do I *say?* My characters' discourse is not necessarily my film's discourse.

There is certainly literary material in my tales, a preestablished novelistic plot that could be developed in writing and that is, in fact, sometimes developed in the form of a commentary. But neither the text of these commentaries, nor that of my dialogues, is my film: rather, they are things that I film, just like the landscapes, faces, behavior, and gestures. And if you say that speech is an impure element, I no longer agree with you. Like images, it is a part of the life I film.

What I say, I do not say with words. I do not say it with images either, with all due respect to the partisans of pure cinema, who would speak with images as a deaf-mute does with his hands. After all, I do not say, I show. I show people who move and speak. That is all I know how to do, but that is my true subject. The rest, I agree, is literature.

It is true that I can write the stories I film. The proof is that I did write them, long ago, before I discovered cinema. But I was not satisfied with them because I was unable to write them well enough. That's why I filmed them. I was searching for a style, but I didn't look to people like Stendhal, Constant, Mérimée, Morand, Chardonne, or others of whom you claim I am a disciple. I read these people very little or not at all, whereas I never stop rereading Balzac, Dostoyevsky, Meredith, or Proust: rich, prolix, involved writers. They present me with a world living its own life. I love them and read them often, just as I go to movies often; they too reveal life to me. And when I film, I try to extract as much from life as possible, in order to fill out the line of my argument. I no longer think about this argument, which is just a framework, but about the material with which I flesh it out, such as the landscapes where I situate my story and the actors I choose to act in it. The choice of these natural elements, and the way I can hold them in my net without altering their momentum, absorbs most of my attention.

Where do I find my subjects? I find them in my imagination. I said that I see cinema as a means, if not to reproduce, at least to represent, to recreate life. Logically, then, I should find my subjects in my own experience. But that's not the case: they are purely invented subjects. I have no special competence in the subjects I treat; I use neither memories nor books. There are no keys to my characters, I use no guinea pigs. As opposed to the novelist in my film (*Claire's*

From *The Taste for Beauty,* trans. Carol Volk (Cambridge: Cambridge University Press, 1989), pp. 80–82.

Knee) I do not discover; I combine some primary elements in small amounts, as a chemist does.

But I will use a musician as an example, instead, as I conceived of my moral tales as six symphonic variations. Like a musician, I vary the initial motif, I slow it down or speed it up, stretch it or shrink it, add to it or purify it. Starting with the idea of showing a man attracted to a woman at the very moment when he is about to marry another, I was able to build my situations, my intrigues, my denouements, right down to my characters. The principal character, for example, is a puritan in one tale (*My Night at Maud's*), a libertine in others (*The Collector, Claire's Knee*), sometimes cold, sometimes exuberant, sometimes cross, sometimes feisty, sometimes younger than his partners, sometimes older, sometimes more naive, sometimes more cunning. I do not do portraits from nature: within my self-imposed limits, I present different possibilities for human types, for both women and men.

My work is thus limited to a vast gathering and sorting operation that I do without a guide, it is true, but that I could very well have given to a computer, as do some of today's musicians.

When I began to film my moral tales, I very naively thought that I could show things—sentiments, intentions, ideas—in a new light, things that until then had received attention only in literature. In the first three I made ample use of commentaries. Was that cheating? Yes, if it contained the main part of my subject matter, relegating the images to the role of illustrations. No, if from the confrontation of this conversation with the characters' conversation and behavior a kind of truth was discovered, a truth entirely different from that of the text or the behavior—and that would be the film's truth.

For example, the filmed action and the words said off-camera were never in the same *tense*. One was in the present or the simple past, and the other almost always in the imperfect. The commentary generalized the individual case shown on the screen, linking it more tightly to preceding or coming events, and also, I admit, destroying some of its uniqueness, its charm of something in the present and only in the present. At the same time, it took away quite a bit of my characters' mystery and the sympathy that the spectators were ready to feel for them. But it would have been an easy mystery, a suspicious sympathy, beyond which, for better or worse, I convinced myself to lead my audience.

In *Ny Night at Maud's,* on the other hand, the protagonist explained too much about himself in the presence of his different partners for us to endure more lengthy confidences on the side. He confirmed himself as narrator only through the title of the film, by two short sentences intended only to keep us from going astray. . . .

Reviews and Commentaries

Reviews

There are scores of reviews of *My Night at Maud's,* if one counts all the newspaper and mass-circulation magazine reviews published around the world. To a great extent they repeat certain themes: an ironic summary of the plot; a reference to the serious topics of the conversation; amazement that such a simple story with so much talk on such lofty subjects could be so engaging; a generally favorable opinion of the direction, the acting, and the film as a whole.

Included are several French reviews from 1969, when the film was premiered at the Cannes Film Festival in May and released in Paris shortly afterward. Jean de Baroncelli's review in *Le Monde* heaps praise on the film, and along the way takes a swipe at other, politically committed and more experimental films; his review typifies the attitude that annoyed Pascal Bonitzer and the *Cahiers du Cinéma* interview team. Bonitzer's own review for *Cahiers* is also included; it devotes most of its energies to exposing Rohmer's barely concealed conservative ideology and denouncing the film as a trap for unwary viewers. Several other more moderate French reviews are also included. Martin Tucker's review, published in the American Catholic journal *Commonweal,* is representative of foreign reaction: instead of politics, the focus is on moral questions and the movie's meaning for the average spectator. Richard Schickel, who reviewed movies for American mass-circulation magazines, explains why he voted for *My Night at Maud's* as the best film of 1970. Peter Cowie, a British critic, acknowledges the film's great charm, but finds the narrator morally blameworthy at the end. In addition, some brief excerpts from other reviews are included, to illustrate the variety of responses to and interpretations of the film.

Le Monde
Jean de Baroncelli

This film is marvelously old-fashioned; I mean that it keeps out of fashion's way or better yet it keeps a suitable distance from fashion. First of all, it takes place in the provinces, in a real French city, a closed field where serious feelings have time to come slowly to maturity. Next it treats problems that are timely only because they are of all times: love (real love, not erotic capers), religion (no joke! the hero is Catholic and accepts the rules of his faith), the difficult search for happiness in the ups and downs of daily life. Last and most important, this film puts on screen intelligent people, capable of thinking, reasoning, making personal decisions—which is a change from the obsessed, insane, or mindless types the cinema so often favors with its attention.

My Night at Maud's belongs to a series of six films (*The Baker's Girl from Monceau, Suzanne's Career,* and *The Collector* were the first three) that Eric Rohmer has baptized *Moral Tales,* a perfect title, which points out the way the director wants to go. Rohmer is connected to that grand old French family of analysts, essayists, and psychologists. Although Pascal is often invoked in the course of the film, the behavior of the characters, a certain seriousness mixed with impertinence, the taste they have for lucid self-examination and intellectual confrontation, show that they are descendants of Montaigne, Diderot, and Valéry.[1] And the elegant off-handedness with which Rohmer tells his story (a sort of sentimental minuet) is equally marked by this classical heritage.

People talk a lot in *My Night at Maud's:* the raw material of the film is as much speeches, thoughts, dialogues, as it is images. But in spite of a few slow spots and repetitions, this gabbiness is never irritating, not only because the author has endowed the characters with his wit and sensitivity, but also because the anecdote that serves as a pretext for these verbal fireworks is directed with enough liveliness (especially throughout the "night at Maud's") that we are constantly interested.

Rohmer's film is obviously not addressed to those who seek only pure action and entertainment in the cinema. It is a work that demands of the spectator a certain amount of attention and participation. He may also be blamed for ignoring the cares and concerns of the age: his *commitment* shuns the day's events. In our opinion, that is its best quality. On the pretext of being up-to-date, so many films prostitute themselves these days that one is grateful to Rohmer for his proud and slightly outdated austerity.

---

1. Michel de Montaigne (1533–1592), Denis Diderot (1713–1784), and Paul Valéry (1871–1945) are three distinguished French writers, "moralistes" like Pascal, but of a more skeptical and rationalist tendency.

Translated by the editor from *Le Monde,* June 7, 1969, p. 11.

The acting is brilliant. Jean-Louis Trintignant gets another role here with the range he had in Z^2 and is just as remarkable. Françoise Fabian's beauty, intelligence, and humor give a special sparkle to Maud's character. And we discover with pleasure Antoine Vitez's talent and Marie-Christine Barrault's pretty face.

2. Z (1969, directed by Costa-Gavras).

Cahiers du Cinéma
Pascal Bonitzer

I
t is understood that *My Night at Maud's* is a film of admirable poetry, of
exceptional erotic richness, of uncommon density, of brilliant writing. But it is
also, and maybe above all, a deliberately ideological film, posing directly to the
spectator the problem of the morality of the couple, and at the highest level: love,
religion(s), and destiny. (As *Humanité*'s note on the film says, "The answer is *each*
of us"[1] [italics added]. One can see right away on what ground the debate would
take place, if there were a debate.) In fact it is the first "moral tale" by Rohmer to
allow its signs, mechanisms, and concepts to reveal themselves as such. Therefore
we will try to point them out.

The Labyrinth. "Under the Company's benevolent influence, our customs are
saturated with chance" (Borges).[2] It seems to us that *Maud* is conceived somewhat
as a trap, and its web is spun like a labyrinth. A labyrinth first of all of the setting,
the setting of the action, and of the discourse, inextricable from each other.
"Wherever you go," says Maud, "you're condemned to the provinces." Let us read
for "provinces" a generic reference to places without a center, but also to *discourses* without a center, derived from other discourses (the slightly "Precious
Ladies"[3] aspect of Rohmerian speakers, from the dandyism of the Tarahumaras[4] to
the Marxism of Pascal) and to films in which the anachronistic notion of Destiny
is disguised in more modern dress as Chance/Probability.

A labyrinth and a trap, like the run of the insane rats of *Pierre et Paul*.[5] An
introductory sequence, cleverly descriptive, puts the elements of the construction
in place: the hermetically sealed space of Clermont-Ferrand and its region; the
closed time of winter; the other time, the narrator's, periodic and without exit,
which takes him from Clermont to Ceyrat and from his job to emptiness; other

1. *Humanité* was the French Communist Party's newspaper.
2. Jorge Luis Borges (1899–1986) was an Argentinian postmodernist poet, novelist, and essayist.
Labyrinths was the title of a 1953 French translation of stories from *El Aleph,* originally published in
1949. This quotation is from the story "The Lottery in Babylon."
3. "Précieuses" was the name given to women in seventeenth-century Paris who, as members of salon
society, sought to purify language and manners.
4. An allusion to a passage in *The Collector,* describing the behavior of Tarahumara beggars who
affect an air of disdain.
5. *Pierre et Paul* (1969, directed by René Allio) deals with the "rat race" of modern society.

Translated by the editor from "Maud et les phagocytes [Maud and the Phagocytes]," *Cahiers du
Cinéma* 214 (July-August 1969): 59. A phagocyte is a blood cell that destroys harmful bacteria, but the
term is used figuratively in French; *phagocyter* means to neutralize, absorb, or swallow up.

sealed spaces: the Michelin factory, the church, by allusion the University, etc.; and, summing them all up, Maud's apartment ("There is no other room": Rohmer's subjects are always a bit claustrophobic; see for example the final sequence of *The Collector* and all of *The Sign of Leo*). Beyond the film itself, there is besides that other sealed space, the darkened movie theater, where the spectator wanders from Maud to Françoise, and from Vidal to Jean-Louis, tied to these discreetly magisterial linkages that are the spice of Rohmerian writing.

It is therefore not surprising that the principal mechanism of the plot should be a system of apparently accidental encounters. To be precise, five encounters in an hour and a half of film, all decisive with regard to Jean-Louis's marriage and/or the revelation of Françoise's secret. Encounters "apparently" accidental (if one excepts the night at Maud's, since it was due to an invitation) because, in such a tightly squeezed time-space, people can only encounter each other. (Once again *The Sign of Leo* supplies the key to the device, if *Maud* reveals the sign: as Jess Hahn [the hero of *The Sign of Leo*] walks through Paris, the probabilities that his shoes will lose their soles, that his clothes will be torn, etc., increase. The dilated, excessive time of *The Sign of Leo* is of the same essence as the hypercompressed time of *Maud* and the absence of time in *The Collector:* a theoretical time, purely intellectual and metaphysical.) And also because accidents in Rohmer are so clearly signified that they cease to be accidents, just as the good luck or bad luck claimed by all the characters in *Maud* is not really good luck or bad luck.

Nothing is by chance. No sign escapes the Rohmerian order.

The Narrative. Therefore, once the physical/ideological frame/labyrinth is in place, the narrative can begin. The narrative, or the game, of love and chance, that is to say, of two loves, as there are two infinites, the atheist and the Christian, and the false accident. If the discourse also rules this game, and not the discourse *of* desire but the discourse (metaphysical-moral) *against* desire, one can designate one loser right off: Vidal, a communist intellectual reading Marx in light of Pascal in a bourgeois drawing room.

Therefore a neutralized communist, recovered by the Rohmerian order. The narrative will, however, remain dependent on this order: what is a moral tale, if not a narrative controlled from one end to the other by a transcendence, a teleology? The least open kind of work that exists. It is a strict linkage of causalities that conducts the film to its dénouement: it is implicit, but certain, that Jean-Louis can marry, and even love, Françoise, only on the condition that he spend the night at Maud's (the two women contrast to each other as exactly as night to day), that he undergo the—brief—temptation of sleeping with Maud, and escape it. If Maud's nose had been shorter . . . ?[6] No, for it is clearly specified that Jean-Louis chooses against desire, for ideology *and* for love. Love is very explicitly contrasted to desire by Jean-Louis: I can love only a woman with the same ideas as mine. And

6. An allusion to Pascal's remark on Cleopatra's nose; see the Introduction.

the immediacy of desire in this perspective is risk itself, temptation, the wrong wager, the wrong infinite.

But "it is in the place of sin that grace abounds."[7] So it is while leaving Maud's—where nothing happened, but where it is "as if" something had happened, whence the subtlety and ambiguity of the double false confession Jean-Louis makes to Françoise—that the narrator meets the one he is to marry. (Grace . . . or the luck of the pick-up artist, for, love or desire, the characters never escape from an essentially erotic aspect of the game they are caught up in. And that is the other pole of Rohmer, a little side irreducibly Roger Vailland,[8] which *The Collector* hid with excess, and which *My Night at Maud's* reveals by lack.)

In fact all the "moral" of the story depends on this contrast: Maud is desirable, Françoise is lovable. Because she keeps to the nontheological law of desire (her atheism is a religion, like the "Marxism" of Vidal: it is just a matter of confronting three lifestyles *on religious grounds*), Maud's life is subject to bad luck, failure, lack of love. Because Françoise has stopped following the law of desire ("I was crazy") for the theological law of love, she attains what conservative thought has always defined as the function and perfection of woman: she becomes wife and mother.[9]

A lack on one side, a plenitude on the other.

Naturally, this contrast permits a double reading of the film, from the left or from the right. In the game of preferences, which will not fail to intervene, the spectator of the left will choose Maud, in the name of desire and freedom, and the spectator of the right will choose Françoise, in the name of love and marriage. And the apologia will have worked perfectly (and the trick will have been played).

7. A reference to Romans 5:20.

8. Roger Vailland (1907–1965), French novelist, cited here because of his interest in somewhat perverse eroticism.

9. And it is not the least diabolical jesuitism of the film that, dragging us along in the game of *its* byzantine judgments (a real water taster's job: which of the three smells the most of holy water?), it makes *us* into formidable casuists. [Bonitzer's note.]

Combat

Henry Chapier

More than his previous *Moral Tales, My Night at Maud's* by Eric Rohmer belongs to the genre of the "chamber movie," an intimate, intelligent, and sensitive cinema in which the word is equal to the gaze, in which dialogue is indispensable. Talkative, analytical, didactic, but only in appearance, behind the seventeenth-century moralist Rohmer is a liberated Jansenist on a little excursion among the freethinkers.

On one of his first escapades Rohmer discovered *The Collector,* one of the rare windows open to the atmosphere of the times, a certain youth culture and characters rather foreign to his habitual universe.

In *My Night at Maud's,* by contrast, the themes and characters return to the fold; we are back among the tormented generation, French in the most classic sense of the term, of the first *Moral Tales.* The action is set in the provinces, the milieu is bourgeois with its religious principles and its social taboos; endless conversations bear upon the eternal war of the sexes, on the problems of the couple, on fidelity, sexual vagaries, and divorce. A marvelous, penetrating, subtle chronicle, an admirable reconstruction of a milieu that resists the pressure of time. Eric Rohmer succeeds in capturing in the cinema the Flaubertian tone of *L'Éducation sentimentale.*[1] It is also Jean-Louis Trintignant's best role to date, an excellent vehicle for Françoise Fabian, and the discovery of Marie-Christine Barrault's beautiful face. A worthy film in all respects, *My Night at Maud's* leaves me cold nonetheless to the degree that its subject is formal, a bit stiff and intellectual.

It is no doubt unfair to give in to one person's taste, to subjective preferences, but, while doing justice to Rohmer's excellent work, I feel free to say that this ultracivilized "chamber movie" does not move me emotionally. I preferred the adolescent romanticism of *The Collector* and, for me, *My Night at Maud's* resembles a television play.

---

1. Gustave Flaubert (1821–1880), French novelist best known for *Madame Bovary* (1857), published *L'Éducation sentimentale* (*The Sentimental Education*) in 1869. This story of an idealistic generation's missed opportunities focused on the Revolution of 1848, which had many parallels in the "events" of 1968.

Translated by the editor from "Cannes 69: du beau 'Cinema de chambre' de Rohmer [Cannes 69: Eric Rohmer's Beautiful 'Chamber Movie']," *Combat,* May 16, 1969, p. 13.

Nouvelles Littéraires
Gilles Jacob

Eric Rohmer's *My Night at Maud's* is the very opposite of a cry for revolution. It touches us with the most classical qualities: pyschological analysis, subtlety, sensitivity, precision. A clear pure note that pierces the surrounding cacophony, this Mozartian cadenza is still being "held." Whether he is showing a mass, cozy provincial life, or the hesitation waltz of an engineer torn between his Christianity, his taste for mathematics, his love affairs, and his aversion to Pascal, Rohmer proves dazzlingly what stature a filmmaker can attain when intelligence rules. Multiplying the traps, the better to avoid them, the film contains the most dangerous scene in French cinema: it brings together in a bedroom/living room a couple who had never met before: Jean-Louis, the engineer, and a young woman doctor, beautiful, divorced. They have dinner. The friend who introduced them leaves. Jean-Louis wants to go home but he lives far out and it is snowing. Maud gets him to stay. The night will go by . . . without anything going on, except discussions and more and more intimate confidences. In the morning, contrary to its wishes, the stray lamb will not have been eaten by the wolf. You can imagine the bawdy farce this encounter could have led to. Here, however, delicacy, spontaneity, and aptness of tone triumph. What Rohmer has drawn from Jean-Louis Trintignant and especially from Françoise Fabian is so miraculous one could wish for the night at Maud's to last forever.

Translated by the editor from *Nouvelles Littéraires*, May 22, 1969, p. 14.

Cinéma 69

Frantz Gevaudan

T his is the fourth of the *Six Moral Tales* of Eric Rohmer. Six films, six
variations on one theme: the search for happiness of a man hesitating
between two women. After the C Major of a St. Tropez summer in *The
Collector,* here is the A Minor of icy winters in the provinces.

He, this time, is Jean-Louis, an engineer at Michelin, recently moved to Clermont-Ferrand, "a shamefaced Christian paired with a shamefaced Don Juan," who
has decided to marry the young girl he passes by in the street every day. Chance—
it plays a big part in this film—leads him to meet a childhood friend who
introduces him to Maud, a beautiful but not-much-given-to-praying mantis. A
subtle minuet of ideas and feelings develops among these four characters, which
only the dénouement, a sort of deliciously ironic epilogue, brings to a close. What
is most striking at first is the great accuracy of the dialogue. A lot of talking is done
during this long night, religion is called into question, paradoxes break out everywhere: we see the Marxist become the apologist for Pascal's wager and the puritan
justify Don-Juanism. Like good bourgeois, they delight in the cheap little thrills of
skin-deep introspection. And yet the film is anything but gabby. There is no
affectation in the oratorical jousts, no tawdriness in this pillow talk, which is both
spirited and spiritual.

This is due to the intrinsic value of the script; also to the dazzling interpretations
of this unlikely foursome, where Françoise Fabian stands out for her sensitive,
intelligent, and strong-willed Maud; and finally to the exceptionally clear direction. Without special effects, without music, by a succession of small touches, Eric
Rohmer sets about depicting his characters and their provincial life composed of
small joys, small pains, and long waits.

And the astonishing presence of that background confers an additional dimen-
sion to this tale, whose moral lies in the difficulty of being an authentic Catholic
in our era.

Translated by the editor from "Le Journal d'un Catho de Province [The Journal of a Catholic from the
Provinces]," *Cinéma 69* 138 (July-August 1969): 26.

Commonweal
Martin Tucker

Since appearing at the Lincoln Center Film Festival last fall, *My Night at Maud's* has been talked about in visually glowing terms, and a persistent if small praise has brought it back to New York for a commercial run. If it succeeds on a popular and financial level, it will be a triumph of the nicest kind.

For the movie is truly a celebration of nicety, of virtue in the kindest and gentlest of ways. It is a story of a man who follows the straight and narrow path and who finds happiness through his restriction of vision. When an insight opens onto a truth for him, he keeps the whole matter in perspective. He will not shake things up just for the knowledge of what lies within the fluid mass. He arranges his vision to fit the proper landscape and milieu. Thus, at the end of the film, when he has had a revelation that his young wife was the mistress of a husband whose middle-aged wife once tried to seduce him, he puts the whole thing out of his mind. He has promised his wife and himself that he will not let the past step out of bounds, intrude into the present.

In this sense the film is characteristic of the new, of the times in which the film was made. For it exhibits in its cavalier rejection of the past a distaste for and dislike of rational and psychological norms. Yet this desire to withdraw from the progressive theory—that is, that the past is meaningful as a fact of progress—is the only connection this film has with the radical mode today. In its isolation from the traditional liberal view that reason can advance knowledge, it is radical on the right. Perhaps this is what makes the film so curiously attractive. For the hero is a gentle, thoughtful man, a mathematical scientist of some proportion. He chooses to regulate his life, to codify his behavior and his vision, and achieve his freedom within the limits of his prescribed area of activity. As the film opens he is going to church in the suburban town of Clermont-Ferrand. He sees a girl in church who fits his ideal of *his* wife; he pursues her through the streets but loses her when another car blocks his way in traffic. He later meets an old friend, a man who represents a less codified approach to life. The friend and the man are bachelors; not having seen each other for fourteen years they talk of old times and the rites of transition. The friend takes him to visit a friend—Maud—and this visit is almost the whole of the film. At least it is the most refreshingly adult view of sex seen in the movies in a long time.

Maud is a doctor, an agnostic, a divorcée. She likes to tease. She maneuvers the hero into staying the night with her in her apartment while getting rid of the friend (who has been her occasional lover). Maud and the hero play a game of seduction—

From "The Screen: Maud's Place," *Commonweal* 92 (May 1, 1970): 169–170.

she tries to seduce him; he tries to resist her. He finally wins, in a battle that shows him to be both honorable and amusing without being priggish or arrogant. In the morning he rushes off to his apartment and finally meets the girl he had seen in church the day before. Later another series of circumstances throws him into the girl's apartment, but here too he resists the idea of seduction. He reads a book instead.

Finally he marries the girl. Five years later he meets Maud on a beach. She has remarried, but the second marriage is going as badly as the first. She is a game but unhappy girl; perhaps because she plays games, the film implies, she is unhappy. The hero on the other hand—a gentle Catholic who may question even his doubt but who never questions authority—is happy. He has a wife he thinks proper: beautiful, intelligent, his own; and a child. He has, in other words, an identity that gives him status (he is wise enough to know that a status that gives him an identity is too fickle a hold on which to base his life-style). The "free" people in the film—Maud and the hero's liberal friend—are the unhappy ones. They are lonely, insecure, tossed about. The hero, however, has a measure of calm and satisfaction because he has striven to achieve recognizable goals: a Catholic girl for a Catholic husband, a seeming virgin for an older bachelor, a respectable bourgeois without any of the modish blasphemies of the intellectual. The hero has to blind himself to his wife's affair with a married man—Maud's first husband—but he is able to obscure this insight in light of a greater vision.

Morality is charity, the film is saying; the greater sin is intellectual gamesmanship with human relationships. The film thus sides with willful, charitable ignorance. The husband tells himself that to see no evil will make evil invisible, therefore nonexistent. This is a charitable and forgiving view of past errors. The intellectuals who discuss the matter—Maud and her occasional lover—are by implication trespassers in the Garden of willed Eden the hero has restored with his new wife.

That the intellectual's delight should be a film celebrating ignorance in a charming, intellectual manner seems extraordinarily perverse as well as extraordinarily significant. It represents a counter-counterrevolution, a return to the sentimental romanticism of assured dogma. The writer-director of the film, Eric Rohmer, calls it a "moral story," one of six in a series of moral tales, and it is clear where his morality lies. That he has been able to achieve his effects by the simplest of means—black-and-white photography, conventional shots and views of provincial towns (even an obvious studio canvas of a hilltop and city background[1] while the lovers talk in a shower of snowflakes), and intelligent conversation—is a wonder that can only be attributed to his talent and to a surfacing need for verities. Rohmer's film is not really a morality play, it is a dream vision, a sentimental view

---

1. Tucker is wrong about this; the hilltop and city background are real, as are all the outdoor scenes, which were shot on location.

that is extremely pleasant as fantasy. It is the other side of romanticizing *la vie bohème;* it romanticizes *la vie bourgeoise.*

The credit for the success of the film's charm and guile also lies with its two stars. Jean-Louis Trintignant, who is probably France's most versatile actor, makes the exasperatingly stubborn hero lovable; he can smile his way out of Maud's embraces without losing his sex appeal. Françoise Fabian, as Maud, is a beautiful mature woman who makes the viewer perfectly aware of her tricks at the very time she is deceiving herself. Every gesture, every line around her beautiful eyes suggests the lost woman willing but unable to give up her frustrating intellectual search. Indeed the two stars and the writer-director almost make the viewer believe again in simplicity, order, and clothing in movies. Such an achievement is not to be belittled—but it must be kept in perspective, for much more than meets the eyes in this visual experience is cracking the surface.

Second Sight
Richard Schickel

"There is," says critic Andrew Sarris, "no greater spectacle in the cinema than a man and a woman talking away their share of eternity together." I happened to read that passage just before seeing *My Night at Maud's,* and it seems to me that at the very least its director, Eric Rohmer, brilliantly proves Sarris's proposition. In so doing, he flies in the face of the prevailing film aesthetic, which offers such warm comfort to all those directors who have been gouging away at our eyeballs with all the very latest instruments of visual torment.

Mr. Rohmer's idea of a really big eye trip is a glimpse in black and white of some rather ordinary scenery passing by outside a car window and his notion of a hot editing technique is to use a reverse angle right where you'd expect to find a reverse angle. Mostly his people just sit around and talk, unaided by Shavian or even Mankiewiczian wit. What they talk around and about is a self-confessed mediocrity (Jean-Louis Trintignant) who takes his minuscule adventures of mind and spirit with desperate seriousness. An engineer working for a large firm in a small town, he is deep into calculus and Pascal, the remarkably dull sermons offered down at the local cathedral, and, most importantly, Jansenism, the theological doctrine that denies free will in favor of predestination. A friend, for devious reasons, introduces him to the lady of the title, and Trintignant passes a couple of ambivalent days with her, fearful that she will upset his conviction that he is predestined to marry a blonde he has glimpsed (but not met) at the cathedral.

Turns out, by God (the phrase is used literally), that he *was* supposed to marry the blonde and that, indeed, she was more closely interwoven into his destiny than anyone suspected and that in the end things work out just as nicely as one hopes they will if Jansen was right. But the details of the story, if one can so dignify the skeleton over which Rohmer has stretched his movie, are of less consequence than the remarkable manner in which these ordinarily pretentious, faintly foolish, incredibly *verbal* people compel our attention—the shifting of a glance or of a position in a chair becomes an event as important as, say, a murder or a cavalry charge in an ordinary movie.

How soberly involved everyone is! How comic is the care with which they examine themselves and each other about their motives and the effect their small statements and actions are having! In particular, how moving it is to watch Trintignant prove himself one of the master screen actors of our time as he studies the life flowing past him to see if it proves or disproves the theories he has been toying with. Years ago D. W. Griffith perceived that one of the unique qualities of

From *Second Sight* (New York: Simon & Schuster, 1972), pp. 306–308.

the movie camera was its ability to "photograph thought," a quality that has not been, by and large, adequately pursued in films of late but which is the principal aim of Rohmer, who is fortunate indeed to have found in Trintignant and friends (Françoise Fabian, Marie-Christine Barrault, Antoine Vitez) actors who can give him some thoughts to shoot.

I doubt that any major American actors would risk such quiet roles in so quiet a picture, and I doubt that, in our present overheated climate, a man like Rohmer could obtain backing for a project containing so little action, so little "youth appeal." Is there, in fact, an American producer who understands that eroticism can be intellectual, may involve neither coupling nor stripping? Is there one who would risk a satire on the modern demi-intellectual's insistence on analyzing everything to death that you do not begin to laugh at until after you have left the theater and the lovely absurdity of the whole enterprise begins ticking like a time bomb in your brain? Is there one who would risk a dollar on a man whose style can only be described as classic formalism? I doubt it. Which means that, if you value these virtues, you're going to have to read a lot of subtitles in order to rediscover them.

Still, *My Night at Maud's* has found a surprisingly large audience in New York among the thoughtfully silent minority, and I'm sure there exist elsewhere enough people of similar bent to give this dry, delicate, elegant novella of a film the audience it deserves.

I ended up voting for My Night at Maud's *as the best film of 1970. The reason was simple—its exemplary simplicity of image combined with its exemplary complexity of thought. The movie had a purity, a wit, a sense of style that were, for me, breathtaking.*

Focus on Film
Peter Cowie

A t first glance *My Night at Maud's* may appear intolerably stuffy, and removed from the realities of life in a French provincial town. *The Collector,* Eric Rohmer's other *conte moral* seen in this country, was altogether too much the work of an aesthete who rigorously eschewed any kind of emotional sympathy with his characters. But in *My Night at Maud's* we are scarcely aware of this intellectual standpoint. The film works simply because it lives up to its pretensions. It "cites" Pascal[1] much as Bergman "cites" Mozart in *Hour of the Wolf* (1968), but it is perfectly comprehensible to the viewer who is unfamiliar with the *Lettres Provinciales* or the *Pensées.*

Reduced to its bare bones, *My Night at Maud's* concerns a devout and fastidious Catholic bachelor, Jean-Louis, who for just one night is persuaded—tempted—to swerve from his rather sanctimonious path through life and to see what may happen should he disobey the calls of reason. Even that summary sounds daunting. We could go on to say that it is about the interacting relationships of a quartet of people—Jean-Louis, Maud, Françoise, and Vidal—and, although the precise balance of the film encourages such mathematical speculations, we have to turn elsewhere to explain both its allusive refinement and its impact on nearly everyone who has seen it so far.

Rohmer allows us to identify with Jean-Louis from the start. He is conspicuously lonely in Clermont-Ferrand, that mournful city in the very center of France. His manner betrays dissatisfaction with his loneliness, and it is this vein of frustration that makes him vulnerable to all the events of the film. Yet secretly we relish identification with a man whose eyes glance eagerly at an attractive blonde during mass; and Rohmer takes this process of identification a stage further when he seats us (the camera) behind Jean-Louis while he hastens in his car through the narrow streets after the service, looking nervously for a sight of the girl.

So to a certain extent we comply with Jean-Louis's decisions from now on. There is the meeting with the long-lost friend, Vidal (a Communist to Jean-Louis's orthodox Catholic) and the wary acceptance of a concert invitation. Vidal's claim to be a stronger puritan than Jean-Louis also gives us confidence. Adventure is in the air; Jean-Louis, like a punter, is calculating the odds, staking part, if not all, of himself on the "possibility of infinite gain."

1. On Pascal, see the Introduction.

From *Focus on Film* 1 (January-February 1970): 11–13.

It is a measure of Rohmer's achievement that we still side with Jean-Louis against the somewhat mocking sophistication of Vidal and his attractive divorcée friend, Maud. His character is meticulously drawn with little touches of behavior—his manners, his sudden boyish smile, his distraught glance round the room for an escape route as he realizes that Maud has inveigled him into staying the night. There is the sense of listening in at a confession as Jean-Louis unburdens his heart to Maud.

With audience identification taken this far, Rohmer can now make a series of melodramatic and largely fortuitous incidents look plausible (and thus give Maud's "That's fate" a bitter significance, as she recalls her lover's death in a car crash). At dawn there is Jean-Louis's sleepy inclination to accept the pleasure that Maud has to offer, followed by his abrupt dismissal of her embrace and her stinging retort as she slams the bathroom door in his face—"I like people who know what they want." There is his engaging "pick-up" of Françoise, the blonde of his dreams, in the town square. There is the convenient car failure outside Françoise's lodgings that enables Jean-Louis to consolidate his relationship with her. And there is, on the beach at the end, the Maugham-like revelation that Françoise was in fact the girl who had broken up Maud's marriage.

But it is when Françoise rejects his belief in predestination, saying "I think that at every moment of our lives we're free to choose," that Jean-Louis is really unmasked. From now on there is no question that he ascribes his fickle conduct to chance when he knows all the time that his instincts—his *humanness*—are to blame. From a position of considerable rapport, we feel cheated and look with disgust on a man who can barely conceal his delight at the revelation, as if the final beach scene proved all his priggish theories about Fate. There is much the same impression at the end of *The Sign of Leo,* an earlier Rohmer film, when Pierre (Jess Hahn), having sunk to the level of a tramp, suddenly reasserts his position with a windfall legacy.

Conversation is vital in *My Night at Maud's.* It lays bare the four characters more cleanly and with less affectation than any violent action could. The long discussions on science, morals, and Pascal are not so rarefied as they might seem. Every argument raised has its counterpart—or its *demonstration*—in the film's proceedings. In Pascal, says Vidal, mathematician and metaphysician are one and it is not long before we perceive why Jean-Louis shrinks from the Jansenist camp. For Pascal despised the relaxed morality of the Jesuits. In the *Pensées* he sided boldly with faith against reason, urging his readers to discipline the body to the outward observance of Christianity. But Jean-Louis is a Jesuit to his fingertips (this accounts for his appeal to our susceptibilities early in the picture). He is self-satisfied. "There's never snow at Christmas", he scoffs to a colleague—but with delicious irony the snow gives Maud her excuse for keeping him overnight. When Vidal suggests that, if left alone with a pretty girl he'd never see again, he might be tempted to sleep with her, Jean-Louis replies with disarming conceit, "Fate, I don't want to say God, has always spared me that kind of circumstance."

Thus religion for Jean-Louis is a convenient cloak of propriety beneath which he may shelter his desires. "My Christianity and my adventures with women are two very different things," he tells Maud when she admits his frankness to be shocking. He is all too keen to maneuver her into a respectable Catholic marriage ("For the church [your previous marriage] doesn't count. I could even marry you with full ceremony. Personally, that would shock me a little, but I see no reason to be more Catholic than the Pope"). Shortly afterward, the sight of the Cross hanging demurely above Françoise's bed gives him an agreeable sense of satisfaction. Françoise is the perfect partner, graceful and devout, without any of Maud's prickly skepticism.

Jean-Louis's moment of truth comes not at the end (when, as we've seen, he can derive a mathematician's arid pleasure from the encounter with Maud), but on the hillside above Clermont, when Françoise tells him brusquely that she has had a lover. For a few moments, as Jean-Louis tries to recover his poise, the snow seems quite palpably cold. The scene shows Rohmer's self-effacing style at its best, and his skill as a writer emerges typically when Jean-Louis turns the situation to his advantage by telling Françoise about his lapse on Christmas Day (without mentioning Maud by name and pretending with suppressed complacency that he had actually slept with her)—"This way we're even."

This uncanny grasp of a character's response to a situation is Rohmer's principal forte here. He has built his film on a *contradiction:* the clash between rationalism and sensitivity-cum-intuition in Pascal. In spite of his disavowal of Jansenism, we can imagine Jean-Louis saying (but not practicing), as Pascal does in the *Pensées,* that unthinking belief—taking holy water, saying masses—is a means of diminishing human passions. Hypocrite that he is, he pretends never to have erred, telling Françoise that he scarcely has problems with his conscience, and gently admonishing her for not obeying Life's Directions for Use ("Don't you ever read what's on the box?" he asks as they make the tea). When talking with Maud, he has criticized the Church's habit of balancing sins against good deeds; but it is precisely this that he practices himself. His "good deed" is his marriage to Françoise, his "sin" the brief liaison with Maud (all the blacker for taking place at Christmas . . .).

As he runs off to bathe with Françoise and his little child in the final shot, he has achieved respectability (grace?) in his own eyes, while Maud is left to climb away through the dunes, trapped in yet another crumbling marriage. In the final analysis, Rohmer challenges our own ambivalent reaction to his film. We respond to Jean-Louis because he is not afraid to abandon his principles for something joyful and worthwhile; we reject him when he continues to assert those principles at the expense of other people's emotions.

A Sampling of Reviews

Revue des Deux Mondes
Reger Régent

My Night at Maud's is an interesting, often very attractive, work by a "cinemato-graphic writer" who may have the failing of writing too much. If he lacked talent, his film would be the illustration of a literary dissertation on Pascal's thought and the light it sheds on relations between men and women in our times.

Translated by the editor from *Revue des Deux Mondes,* June 1, 1969, pp. 624–625.

Image et Son
Jacqueline Lajeunesse

Catholicism [and] Marxism apparently pose no real existential problems. . . . Only Maud seems truly alive, endowed with curiosity and desires, and probably in-capable of living a happy and balanced life. . . . A 1968 "Marivaudage."[1] Its interest is very limited.

Translated by the editor from *Image et Son* 230–231 (September-October 1969): 186.

L'Express
Pierre Billard

This night at Maud's is a night of fiascoes with humor and dignity. Jean-Louis learns that in the wager of love, unlike Pascal's, if you win, you win nothing, but if you lose, you lose everything. The most misplaced word to describe the pitfalls of love constructed by Eric Rohmer would be "Marivaudage." His characters put themselves completely into the words and acts of everyday life. They have an "existential" quality one would seek in vain in the many film heroes—photog-raphers, CEOs, and weary fashion designers—who suffer to the hilt from the angst of modern living in the psychedelic tea parties of Parisian high society. The

1. Pierre de Marivaux (1688–1763) wrote comedies based largely on subtle nuances of language; the term "marivaudage" means "overly refined talk about love."

characters of *My Night at Maud's* are indeed modern, more than all the others, since they are in direct contact with the real morality and the real sensibilities of France today.

Translated by the editor from "Sous le signe de Pascal [Under the sign of Pascal]," *L'Express,* June 9–15, 1969, p. 52.

The Observer
Penelope Mortimer

No marriage, it is implied, can go well with an intellectual brunette atheist. Maud and Françoise recognize each other. The simple Catholic, without really meaning to, has triumphed over Maud with two men. They say good-bye, friendly, at ease, only a little sad. Jean-Louis has gotten what he wants—which is not, perhaps, very much. Maud, demanding more, will forever remain unsatisfied.

From *The Observer* (London), November 23, 1969.

The Nation
Robert Hatch

My Night at Maud's is a four-sided conversation, a mathematical working out of relationships, in which much consideration is given to prudent gambles, human morality and divine sanction, predestination, the irony of coincidence, and the thoughts of Pascal. It is not at all what a movie is supposed to be. . . . Mlle. Fabian (Maud) and Vitez clearly represent the brighter pair in the quartet. They are the more attractive, the more self-reliant, the more inventive and fun to be with. Trintignant and Mlle. Barrault, whose characters are both believing Catholics, are self-justifying, morally apprehensive, smart but intellectually unenterprising. Unlike the other two, they are little given to laughter. But Trintignant's rather priggish code sustains him in real generosity and Mlle. Barrault's conventionality includes loyalty. They make a go of it together, whereas Maud and her friend, the somewhat radical, somewhat mocking teacher—about whom one really cares a lot more—make a go of it with no one.

From *The Nation,* April 27, 1970, p. 509.

Commentaries

Although there are many interesting works on Rohmer's work as a whole, and on the history of French cinema during the past thirty years, extended critical writing on *My Night at Maud's* by itself is relatively rare. C. G. Crisp has written an excellent book on Rohmer, with a chapter devoted to *My Night at Maud's,* published in 1988; a portion of it is reprinted here. Crisp develops an interpretation grounded in Rohmer's own ideas, as expressed in the other films, in interviews, and in his critical writing. Basically, he argues that Maud represents a false promise for the narrator, who makes the right choice in preferring Françoise. It is noteworthy that, in presenting the argument, Crisp does not find it necessary to respond to any previous criticism. Just two years earlier (and therefore too late to be cited by Crisp), Frank R. Cunningham had argued an opposite case in his article, "Pascal's Wager and the Feminist Dilemma in Eric Rohmer's *My Night at Maud's*." He devotes a paragraph to previous scholarly comment, but in fact most of the works cited are either reviews or general works on the cinema. A portion of Cunningham's article is also reprinted.

Going back to 1977, Marion Vidal's *Les Contes moraux d'Eric Rohmer* also contains a chapter on *My Night at Maud's,* focusing on an analysis of the characters, and concluding that the narrator's marriage to Françoise is based on lies and deception, and therefore not the happy ending it may seem. Vidal's study is not widely available in the United States, even in French; a generous excerpt is therefore provided. Vidal, like Crisp, relies entirely on internal evidence and careful reading; no previous criticism is cited.

The earliest selection is Jean Collet's essay, "Eric Rohmer, the Passionate Architect," a chapter from his book *Le cinéma en question* (1972); Collet argues for a parallel between Rohmer's cinema and architecture, in that both strive to reveal the hidden beauty of the world. The characters' struggle to find moral order is equivalent to the director's effort to film a narrative.

My Night at Maud's
Marion Vidal

I f there was ever a film in which the use of black and white was justified, this is
the one. *My Night at Maud's* is a work of snow and night. Most of the sequences
are nocturnal. The evening at Maud's by itself takes up nearly half the film. The
costumes and sets were conceived and constructed in black and white, right down
to the white fur cover on Maud's bed, a practical idea of Françoise Fabian's,
"because it was so cold in the studio," which Rohmer immediately adopted for, he
said, "it brought snow to mind again." Ubiquitous snow, which seems to link the
characters' past and future since it evokes childhood ("I don't like snow much,"
Vidal proclaims, "it looks phony, it looks like kid stuff") and it will be, as we shall
see, the instrument of fate.

My Night at Maud's can be considered the most representative of the *Moral
Tales*. The traditional scheme is illustrated in exemplary fashion: the encounter
with the chosen one, the search for her, the intervention of the seductress, then the
return of the chosen one, all just as in *The Baker's Girl from Monceau,* but with
more clarity and more elaboration. No hesitation or ambiguity here. Françoise is
felt right away by the narrator to be "the One and Only, the Person you never
expected to find, the Summa of all perfections ever imagined and wished for."
Maud, the first active-type seductress, is, by her beauty, her intelligence, her
elegance, a dream temptress. Maud the dark lady, Françoise the fair, opposite in
every respect and for once in an equal combat, where the undeniable superiority of
the seductress effectively compensates for the handicap constituted by the narrator's
bias in favor of the chosen one. Finally, the role of fate and chance in the hero's
life, the moral implications of his acts, are studied in depth. The thoughtful
analysis, situated on a metaphysical and religious plane, reaches a level heretofore
unequaled. For all these reasons—to which may be added the professionalism of
the actors (Jean-Louis Trintignant, Françoise Fabian, Marie-Christine Barrault
and Antoine Vitez), the masterful direction, and the superb photography of Nestor
Almendros—*My Night at Maud's,* the "third" moral tale, appears more controlled,
and certainly more mature, than the "fourth," *The Collector.*

The main reason for the delayed shooting of *My Night at Maud's* was that
Rohmer had to wait two years for Trintignant to be free to interpret the role of the
narrator. It would take no less than his charm, thought Rohmer, to make this
thankless part tolerable. The fact is that the narrator—we will call him Jean-Louis
henceforth since he has no name—is often irritating. His Catholicism seems out of
date, his scruples sometimes ridiculous. Maud sees in him "a shamefaced Christian

Translated by the editor from *Les Contes moraux d'Eric Rohmer* (Paris: Lherminier, 1977),
pp. 83–105.

paired with a shamefaced Don Juan." He appears as a weakling, a man of impulses, constantly dodging behind a moving wall of hesitations, procrastinations, and little lies. "I won't tell everything in this story" he announces coyly at the start of the short story. An understatement, if one reflects that he lies all the time, especially about insignificant things: the fact that he prefers to cook rather than eat out, that he does or does not know how to make tea. . . . Furthermore, he uses lies to protect himself against the curiosity of others: Maud and Vidal, for example, when they interrogate him about the existence of the mysterious blond girl. Sometimes he also adapts his lies to the personality of his partner: regarding his past conquests, he talks to Maud of passion and reciprocity, and affirms that circumstances alone caused the end of these liaisons. To Françoise by contrast he says that he had been left for another man by a girl he loved and who did not love him. Partial truths? Outright untruths? It is certain in any case that Jean-Louis is a master of mental restriction and lie by omission. Trintignant's sincere manners, soothing voice, and honeyed smile as he plays the hypocrite are marvels to behold.

Perhaps these lies stem from a great timidity? Perhaps the narrator is trying to hide his real personality behind false appearances and false confessions? As a precaution, Jean-Louis, like all Rohmer's heroes, tends to avoid too-intimate contacts with his peers, to reject a priori any emotional or even friendly commitment. Careful with his feelings, he hesitates to invest them in troublesome or cumbersome relationships. Overseas, he made friends easily, for he knew the bonds were fragile. Back in Clermont-Ferrand, where he is thinking of settling, he keeps his distance and does not try to meet new people. In the course of their last meeting, he admits to Maud, with a rudeness one hopes is unconscious, "If I'm cheerful around you, it's because I know we're not going to see each other again." All things considered, he is not so different from Vidal, who declared himself somewhat provocatively in favor of business trip love affairs and summer romances, limited in time and stripped of consequences. More than modesty, this attitude signals in the narrator a certain cowardice and a total lack of spontaneity, a fact neither Maud nor Françoise fails to notice. His very faithfulness ("It's odd how I don't like to leave people," he tells Maud, "I'm faithful, even to you.") is a fear and refusal of adventure. In the absolute, he explains, one ought to love only one woman and no other, even platonically. A good way to calm his fear of risk and satisfy his moral demands at the same time.

Let us, however, lighten up this slightly dark portrait. Let's give the narrator the benefit of the doubt where his protestations of modesty are concerned: perhaps they are partly sincere. Let's also give him credit for the odd moment of shame before his weaknesses and cowardice. Let's recognize finally that he has the virtues of his vices. Knowing himself imperfect, he is indulgent toward others. A lukewarm Catholic, little inclined toward saintliness, he at least has the merit of tolerance and accepts all religions, "even the one of people without any." Thus he does not condemn Maud's divorce, even though in his own case such a solution would be radically excluded. . . .

The places where the two heroines of *My Night at Maud's* live are in their image. To the prudish Françoise's austere and impersonal cell corresponds Maud's elegant and comfortable apartment. Prints on the wall, shelves full of books, tasteful modern furniture, hospitable fur rugs and cushions. Maud is beautiful, gracious, sensual, intelligent, and direct. Liberated in sexual as well as religious matters, she contrasts not only with Françoise, introverted and maybe frigid, but also with Vidal and Jean-Louis, who seem a bit like "boy scouts" and "arrested adolescents" next to her. Unsure of himself, Vidal brings Jean-Louis as a chaperone to go to Maud's. When he throws Jean-Louis into Maud's arms, it is to protect himself against himself and to have a pretext to "despise and hate" a woman he loves and admires, but whose evident superiority he cannot tolerate.

An atheist and freethinker, Maud is not amoral. She has many principles, some of them very strict. But they are not the same as Jean-Louis's. Whereas he cannot conceive of sexual relations outside marriage (or at least without the idea of marriage in the background), Maud could very well envisage an affair with Jean-Louis without having the least intention of marrying him. On the other hand, she is as choosy as he is regarding her partners, and just as capable of abstinence when nothing worth the trouble is available. She refuses, for example, to take up with Vidal again, their previous affair having seemed rather futile to her. In many regards, moreover, she gives evidence of a moral rigor infinitely more demanding than Jean-Louis's. Her candor and sincerity, in particular, contrast with the narrator's puerile lies and his petty compromises with his conscience. Maud is loyal and wholehearted: "When I say yes, it's yes, and when it's no, it's no." She declares herself *scandalized* by Jean-Louis's jesuitism. This term must be taken in its strong, almost biblical sense: Jean-Louis, the "good Catholic," is by his laziness and lack of fervor an object of scandal for Maud the nonbeliever, who has a high opinion of Christian values, if only as an outsider. And yet Jean-Louis, so different from her, so lacking in the qualities she most values, is the one Maud fixes her choice on. . . .

The way Maud gets around the narrator is undoubtedly a masterpiece of strategy. Having deliberately immobilized herself in the bed, she gets him to serve her, asking now for cigarettes, now for a glass of water, and thus tames and domesticates him. She turns back against him the reasons he brings up for leaving her: he says he should leave out of politeness and consideration, she proves to him that he is only worried about respectability and he should keep her company, if only out of compassion and Christian charity. Does she really want to seduce him? Doesn't she just need a little companionship and human warmth in these difficult days after her divorce? The pathetic moment when she talks about her lover, dead in an accident on an icy road, casts a different light on her plea about the snow, which she had used to persuade Jean-Louis to stay, and which we had taken for a convenient pretext. Above all, and this fact is important, between the moment when Jean-Louis and Maud fall asleep lying beside each other and the moment in the light of early dawn when the still-sleepy Maud puts her arms around Jean-Louis, only several hours have passed; and during this time the seductress has slept calmly next to her companion. So what should we make of this overture to flirtation? Is it the natural reaction of a sensual and sensible woman responding, in the mists of a half-sleep, to the attraction of a masculine body? Or is it the climax of a concerted plan of seduction? Did she then want to seduce him? If so, why? Love? To toy with Vidal? As a challenge, to prove that the atheist's charms could overcome the believer's scruples? As retaliation against the mysterious blond girl who reminds her, for good reason, of her rival for her ex-husband's love? As always, the mystery is far from being solved. The only case in which the seductress openly admits her intention to seduce the narrator is in *Chloe in the Afternoon,* when Chloe announces to Frédéric that she wants to have his baby. In this case, her motives remain hidden and we never know whether the narrator's ultimate capitulation results from circumstances, the seductress's skill, or his own autosuggestion, making him a victim of his own fantasies. The contrast, much beloved by Rohmer, between the behavior of characters and a whole background of veiled intentions and unconfessed motives that we suspect, takes on its full meaning in *My Night at Maud's.* Maud, in fact, is a frank and spontaneous person. More than the baker's girl, Suzanne, or Haydée, she needs to talk about herself and explain herself. We learn many things about her past and her feelings. The mystery surrounding certain of her actions is not artificial or willfully exaggerated by the author. It is only the reflection of the complexity of human souls, of the enigma represented by every human being, even the most forthright and the most sincere.

Another peculiarity of this tale is that we don't find the narrator's usual condescension toward the seductress, the kind of contempt for her modest origins and lack of education (the baker's girl), her lack of dignity (Suzanne), her "vulgarity" and dissolute life-style (Haydée). On the contrary, it is clear that Jean-Louis appreciates Maud intellectually, he is stirred by her beauty, and he does not condemn her liberated way of life or her lack of religion. The narrator's seduction will thus not have as its only result, as in the first three tales, his recognition of the physical and moral qualities of the seductress, but rather, his acceptance of a philosophy of existence totally different from his own. "Women", says Jean-Louis, "have always contributed to my moral progress." He could not be more right about Maud, since she pushes him to question his own conduct and way of life. When he leaves her hastily after their night together, he feels all at sea: "Outside, the cold, the white snow, far from comforting me, brought me back to myself and to my shame for having lacked the courage either to refuse absolutely or, having gone so far, to have followed through." He thinks he can congratulate himself on having remained faithful to his principles and on not having betrayed the chosen one, but he feels only shame and bitterness at having been a boor and a cad with a woman who deserved his esteem. For the first time, Jean-Louis doubts himself: he has lost his lodestar. "I was the one who didn't seem to be myself anymore, or, more precisely, I felt available to almost anything, without ideas, without principles, without character, without will, without morality, without anything. . . ." Here we are a long way from the thoughtlessness and relief with which the narrators of *The Baker's Girl from Monceau* and *The Collector* abandon the seductress to run back into the arms of the chosen one. Here we find on the contrary a situation that foreshadows Frédéric's in *Chloe in the Afternoon,* torn between his bourgeois marriage and the adventurous existence Chloe offers him, with Frédéric escaping ingloriously and in complete disarray to take refuge beside his wife.

The evening at Maud's occupies the center of the film and almost half its total length. Keystone of the work, it is also one of the most beautiful examples of Rohmer's direction one can cite. Classic direction by the sobriety of camera movements, the choice of frames compatible with the natural points of view of the protagonists. Direction with soul where the important thing is not so much what the characters do or say but the immaterial network of feelings, sensations, impulses, and dislikes that is woven bit by bit between them. If in the conversations the camera is often on the listener and not the speaker, it's because Rohmer is more interested in describing the repercussions of a character's words or gestures on the faces and attitudes of the witnesses. The dinner sequence is a game of hide-and-seek where Vidal, Maud, and Jean-Louis observe and try to unmask each other without giving themselves away. The way the filmmaker frames the character who is talking, moves to the one who is listening, lingers on him while he answers and still longer while the first one begins to speak again, then returns to the first to record the end of his speech and stays on him while the second one answers, again off-camera—this frequent camera lag with regard to the speaker and slippage toward the listener gives to the scenes of conversation an incomparable cohesiveness, which would be hard to obtain with classical Hollywood editing, where one shifts more automatically with each speech, from shot to countershot and back again.

In the shift from one character to another, the use of pans instead of a succession of abrupt cuts accentuates still more the flowing effect. When Rohmer uses a cut, it is in contrast to this flowing style to mark a pause or turning point in the conversation. After Vidal's departure, Maud and Jean-Louis exchange remarks about their friend. Maud is shot in a close-up, with Jean-Louis just visible at the edge of the frame. Suddenly, Maud signals a change of pace: "So, where were we?" Cut to Maud and Jean-Louis seen in profile and the conversation moves in the direction of Jean-Louis's confidences.

Another example of this style, both rigorous and fluid, economical and emotional, is the shot in which Maud reframes herself after having related her lover's accident. Sitting on her bed, she leans forward and grasps her knees with a pensive look: without any camera movement, we go from a detached and objective general shot to a close-up full of feelings.

During the first part of the evening, before Vidal's departure, the pans favor Maud, the center of attraction and the stakes of the men's game. While Vidal and

Jean-Louis exchange repartee off-camera, a "fascinated" camera, complicitous with their desire, follows her movements. In the second part of the evening, on the contrary, when Maud remains alone with Jean-Louis, he is the one supposed to be the object of curiosity and longing and he is the subject of most of the pans, with Maud off-camera. In the first part of the evening, Maud was escaping from Vidal, whereas in the second part Jean-Louis is escaping from her. Whence the evasive, unstable, elusive aspect, admirably translated by camera movements.

Another difference results from the use of general or American shots in the first part, the close-ups being almost always saved for Maud and Jean-Louis when they succeed in getting away from the burdensome presence of Vidal. In the second part, by contrast, close-ups are more frequent, underscoring the increased intimacy of the two characters. . . .

The epilogue of *My Night at Maud's* contains a dramatic shock: Françoise's lover was none other than Maud's husband. This stunning disclosure is revealing both of Rohmer's attitude toward his heroines and of the moral ambiguity of the tales.

On one side, the author's justice strikes down on the seductress who was guilty of challenging the quasidivine order he has founded: Maud's first husband and Jean-Louis both leave her for Françoise. On the other side, the narrator's progress on the road to sainthood—or at least toward self-fulfillment—is debatable to say the least. To be sure Jean-Louis has found his guiding star again. But what has come of all these lucky breaks, these happy accidents, and the divine assistance the narrator had the benefit of in his search for the chosen one? A fantasy marriage, founded on lies and secrecy. Secrecy on Françoise's part, in hiding her former lover's identity from her husband for five years. Repeated lies on Jean-Louis's part, meant to preserve a union that apparently can survive only thanks to the illusions and the climate of duplicity maintained by the couple. At the beginning of his life with Françoise, Jean-Louis tells her that the very morning he met her he was coming from the bed of a woman with whom he had slept. Five years later he persists in the same lie, adding that the woman was Maud. In the first case, it was a question of overcoming Françoise's scruples; in the second, of softening her remorse by proving to her that despite her guilty affair she must not feel unworthy of him. The narrator's moral progress has therefore consisted essentially of swapping the gratuitous little white lies of the past for "pious" lies motivated by pity. In this transition from a thoroughgoing mythomania to a dubious compassion, morality loses what religion is not sure of gaining.

Eric Rohmer, the Passionate Architect
Jean Collet

I t took three years and the discovery of *My Night at Maud's* to clear up the uncertainty about *The Collector.* Many viewers had taken this film for a libertine rather than a moral tale. However, the relations between Adrian and Haydée do not differ so much from the ones Rohmer sets up between Maud and the very Catholic hero of his last film, the young engineer played by Jean-Louis Trintignant.

Both characters are manifestations of *conscience*—or clear conscience—in very real situations that are ambiguous to say the least. And conscience in both films is experienced as resistance. Resistance to seduction, to temptation, to evil, but still more to the real. It is very clear in *My Night at Maud's,* in which the first woman, Françoise, is presented right away as an image (the engineer sees her at mass and follows her in the street), whereas the second woman, Maud, bursts in and imposes herself as a very carnal being, with her weight of experience and life, her past.[1] In short, out of the imaginary creature glimpsed in the church, the engineer can make "his wife"—that is, he can experience in the highest degree the exalting dizziness of a free choice in her regard: "The sudden, precise, definitive idea came to me that she would be my wife." Of course, later on, Françoise will cease to be an image, will manifest her own resistance, and her freedom. But she will marry the engineer as he had decided. It is only in the very last minute of the film, long after his marriage, in a stupefying revelation worthy of *Les dames du Bois de Boulogne* (*Ladies of the Park*),[2] that the engineer will learn whom he has married: not the ideal blond girl, the practicing Catholic, who haunted his imagination. Françoise was Maud's husband's mistress. And it is in Maud's presence, by a fortuitous meeting, that he discovers this truth. And so the moral distance between the two women will somewhat collapse, at least the distance the engineer thought he saw. That distance, that difference between the brunette Maud and the blond Françoise, was at most the difference between the real and the imaginary. Maud had really given herself, whole, body and soul, *transparent,* from the first meeting. The day after that night, the engineer will confide to her: "I have the impression I've known you for an eternity." Françoise, by contrast, exists only as the stakes of a wager. She is marked with the sign of the arbitrary. What is more,

---

1. Collet quotes the short story here.
2. Collet explains that the hero learns he has married a prostitute. The film was directed by Robert Bresson in 1945 and based on a story in Denis Diderot's novel *Jacques le Fataliste.*

Translated by the editor from *Le cinéma en question* (Paris: Éditions du Cerf, 1972), pp. 172–183.

this arbitrary choice, this sudden decision, is rooted in a religious faith. It is because Françoise was seen there, at that mass, in this moment of spiritual communion, that the hero blindly chose her as a wife. And it is perhaps because Maud has been discovered, outside any mystery, in the frank and simple climate of an open-hearted dialogue, that the hero—whatever he may say—refuses to take her as a wife, despite his evident love for her.

One can discuss forever such a Christian (?) concept of marriage, such an idea of predestination or of providential encounters. The film encourages it. It is not for nothing that the shade of Pascal hovers over all the conversations, and that mathematics, the calculation of probabilities, the notions of chance and luck, are frequently evoked.[3] Paradoxically, one may find more Christian, because more human, more painfully incarnate in life, the two characters in the film who do not claim to be Christian: Vidal, the Marxist professor, and Maud, the wounded woman who can still love. Before these two anxious and unfulfilled beings the young Catholic engineer boasts of his luck with a clear conscience and a smugness that come close to boorishness. He may have Faith, but not Love. And if, despite his spinelessness and his passivity, he has the stronger role in life, if he has a power over events that brings him success, is it not precisely to the degree that he is uncommitted in the event, that is, in reality? He is closed to encounters, but not to luck. . . .

The heroes of the moral tales maintain with those around them the same dialectical relationship that Rohmer's cinema maintains with reality. If these characters talk abundantly—among themselves or even more in confessing to us—one would be wrong to reproach them for it, since it is the very object of these moral tales: the problem is that they narrate existence instead of living it. Speech, narration, is the refuge of consciousness, a flight from lived experience. But paradoxically it is because this narrative exists, in its firmest and most arbitrary layout—as arbitrary as the theme of the six tales—that nature is revealed in its transparence and wild brilliance. Without this contradiction, no work of art. Without it, moreover, no possible moral life, no Grace. That is where Rohmer's entire work meets Pascal, touches him, and moves away. On the artist's part there is no abandonment to an aesthetic grace, a sort of primary innocence that would lead naturally to success. There is struggle. One is not transparent. One decides to become transparent.[4] This initial stiffness, this awkwardness of the will, must be softened by a long wrestling match with things, a slow saturation, a patient education, such as the one Maud could give the engineer, or the one Haydée imposes on Adrien, despite (or because of) all the rigor of his principles. . . .

[Collet quotes a remark Rohmer made about another film:] "What bothers me is you can smell the cinema too much."

3. Collet remarks that Rohmer made a television film on Pascal, with a dialogue similar to the one in *My Night at Maud's.*
4. Collet notes that the choice may be wrong.

Thus is set the debate, more timely than ever, to which *My Night at Maud's* forces us back: on one side are those who film the cinema, who expose its constantly reborn mirages, who constrain the spectators to recognize themselves as spectators, voyeurs, consumers. In brief, to use the trendy jargon, who defamiliarize by "deconstructing" films. Facing them are those who modestly take up the cause of things, once supported and then betrayed by Godard. Those who try to make their act transparent, to make us forget that they are filming to let us look at what they see. For his part, Rohmer has never hesitated about what side to take. Already in 1955 he wrote: "What a filmmaker worthy of the name intends to have us share is not his admiration for museums but the fascination the things themselves exert on him."[5]

Today this aesthetic choice can also be analyzed in political terms: to unmask the cinema is to be on the left. To tend toward transparence is to be on the side of the conjurers, to be a reactionary. . . .

What touches me here is that Rohmer filmed as simply as possible infinitely complex beings. He filmed from the most realistic point of view characters who live in their imagination and try to stay there in spite of everything. Jean-Louis had decided that his wife will be this *image* glimpsed one Sunday at mass. Vidal moves us by weaving around himself the fine cloth of a discourse in which, with modest humor, he wraps up the drama of his loneliness. Maud, like Haydée of *The Collector,* is between these two men, so sensual, so available, so "transparent" that she chases Vidal away without being able to keep Jean-Louis around.

Rohmer films these dreamers as he recorded the nightmare of a pedestrian on the Place de l'Étoile (*Paris vu par. . .*) with the camera of Rossellini, Hawks, Dreyer, or Murnau. A camera that refuses to go against appearances, that takes down the reality of the imagination, the trace of our tastes and our desires. *My Night at Maud's* is a documentary on beings walled up inside their ideologies.

Everything here leads toward rumination about the ideas and toward speculation. *My Night at Maud's* is a wintry film, under the sign of Saturn. Nothing is missing from this tale, neither snow, nor Christmas Eve, nor the frozen mountain, nor the city huddled down, nor the moral to end the story.

In the euphoria of a good meal, Jean-Louis makes fun of Pascal because he did not know how to *taste* the Chanturgues wine, to be attentive to its quality. One smiles. But for Jean-Louis, too, and for Vidal, it is a long way from life to lip, from existence to word. This false Christian and this false Marxist slide past things without seeing them. They talk and talk and the talking keeps on the edge of the encounter.

But this resistance of the characters to the appeal of the real—how can we fail to see that it expresses the fundamental problem of any filmmaker? The availability, the

5. "Le Celluloïd et le marbre," *Cahiers du Cinéma* 49 (August 1955): 13.

transparence of the gaze, Rohmer's attentiveness, all obvious qualities in the film, far from being the fruits of a lazy abandon to whatever happens to come before our eyes, are the conquests of that resistance. It is Jean-Louis's resistance to Maud that brings him to Françoise.

It is the filmmaker's resistance to events that leads him to the real. This dialectic of creation—resistance, transparence—has become the subject of the film. And its power of provocation, at least equal to that of the films of Godard or Straub,[6] depends on the permanent mastery of events, on that construction of the narrative, on that direction that brings together their arbitrary aspects and then disappears unnoticed for the benefit of the things.

Then one can—and one should—discuss endlessly: about will and luck, Marxism and Christianity, work and grace, calculation and chance, love affairs and marriage, travel and the provinces. . . . Useless to ask what Rohmer thinks. He does not think, he films. It is up to us to think. With a superb and magnificently invisible insolence, he gives us an extraordinary lesson in freedom. A freedom that scares us because it calls on us irresistibly to choose for ourselves, therefore to be free. On the most closed world, Rohmer casts the most open gaze.

6. Like Godard, Jean-Marie Straub is an avant-garde director.

My Night at Maud's
C. G. Crisp

L ike Rohmer's previous temptresses, Maud is associated with desire and appetite. Consider the elegance, the good food, the fine wine of the central scene in her flat. In her company, and under her influence, the narrator is moved to exalt the pleasures of this world in the form of a good wine—Chanturgue. It's a sin, he says, not to appreciate it fully—a sin to gulp it down without noticing what you're drinking. This is what he holds against Pascal, who had never leaned back in a chair and said expansively of something of this world, "This is good."

Later, Vidal picks him up on this point:

"Is that what you believe? . . . And yet, you don't wager, you don't risk
   anything, you don't give up anything."
"There are things I give up."
"Not the Chanturgue."
"But the Chanturgue isn't at stake."
"Yes it is."

All appetites are one appetite, and that one appetite is for the things of this world, represented by Maud and the wine she offers him; it is this sort of self-indulgence he must learn to suspect. As Vidal goes on to say, putting the opposition in more general terms, "one must choose between the finite and the infinite."

The narrator protests that his casual remark about the wine is being inflated out of all proportion: "When I choose the Chanturgue, I don't choose it rather than God. . . . That's not what the choice is." But it is. The lesson of the film is that one must choose between a glass of wine and God; and that this choice is remarkably difficult to make.

It's clear already that our narrator is cast in the mold of Rohmer's hypocritical "unreliable" narrators, and very limited in his self-awareness. Vidal is always more perceptive about him than he is himself; so is Maud. He is somewhat smug and complacent, and it is this unhealthy smugness that the events of the film are destined to undermine. Before the film ends he will be forced, for instance, to reevaluate his glib judgment of Pascal.

But Pascal's *Pensées* is not the only book to figure in the film. In a striking parallel with Godard's *Pierrot le fou* (1965), our protagonist buys two books at the beginning of the film that define the poles of the argument to be carried on over the next ninety minutes. The other is a mathematical text on *The Calculation of*

From *Eric Rohmer* (Bloomington: Indiana University Press, 1988), pp. 52–59.

Probabilities: mathematics and theology, the two studies that Vidal talks of as intimately related and of ultimate importance. Mathematics is presented as an internally coherent system, based on reason, on logic, permitting the accurate calculation and measurement of all material objects, and implying an ability to comprehend and master both Nature and ourselves. Pascal too was a mathematician, we are told, but toward the end of his life he rejected that study in favor of a more mystical insistence on faith. The implication of his stand is that reason will get you nowhere (except into blind alleys), that the material world is relatively insignificant, and that there is no possibility of comprehending rationally the ultimate truths. Faced with this situation, man's only recourse is blind unquestioning faith.

Reason and faith, then, are the two poles of the film, and synonymous with that other opposition we have seen as central to all Rohmer's films—unity and diversity, this world and the next, the relative and the absolute. And reason is yet another of those ghostly lights that his protagonists follow in their attempts to find a way through the mire of desire and appetite, in their search for certainties. Astrology, superstition, table-turning, all proved illusory; and no less so will this apparently more substantial path of calculating statistical probabilities to which our narrator is devoted at the beginning of the film.

The narrator's moment of triumph—of triumph over himself—will come when he rejects Maud and chooses Françoise. This is the moment of conversion from being a 'false' Catholic to being a true one; and at this moment he comes across a book in Françoise's flat entitled *Concerning True and False Conversion;* he goes to a second church service, complementing the first, during which the priest asserts what he has had to learn so painfully: one must be a saint.

This then is the surface argument of *My Night at Maud's*—the particular instance of the general argument around which the *Moral Tales* are fashioned, and perhaps the instance in which the underlying ideology is most overtly discussed. In itself, the argument could easily seem long-winded, irrelevant, or frankly antipathetic to the bulk of the spectators. If it seldom does, the reason should be sought in the series of subtle oppositions, many of which we have met in Rohmer's earlier films, which serve not only to generate the meaning but, more important, to invest a morale that could be described as austere with all the connotations of exhilaration and liberation.

The whole struggle has taken place in the depths of winter, the bleakest hour, when life is at its lowest ebb, but enlightened by a sign of hope in the form of Christmas Day, a day of rebirth and regeneration. As the priest says, "Something must be born in each one of us this night;" and it is.

The film is not only set in winter, it is set in the provinces—in Clermont-Ferrand, high in the central plateau of France, where Rohmer himself lived for a time. France is perhaps the most centralized country in the world, both physically and psychologically. Everything of significance happens or is felt to happen in Paris. Provincials, more so in France than elsewhere, can seem to be living on the fringe of things, excluded from meaningful participation, grubby faces peering into the window at an elegant festivity. It's logical, then, in an age when the center doesn't hold, that the generalized sense of a loss of belonging should be translated in book and film into images of provincials who know themselves to be such—outcasts, travelers who like our narrator are as much at home in Vancouver, Canada, or in Valparaiso, Chile; and this principally because they are truly at home nowhere. As Maud says, "Wherever you go, these days, you're condemned to the provinces." Though, as she hastens to add, she prefers it that way: she, at least, has learned to live in a relative world. The narrator has not, and will not. He is forced toward a religious commitment in order to regain a focus, a center to his existence, in order to transcend his provincialism.

The two nights characterize the respective halves of the film: after his night with Maud, and his humiliating flight, which in fact (though he doesn't realize it at the time) is a blessed escape, he returns to his aerie, and the film begins over again. We see almost identical images of him fussing about the house and driving away from it down into the valley, with lateral shots of the surrounding country-side from the moving car, then into a café, whereupon he sees Françoise on her bicycle again. He had taken a wrong turn the first time, and the whole first half of the film has been a dead end. Now he is being given a chance to start over again, knowing where he has gone wrong. And this time he makes no mistake: treating Maud, her dark powers sapped by daylight, snow, and mountain heights, as an affectionate friend, he chooses Françoise, Faith, and Nature.

But in the course of acquiring a greater complexity through association with these other vertical and climatic oppositions, the nature/antinature theme already explored in *The Collector* suggests broader cultural connotations: linked to and extended by the axes of mountain heights/industrial depths, countryside/city, religion/commerce, it develops into a contemporary reminiscence of that theme so familiar to Western civilization since the sixteenth century (and for that matter since Roman times)—but reinvigorated by the cinema, from *Metropolis* [1926, directed by Fritz Lang] and *Tabou* [1931, directed by F. W. Murnau and Robert Flaherty] to *Fahrenheit 451* [1966, directed by François Truffaut] and *Pierrot le fou* [1965, directed by Jean-Luc Godard]—the reactionary nostalgia for a preindustrial age of innocence, the condemnation of civilization as a corrupting force, the regret for a Paradise Lost. If Maud is antinatural in her preference for night-time and its related activities, she is doubly so because of her sophisticated urban life-style, her self-indulgent industry-born comforts.

The narrator's escape to Nature, then, is an escape from the unrewarding complexities of an urban mechanized world to a Rousseauesque dream of rural peace and permanence. The projected title for the film was *The Girl on the Bicycle,* and it is no accident that the heroine affects a somewhat primitive form of transport, nor that the narrator has to quit his car and catch up with her on foot. Rohmer has described himself as "a man fond of walking. I don't like cars. Even in *Maud* this theme recurs: so what if the hero *is* an engineer with Michelin; the moral of the film is nevertheless that a velo-solex goes faster than a car, and that you can go faster still on foot."[1]

This rejection of a mechanized world in favor of Nature attains its apotheosis in the final images of the film, when the protagonist turns away from Maud and prances off toward a wide horizon of sea and sky. The implication is that in choosing Françoise he is choosing liberty, and as a reward the world is opening up before him. And this serves to remind us how enclosed he has been up to this point, whether during that extraordinary long scene in Maud's apartment or constantly peering out from behind the glass wall of his windshield; and this reminds us too why Françoise should have initially seemed so attractive to him, sailing along so freely on her bicycle.

That the world should be presented as opening up before the narrator at the moment of his commitment to Françoise is the more interesting because, even more than in the case of the oppositions mentioned earlier, this imagery works subconsciously to contradict the *apparent* nature of the choice. The narrator is, after all, choosing a rigid code of religious doctrine, a tightly structured system—a "prison"—in preference to the looser, more liberal system of the freethinker, Maud. Yet the visual imagery works in the opposite direction, to suggest the ultimate *escape* from such a prison.

This paradox is continued in another; Maud, the sensual 'animal,' who might well in a different context (*L'Enfant sauvage* [*The Wild Child,* 1970, directed by François Truffaut], say, or *Lady Chatterley's Lover* [1955, directed by Marc Allégret, or 1982, directed by Just Jaeckin]) have been associated with forests, nature, and the countryside, is only truly at home in urban apartments; it is the spiritual one who understands the open spaces. Clearly, the impression that these images contribute to create is that, *despite appearances,* true liberty lies with Françoise rather than with Maud; *despite appearances,* to give way to animality is perverse rather than natural. In a sense, these paradoxes echo another and older paradox: only by sacrificing yourself can you attain the Kingdom of Heaven, only by losing your life can you hope to gain life. As they stand, these statements would no longer attract widespread agreement; they are not therefore made openly, but implied through a sensation of constriction and claustrophobia that gives way ultimately to a sensation of expansiveness and exhilaration. So that it is *this* world—Maud's world, of desire, appetite, and animality—that comes to seem artificial, perverse, a prison ruled by mechanistic logic, and the other—Françoise's— that comes to seem a release into the natural fluent order of things, attained through a grace that passeth all understanding.

1. In an interview with Claude Beylie, *Écran* 24 (April 1974).

Pascal's Wager and the Feminist Dilemma in Eric Rohmer's *My Night at Maud's*

Frank R. Cunningham

I wish to discuss the relationship established by Rohmer between the philosophy of Pascal, discussed often by the narrator and his acquaintances, and the problems caused by these concepts for Maud, whom I consider by far the most sympathetic and admirable character in the work. I contend that Maud's dream, her wish for a sustained and sustaining dynamic relationship with a man combining intellectual, ethical, and sensual levels of experience, is rendered impossible in the spiritual world of Clermont-Ferrand because of values characterized by a fear of risk and involvement on the part of the narrator. Because of the engineer's geometric certitudes and conventional propensities, Maud and he are cheated of far more than their "night" together, but of a potentially comprehensively passionate relationship that could be greatly fulfilling to them both, but which he evades out of fear and ignorance. Many modern writers—Lawrence and Faulkner come immediately to mind—have depicted the defeat of women's relational dreams because of moral shallowness and lack of courage in the male, but Rohmer breaks new ground in narrative film in his suggestion that men frequently "prefer to emphasize the possibility of choice rather than the activity of it."[1]

Since man must choose—not to make the wager in favor of God's existence and benevolence is still a choice—"if, therefore, a man cannot help choosing one way or the other, he should consider *where his interest lies*"[2] For those straining to believe, says Copleston, Pascal's view is that it is to their advantage to believe. Pascal is inconsistent in that he sometimes states that this process is itself a risk, but as often falls back into the vein of spiritual utilitarianism: "If you win, you win all; if you lose, you lose nothing. . . . At each step you take in this path, you will see such a certitude of gain and such a nothingness in what you hazard that you will recognize at the end that you have wagered for something certain and definite *and for which you have given nothing.*"[3]

It is not surprising that Maud despises as inauthentic and morally slack such a vision of a spiritually corporate insurance policy, or that the narrator essentially

---

1. James Monaco, *The New Wave* (New York: Oxford University Press, 1976), p. 295.
2. Frederick Copleston, *A History of Philosophy,* vol. 4 (London: Burns, Oates and Washbourne, 1958), p. 170; emphasis added by Cunningham.
3. Ibid., emphasis added by Cunningham.

From *The Kingdom of Dreams in Literature and Film,* ed. Douglas Fowler (Tallahassee: Florida State University Press, 1986), pp. 85–89.

endorses it through his actions, if he partially doubts it in what he states at times during his night with Maud. (It must seem to her somewhat akin to a television jingle: "You're in good hands with Pascal. . . .") When we look with closer scrutiny and criticality at some formal and visual details in *My Night at Maud's,* we shall see that although Maud likes the engineer, she does not admire his rigidity or his vacillation, and she recognizes that "she presents him with a problem vexingly Pascalian . . . beyond his wits, since the oppressive possibility of making love to her represents a bet in which there is nothing to be lost and perhaps a kingdom to be won."[4] Our initial view of him in the film is on his balcony, solitary; Rohmer depicts him visually "pinned" against iron bars in deep background as he drives into the city to attend mass. The first dialogue line, spoken by the kindly priest, is "Mercy upon us all," perhaps ironically directed at those who so fear risk that they idealize the world and live mainly in their own ego-constructions (Rohmer's last shot of the priest reveals him framed by twin stone pillars, symbols of his absolute certitude—and spiritual safety). This dependence upon an outward God-figure is a fine commentary visually on the engineer as he begins his pilgrimage to find the ideal blond, Catholic mate. When the camera first turns to contemplate the object of his gaze, during the opening mass, Françoise is presented in an ethereal, nonsexual image; in extreme close-up she seems a Madonna figure as we see behind her the blurry reflection of six altar lights. (Interestingly, Françoise is never depicted as though she possesses a bodily, sensual reality; even during the final sequence at the beach, she seems entirely removed from erotic context—even in her attractive bathing suit—the veritable image of a good wife and mother figure.)

When we next see the engineer, he is again in his dark, spare apartment, studying probability theory. (He is, after all, an engineer with Michelin.[5]) We see him framed, and symbolically imprisoned, between three geometrically patterned windows. In the next two sequences he is seen at Michelin, saying to a colleague who suggests a social engagement that "my family is Catholic and so am I," as if to present himself to his new co-workers only in a predefined social role; and then in two bookshops, where he is seen avidly reading some works by Pascal. Frequently during these early scenes, the narrator is juxtaposed against or near huge white buildings or other structural abutments, concrete monoliths that prefigure the stolidity (and unimaginativeness) of his religious self-definition during the rest of the action. In his night at Maud's he at times rails against Pascal for his alleged "rigidity," yet his actions speak much more eloquently about his character than his words. Austere to a fault,

4. Penelope Gilliatt, "A Good Night," in *Film 1970–71,* ed. David Denby (New York: Simon & Schuster, 1971), p. 126.

5. A corporation whose rubber trees in Indochina during the early decades of this century reportedly were planted atop the bodies of the peasants who tended them (but such psychological imperialism must be a part of another study of the narrator). [Cunningham's note].

he expresses with dismay to Maud and Vidal the opinion that he opposes Pascal because the philosopher's ideas were condemned by the institutional church—it is this that seems to bother him more than the truth or falsity of Pascal's thought. Of course, the most revealing action is his ambivalent reaction to Maud's offer of intimacy. Repressing the attraction and admiration he really feels for this remarkable woman, he richly earns her gentle but firm censure. (She has earlier chided him humorously by commenting that she could easily see him as a boy scout.) And perhaps most tellingly, he had earlier said of the "wager": "What I don't like in the wager is the idea of giving in exchange."

After his night with Maud, he meets his idealized wife-candidate, parodied by Maud in the days before "personals" columns as "Catholic engineer seeks blond girl, Catholic—correct that to 'practicing Catholic.' . . ."[6] She is a lesser woman than Maud intellectually, in terms of worldly experience and professional attainments, even sexual attractiveness (although perhaps the narrator finds the mythic figure of the blonde to be spiritually safer than the unfortunate Maud, possessor of dark hair!). Françoise, however, fulfills his unconsidered and largely irrational image of Woman; perhaps also part of her appeal is that she is very young and (he wrongly assumes) inexperienced in the world's ways. (We are to learn that another weak man, Maud's former husband, has had his affair with this very blonde.) Younger at twenty-two by eight years than Maud and by twelve years than the narrator, Françoise is wise enough to see that "[your] principles come before love," during their discussion over tea, and that a previous liaison with a woman ended because the narrator didn't have to make a choice. Later the next day, when Françoise and the engineer attend mass together, the sincere, kindly priest speaks of Christianity as "a way of life, an adventure," and the new lovers listen, seemingly rapt. But this aspect of Pascal's wisdom, though understood by the skeptical, freethinking Maud, lies far beyond the capacity of the humble narrator.

In the next-to-last sequence of the film, the two stand on a hill overlooking the city and Françoise courageously tells him of her affair while keeping the identity of her former lover a secret. A geometer to the end, the narrator, while kind in his attempts to assuage her guilt over the concluded affair, can only say with incredible naiveté that he's happy at these events because, after all, he has had previous sexual experience and "this way we're even." Further, he lies to her that he has recently slept with a woman (he means Maud though he, too, keeps her name a secret); rather than treating a woman he loves with honesty—treatment that a woman of Maud's nature demands—he is content merely to use the situation to puff up his ego.

---

6. Cunningham misquotes and somewhat misrepresents the incident; see shot 125. It is the narrator who self-mockingly suggests a personal ad.

The final sequence at the beach is one of film's great moments. Five years have passed, and the young marrieds bring their little boy for the conventional day at the beach. Striding up the path toward the road is Maud (symbolically, the couple is on the downward path, with the narrator a pace or two in front of his wife and son, in the traditional male place). As they talk with Maud, Rohmer cuts from Maud to the narrator; very rarely are these two shown in two-shot composition, as if to emphasize the moral and spiritual distance between them.[7] Maud says he lied about his promise to call her to say good-bye after a promise in supposed friendship had been made to that effect; she seems unsurprised at these omissions, as she is about the identity of his wife. Evasions pile up, as the narrator refers to his former "evening" with Maud, but Maud, ever ready for the unsparing truth, reminds him that it was a night, not an evening. She confides that she has married again, but that it isn't going too well—perhaps she again has met a man without the moral strength and spiritual integrity that she deserves. "I've never had any luck with men," says this strong woman mourning the lack of strong men. Rohmer photographs her clad in a simple black bathing suit, the wind whipping through her long, black hair.[8] Her last thought is to consider his feelings, lest his wife be jealous of their talking together too long. She breaks off the conversation, and the final shot of her is as she walks slowly and confidently up, up the slope toward the road, secure in her Nietzschean will-to-assertion,[9] if saddened at the perennial outcome of her feminist dilemma, her dream unfulfilled.

The film ends with the narrator's going down to his wife as she kneels in the sand. By sparing her feelings, by keeping from her the knowledge that he possesses about his noninvolvement with Maud, by lying that she was his affair, he at least gives her an illusion to cling to, their reed in a swirling wind. Hand in hand, holding their child, they run from the prying camera's eye into the sea, secure in their illusions, their conventional marriage, their need not to be honest with one another, far from the moral struggle and ambiguity faced daily by Maud. Their institutional Christianity is sterile when compared to Maud's ceaseless creation of value, her spontaneous and perennial openness to risk and social and intellectual involvement. True to the vision of the Christian existentialist, Maud envisions other human beings as ends-in-themselves, whereas the narrator tends to see them as means, such is his utilitarian view of Pascal and Christianity. Perhaps the film's most incisive irony is that Maud is even truer to the totality of Pascal's vision than is the narrator; contemptuous of the values of comfort-seeking and security-striving as ends-in-themselves, Maud is instead the free spirit who

---

7. Graham Petrie, *Film Quarterly* 23 (Winter 1969): 57.

8. It is in fact Françoise who wears the black bathing suit in the final shot; Maud is wearing a light-colored beach dress in her last scene.

9. See Friedrich Nietzsche, *The Joyful Wisdom* (1887), trans. W. Kaufman (New York: Vintage, 1974), book 4, aphorism no. 341; book 1, aphorism no. 58.

comes close to fulfilling Pascal's human ideal in his memorable "Grandeur of Man" passage in the *Pensées:*

> Man is but a reed, the weakest thing in nature; but a thinking reed. It does not need the universe to take up arms to crush him; a vapor, a drop of water, is enough to kill him. But, though the universe should crush him, man would still be nobler than his destroyer, because he knows that he is dying, knows that the universe has got the better of him; the universe knows naught of that.
>
> All our dignity, then, consists in thought. We must look to that in order to rise aloft; not to space or time which we can never fill. Strive we then to think aright: that is the first principle of moral life.[10]

10. Blaise Pascal, *Pensées,* trans. H. F. Stewart (New York: Pantheon, 1965), p. 83.

Filmography and Bibliography

Rohmer Filmography, 1950–1992

1950 *Journal d'un scélérat* (short subject)
Screenplay by Rohmer.

1951 *Présentation* (short subject) (as *Charlotte et son steak*, part of *Charlotte et Véronique*, 1961
Screenplay by Rohmer.

1952 *Les Petites Filles modèles* (short subject, unfinished)
Screenplay and direction by Rohmer and P. Guilbaud, from the story by Sophie Rostopchine, comtesse de Ségur.

1954 *Bérénice* (short subject)
Screenplay by Rohmer, from a story by Edgar Allan Poe.

1956 *La Sonate à Kreutzer* (*The Kreutzer Sonata*)
Screenplay by Rohmer, from the story by Leo Tolstoy.

1957 *Tous les garçons s'appellent Patrick* (*All the Boys Are Called Patrick*, short subject) (later part of *Charlotte et Véronique*, 1961)
Screenplay by Rohmer.

1958 *Véronique et son cancre* (short subject) (later part of *Charlotte et Véronique*, 1961)
Screenplay by Rohmer.

1959 *Le Signe du lion* (*The Sign of Leo*, released in 1962)
Screenplay by Rohmer.

1961 *Charlotte et Véronique*, (a compilation of short subjects by Rohmer and Jean-Luc Godard, including Rohmer's *Présentation* [1951], reedited; *Tous les garçons s'appellent Patrick* [1957]; and *Véronique et son cancre* [1958]).

1962 *La Boulangère de Monceau* (*The Baker's Girl from Monceau; Six Moral Tales*, I)
Screenplay by Rohmer.

1963 *La Carrière de Suzanne* (*Suzanne's Career; Six Moral Tales*, II)
Screenplay by Rohmer.

1964 *Nadja à Paris* (short subject)
Screenplay by Rohmer.

1965 "Place de l'Étoile," an episode in *Paris vu par. . .* (*Six in Paris*)
Screenplay by Rohmer.

1966 *Une Étudiante d' aujourd' hui* (short subject)
Screenplay by Rohmer, based on a text by Denise Basdevant.

1967 *La Collectionneuse* (*The Collector; Six Moral Tales,* IV)
Screenplay by Rohmer.

1968 *Fermière à Montfaucon* (short subject)
Screenplay by Rohmer.

1969 *Ma Nuit chez Maud* (*My Night at Maud's, Six Moral Tales,* III)
Screenplay by Rohmer.

1970 *Le Genou de Claire* (*Claire's Knee, Six Moral Tales,* V)
Screenplay by Rohmer.

1972 *L'Amour l' après-midi* (*Chloe in the Afternoon, Six Moral Tales,* VI)
Screenplay by Rohmer.

1975 *La Marquise d' O. . .* (*The Marquise of O. . .*)
Screenplay by Rohmer, based on the novella *Die Marquise von O. . .* by Heinrich von Kleist.

1979 *Perceval le gallois* (*Perceval*)
Screenplay by Rohmer, based on the medieval romance by Chrétien de Troyes.

1981 *La Femme de l' aviateur, ou on ne saurait penser à rien* (*The Aviator's Wife, Comedies and Proverbs,* I)
Screenplay by Rohmer.

1982 *Le Beau Mariage* (*A Good Marriage, Comedies and Proverbs,* II)
Screenplay by Rohmer.

1983 *Pauline à la plage* (*Pauline at the Beach, Comedies and Proverbs,* III)
Screenplay by Rohmer.

1984 *Les Nuits de la pleine lune* (*Full Moon in Paris, Comedies and Proverbs,* IV)
Screenplay by Rohmer.

1986 *Le Rayon vert* (*The Green Ray* [U.K.]; *Summer* [U.S.A.]; *Comedies and Proverbs,* V)
Screenplay by Rohmer.

1987 *L'Ami de mon amie* (*Boyfriends and Girlfriends, Comedies and Proverbs,* VI)
Screenplay by Rohmer.

1987 *Quatre Aventures de Reinette et Mirabelle* (*Four Adventures of Reinette and Mirabelle*)
Screenplay by Rohmer.

1990 *Conte de printemps* (*A Tale of Spring, Tales of the Seasons,* I)
Screenplay by Rohmer.

1992 *Conte d' hiver* (*A Winter's Tale, Tales of the Seasons,* II)
Screenplay by Rohmer, loosely based on the play by Shakespeare.

Selected Bibliography

Baroncelli, Jean de. Review. *Le Monde,* June 7, 1969; p. 11.

Bedouelle, Guy. "Eric Rohmer, ou les aventures d'un moraliste." In *Du spirituel dans le cinéma,* pp. 47–62. Paris: Cerf, 1985.

Bellot-Antony, Michel. "Les Constantes d'un genre: Le Conte moral de Marmontel à Eric Rohmer." In *Frontières du conte,* ed. François Marotin, pp. 79–88. Paris: CNRS, 1982.

Crisp, C[olin] G. "The Ideology of Realism. Eric Rohmer: *Celluloid and Marble* and *My Night with Maud.*" *Australian Journal of Screen Theory* 2 (1977): 3–32.

———. *Eric Rohmer: Realist and Moralist.* Bloomington and Indianapolis: Indiana University Press, 1988.

Davis, Melton S. "Boy Talks with Girl, Boy Argues with Girl, Boy Says. . . ." *New York Times Magazine,* November 21, 1971, pp. 38ff.

Gardner, Paul. "My Night with Rohmer." *New York Magazine,* November 8, 1976, pp. 64–69.

Hammond, Robert, and Jean-Pierre Pagliano. "Eric Rohmer on Filmscripts and Filmplans." *Literature/Film Quarterly* 10, no. 4 (1982): 219–225.

King, Norman. "Eye for Irony: Eric Rohmer's *Ma nuit chez Maud.*" In *French Film: Texts and Contexts,* ed. Susan Hayward and Ginette Vincendeau, pp. 231–240. London and New York: Routledge, 1990.

Magny, Joël. *Eric Rohmer.* Paris: Rivages, 1986.

Monaco, James. *The New Wave.* New York: Oxford University Press, 1976.

———. *How to Read a Film.* New York: Oxford University Press, 1981.

Pascal, Blaise. *Pensées,* trans. and ed. H. F. Stewart. New York: Pantheon, 1965.

Rohmer, Eric. *Six Contes moraux.* Paris: L'Herne, 1974. [*Six Moral Tales,* trans. Sabine d'Estrée. New York: Viking, 1980.]

———. *Le Goût de la beauté.* Paris: Éditions de l'étoile, 1984. [*The Taste for Beauty,* trans. Carol Volk.

Cambridge: Cambridge University Press, 1989.]

Séry, Patrick. *"Le Genou de Claire, d' Eric Rohmer: Un homme mûr entre deux adolescentes"* [interview]. *Le Monde,* December 10, 1970, p. 17.

Sourian, Peter. "Eric Rohmer: Starring Blaise Pascal." *Transatlantic Review* 48 (Winter 1973–1974): 132–142.

Vidal, Marion. *Les "Contes moraux" d' Eric Rohmer.* Paris: Lherminier, 1977.